GROWING UP holy & WHOLLY

GROWING UP holy & WHOLLY

Understanding And Hope For Adult Children Of Evangelicals

Donald E. Sloat, Ph.D.

Wolgemuth & Hyatt, Publishers, Inc.
Brentwood, Tennessee

The mission of Wolgemuth & Hyatt, Publishers, Inc. is to publish and distribute books that lead individuals toward:

• A personal faith in the one true God: Father, Son, and Holy Spirit;

• A life-style of practical discipleship; and

• A worldview that is consistent with the historic, Christian faith.

Moreover, the Company endeavors to accomplish this mission at a reasonable profit and in a manner which glorifies God and serves His Kingdom.

Wolgemuth & Hyatt, Publishers, Inc.
1749 Mallory Lane, Suite 110, Brentwood, Tennessee 37027.

Library of Congress Cataloging-in-Publication Data

Sloat, Donald, 1941 —
    Growing up holy and wholly : understanding and hope for
adult children of evangelicals / Donald Sloat. — 1st ed.
        p. cm.
    ISBN 0-943497-87-6
    1. Evangelicalism — United States. 2. Adult children of
dysfunctional families — United States — Pastoral counseling of.
3. Adult children of dysfunctional families — United States —
Religious life. 4. Family — United States — Religious life.
I. Title. II. Title: Adult children of evangelicals.
BR1642.U5S46 1990
248.8'4 — dc20   90-34747
                                                              CIP

To my wife, Linda

CONTENTS

Part Two: The Foundation for "Holy" vs. Wholly

Part Three: The Evangelical Rules

PREFACE

I n November of 1988, a historic event took place in Atlanta, Georgia. The First International Congress on Christian Counseling convened with over 1,300 registrants representing the United States, Canada, Australia, South Africa, Switzerland, and other countries. It was an inspiring, energizing event as I experienced the excitement and the stimulation of ideas being expressed and exchanged. It also had an additional significant effect on me.

Atlanta '88, as the congress was also called, offered a day of precongress institutes, and I organized a workshop entitled "Moving from 'Holiness' to Wholeness: Treating Individuals from Dysfunctional Christian Backgrounds," which was attended by professionals from all over the United States and one person from South Africa. The workshop participants responded positively to the ideas presented, and I also tested the phrase "Adult Children of Evangelicals" on them. Their enthusiastic encouragement was valuable support for my budding ideas. By listening to the professionals in the workshop, I also realized that many of us had individually made the same discovery: many of the Adult Children of Alcoholics (ACA) concepts also fit dysfunctional Christian families, except the crossover breaks down when there is no alcohol involved. Although the ACA ideas were helpful, there was an incomplete fit between the two sets of dynamics. Nevertheless, we had begun to notice a syndrome of behavior that was peculiar to Adult Children of Evangelicals in a way that certain behaviors were peculiar to Adult Children of Alcoholics. This reinforced my developing notion of Adult Children of Evangelicals (ACE).

As the congress progressed, I listened, watched, talked, and tried to learn as much as I could about the issues that Christians and Christian counselors were facing. The air was filled with talk about dysfunctional homes, physical abuse, sexual abuse, co-dependence, drug abuse, and so on. The book tables were covered with books on these same topics. It gradually occurred to me that a modified version of the three alcoholic rules (Don't Talk, Don't Trust, and Don't Feel) could serve as a model for understanding the dysfunctional evangelical Christian home and the problems that Christian counselors were seeing in the lives of struggling Christians. As I was pondering all of this in Atlanta, the evangelical version of the three alcoholic rules and their unique ability to create an emotional split in people suddenly flashed in my mind.

I have used the alcoholic model of dysfunction as a jumping-off point for the evangelical version of the three rules since many laypeople as well as professional therapists are already familiar with the ACA concepts. The phrase, "Adult Children of . . . " has become a common term that is used to describe survivors of various dysfunctional family situations and experiences, and many evangelical homes have produced their share of survivors who are now "Adult Children of Evangelicals." The Adult Children of Evangelicals (ACE) syndrome as conceptualized here is broader than *co-dependence,* another current term. Although the dynamics that produce ACEs are fertile soil for co-dependent behaviors to develop, not all ACEs are going to be co-dependent. If you are not familiar with the ACA concepts and rules, enough material is provided to give you a basic idea of their meaning.

Before we go any further, let me also explain what I mean by *evangelical.* Historically and theologically, the term has been used to describe Christians who emphasize the importance of *personally* embracing the gospel. In spite of other theological differences, the emphasis on personal experience is the common denominator that has defined the evangelical identity. This traditional definition certainly applies to the concepts being discussed here.

Through the years of working with people from varied denominations, however, I have discovered that these ACE conflicts are not the exclusive property of evangelicals. Christians from denominations who resist the evangelical label also experience similar struggles and problems. In fact, any legalistic religious belief system that emphasizes control and personal stifling is going to create the climate for personal repression. Since there are also wide differences among congregations across the same denomination due to the pastor's emphasis or the community's local culture, some churches may or may not fit the qualities described in this book. The critical component that results in the problems under discussion here is the rule-based approach to the Christian life, and although I realize there are churches and groups of believers who do not emphasize this type of Christian system, there are many who do.

In light of this, I am using *evangelical* loosely as a broad-brush term to cover general Christendom and those who take the Bible's teachings seriously. This includes the major denominations as well as the independent churches, and the Calvinists as well as the Arminians and the Catholics. The term *fundamental* is too restrictive since there are many Christians who do not identify with the fundamentalist movement, but evidence the disorder under discussion here. Not everyone fits the historical evangelical definition, either, but it seems to be more adequate than other terms that are available.

It is my hope and prayer that this book will fill the niche that exists between the ACA concepts and the dysfunctional evangelical family as we all work together as Christians in striving toward the true holiness and wholeness that God intends for us.

Donald E. Sloat, Ph.D.
April 14, 1990

ACKNOWLEDGMENTS

There are a number of persons who have made valuable contributions and offered support for this project. In addition to being a sounding board for my ideas, John Stapert, Ph.D., utilized his training in theology and psychology to be my consultant when I needed constructive input for the manuscript. My concept of grace has been deepened through my relationship with Harold J. Ellens, Ph.D., who has become a valued friend in the past several years. I appreciate his graciousness in allowing me to include his material in Appendix C. Henry Cloud's presentation at *Atlanta '88* stimulated my thoughts about splitting and also contributed to my developing concepts. The other persons who have contributed to this book are the many struggling Christians who have trusted me with their deepest pain and shameful secrets as they journeyed from "holiness" toward wholeness.

The special people in my life are my family. Linda, my wife, is the one person who helped me experience the true feelings of grace, and she has been my number one supporter through the years. Her support is the basis for many of my ideas and projects. Amanda and Molly, my two beautiful daughters, have added dimensions and a richness to my life that I could never have imagined years ago. Their bright smiles, dancing eyes, contagious laughter, and unending love have touched me more deeply than words can ever say. Thank you, Linda, Amanda, and Molly, for being yourselves and encouraging me toward my own wholeness.

PART ONE

A PERSPECTIVE ON THE ISSUES

1

"HOLINESS" CAN STIFLE YOU

I don't feel good about my life, but I don't know how it can be changed. I didn't know I was depressed until a friend of mine helped me see it. I guess I'm angry for what the church did to me."

The voice belonged to Treva, a fifty-one-year-old woman who was sitting in my office for her first session. As I listened to her words and observed her appearance, I saw a drawn face that indeed looked taut and unhappy. Tension was obvious as she spoke through pursed lips and occasionally glanced at me with uneasiness, slowly describing her reasons for coming to see me.

"Did you grow up in the church?" I asked, encouraging her to continue talking although I was quite sure of the answer.

"I was born and raised in a holiness church," she replied. "There was so much I couldn't do. I always liked music, but I couldn't be in the school band because the uniforms included slacks, which I couldn't wear. In high school I had to braid my hair and wear those funny brown cotton stockings. I had to look so funny." Her disgust and bitterness showed in her voice.

"What about the church you attend now?" I wondered aloud.

"Oh, we go to a different one now, and there are not many demands. But it is still hard. You know, I studied the Bible about wearing jewelry, and I can't see that it's as sinful as they make it. Scripture doesn't bear it out, but I can't bring myself to wear it. In the back of my mind I keep thinking, *What if they are right, and God really doesn't like it? Then I'd get it!"*

"What about your feelings? What do you do with your emotions?" I asked, trying to develop a feel for the way she handled her inner life.

"In our church we were not supposed to have any. If we did, we were not supposed to let anybody know it. I don't know whether there is any connection, but I have had migraine headaches for years, but not as often lately — I'm not taking any medication for them. I could never be good enough. We had a long list of rules at home, and when I married, my husband had his own list. He'd laugh at me and say, 'Here's the new list.' He'd read the Bible and see that they wore slacks, 'But get those blue jeans off!' he'd say."

As I listened to Treva's description of her life and became more deeply acquainted with her, I was struck by how well she had adhered to the rules espoused by her parents and their evangelical holiness church. Her teen years and adult life had been dominated by the "master-list" of what she could and could not do, despite her inner feelings to the contrary. She had consistently obeyed the rules, believing it was what God wanted for her. She systematically suppressed any contrary inclinations.

Treva had denied herself jewelry, stylish clothes, personal interests, and other pursuits that seemed worldly. She had been a submissive daughter and wife. Her church attendance would have pleased any pastor, and she used her musical ability as church pianist. When she was elected to other offices in the church, she handled the responsibilities with conscientious effort. Her morals were above reproach. Alcohol, tobacco, and filthy language were foreign to her lips. Money was spent frugally, and her tithe was as regular as clockwork. By all appearances she had been a successful Christian woman in the holiness pattern.

However, a second, conflicting observation began to emerge as I listened to her story. Despite her Christian life-style, Treva was not a happy woman. I could sense her pain as she vented her frustration. She presented the living picture of an adult child of evangelical parents — a woman who grew up living by the rules but had no joy in her life. She was unhappy, bitter, unfulfilled, and angry. She knew the right words and could recite her church's theology, but her life was empty, and emotionally she was not a whole person. She had given up a good job with career promise to be a housewife and please her husband, but now she wondered wistfully what might have been if she had continued working. Now middle-aged, she struggles with an inner desire to grow beyond her religion-enforced boundaries and toward wholeness, but fears she will lose her holiness and good standing with God in the process.

What Is Holiness?

"Isn't holiness a quality for which Christians should strive?" you may wonder. Yes, I believe it is. The Bible refers to it often, and God's holiness is one of His essential attributes. But I believe the "holiness" Treva was trying to achieve (the type referred to hereafter with quotation marks) is not really what God intends for us. The concept of "holiness" as used here is the false sense of holiness that comes from carefully living a Christian life based on keeping the rules on the master-list.

As a psychologist I could see that, even though Treva had been able to live a "holy" life, her life lacked wholeness. She was depressed and unhappy; her spirit was bitter and her heart filled with anger toward her father, toward God, toward "men preachers who stand up there like big shots telling all of us what to believe," and toward her husband. She lacked confidence in her own understanding of Scripture, and her inner spirit was tense and on edge. In order to live by the master-list, she had systematically trained herself to deny or repress her emotions, and she had been so successful that it was difficult for her to express any feelings freely and without guilt. In fact, when she did approach her emotions, she told me *about* them, rather than actually feeling and expressing them to me.

To live by the rules, she had disowned the parts of herself that were in conflict with them. For example, to keep the rule that required her to look plain in order to please God, she had to dispel any desire to dress in an attractive, fashionable manner. If she was unable to get rid of the desire, she at least had to want to banish it. She was not free to be totally herself, to include her thoughts, feeling, desires, urges, etc., as part of her person.

The "holiness" that comes from adhering closely to a set of rules is a false one based on performance and doing all the right things. It is an external system of behavior that appears to measure up to the expected standards, but it does not deal with the issues of the heart. Treva's life illustrates how it is possible to live by the rules and, by that definition, to be "holy." But such a life is incomplete.

The conflict between the Pharisees and Jesus was over this identical issue. The Pharisees had developed an extensive system of rules for spiritual living, and meticulously following them gave them a sense of self-righteousness and "holiness." Jesus was disgusted with this form of "holiness" and described it as superficial spirituality. "For you are like whitewashed tombs which appear beautiful outwardly, but inside are full of dead men's bones and all uncleanness" (Matthew 23:27).

Too often our evangelical churches apply a similar system of rules for Christian living. In *The Dangers of Growing Up in a Christian Home* (Nashville: Thomas Nelson, 1986), I discuss this master-list of sins that many churches adopt. It includes many activities Christians are not supposed to engage in and thoughts they are not supposed to have. The state of one's spirituality is calculated by how well one follows the list. Those people who are able to conform are regarded as having achieved "holy" lives, although their hearts may hide many secrets and unholy thoughts. These thoughts and feelings must remain hidden because they are not supposed to exist. So to be in compliance with the rules, a person has to deny many honest motives and feelings.

We can see from Treva's description of her life that living by the rules can be a stifling experience, producing a superficial, external sense of "holiness," while the internal experience is one of depression, fear, and anxiety.

What Is Wholeness?

Wholeness, on the other hand, is an inner state of being, a certain attitude toward oneself and others. It is rooted in safe attachments with significant others and a confidence that one is a worthwhile person in spite of imperfections. Those who can accept and love themselves can affirm, encourage, and support others whether or not they are of like disposition. One can accept them where they are and respect their boundaries without detaching from them. A whole person is able to trust his or her own feelings and judgments about ideas and situations and still remain open to other ideas. Wholeness enables one to be open to new experiences and to take appropriate risks that enhance personal growth. The qualities of self-care, setting limits, assertion and renunciation, reaching out to others, and sacrificial service are neatly balanced. Wholeness is also grounded in the Christian faith, for its basis is love. The whole person is characterized by love for God, for himself or herself, and by love for others.

From a Biblical perspective, wholeness means having the qualities Christ had. He was His own person with a clear set of inner values that He used in a positive, active way. There was no defensive live-by-the-rules-to-feel-safe life-style. He balanced His need for solitude with the pressing need to minister and was able to love and attach to even the worst people as He maintained His own focus and identity. He was able to love Himself and others because He was a whole person.

"Holiness" vs. Wholeness

Unfortunately, the rule-based system clouds the Biblical concept of wholeness and the pervasive quality of love and freedom available through grace. Unfortunately, this clouding takes place too frequently in the church and creates a dilemma, not only for those who have grown up as second- and third-generation Christians, but also for new converts. Churches and parents often depict the Christian life as a program for living based primarily on rules of behavior, and they emphasize that one must keep the rules in order to remain in God's good graces. They establish fear as a motivational system to make sure people do not stray too far from the acceptable ways. It is difficult for most children to reject such a plan for their lives when it involves so weighty an issue as one's eternal destiny.

The implicit message is, "If you want to see God, live by the rules. If you fool around with your own thoughts and feelings, you are going to incur God's anger because those feelings are wrong, and you will be a selfish, sinful person." "Holiness" and wholeness are perceived as mutually exclusive opposites. "Holiness" is presented as the only spiritual choice; whereas, those who choose wholeness risk God's wrath in the process. It seems impossible for one to have wholeness and God's blessing at the same time. In order to embrace the blessing of "holiness," one must reject the parts of oneself that conflict with the rules and must consequently reject wholeness.

After listening to my discussion of several of the problems associated with growing up in a Christian environment, a woman in her late twenties approached me after the Sunday morning class. "My father abused me, physically, not sexually, and we were a Christian family. My mother, I realize now, was more spiritual than my dad, but I didn't know it because she was so quiet about it. I just really have a hard time in church. I find that I am afraid of God, and when I talked to a minister about it, he said, 'That is good. Too many people are not afraid of God,' and he gave me a bunch of Bible verses."

As I listened to her story, I realized she had experienced more fear than trust in her family, and her fear-filled experiences had made all relationships difficult for her, not only with God, but with people as well. In telling me her background, she revealed the struggle she had with the legalism in churches she had been attending.

"My husband grew up in the church, and all of it is no problem for him. I stayed away from the church for about eight years because I couldn't take it, and now that we are back in church, I feel so closed in by all the rules. Everything has to be just so. I think I really do want to have a relationship with God, and I don't want to dump everything, but I am afraid. It's just all these little things you can and can't do. I get to the place where I don't know if I can take it anymore." Although she had grown up in a church and had trained by all the rules, now that she had returned to active involvement as an adult, she found herself still struggling and fearful.

This same problem faces those coming into the church as new Christians when they are suddenly hit with the bewildering master-list of things one can and cannot do. One young man in his late twenties told me, "I really didn't expect all this in the church. I just became a Christian a year or so ago, and I expected people to be really happy because they know the Lord and love each other. I find myself thinking, *It isn't supposed to be this way. All these rules and stuff?* After a while it starts to get me down, and I'm afraid if I stay in this church I am going to become just like them."

This fellow's first-generation Christian enthusiasm and excitement were being slowly chilled by the stifling nature of the teaching he received. In some instances it can be easy for new Christians to adopt the prevailing attitudes about the way Christianity is supposed to be lived, and since they have a limited perspective, they tend to go along with the system even when they feel something is not right about it. This intuitive sense that something does not fit has often been reported to me by Christians. This feeling should not be ignored. If you have such an intuition, do not squelch it; check it out.

Whether to choose "holiness" or wholeness is a dilemma that faces many who grow up in an evangelical church or new Christians entering an organized church for the first time. Is it really possible to choose wholeness and also become holy in God's eyes? Does God intend for us to choose between holiness and wholeness? Is there a true dilemma? The purpose of this book is to examine the apparent conflict between growing up "holy" and growing up wholly, especially in evangelical churches and homes.

We will discover problems similar to those in alcoholic families. At first glance this may seem surprising, but I have noticed many similarities, and the conceptual model for Adult Children of Alcoholics (whom we will refer to as ACAs) partially conforms to the evangelical situation. We will look at the dysfunctional practices in many Christian homes and churches that create Adult Children of Evangelical Christians (whom we will refer to as ACEs). We will examine the rules that set the tone in many Christian homes and see how these compare to the "rules" in an alcoholic home. This will help put into perspective the conflicts that many Christians experience.

There is a tendency to think of the fundamentalists when one thinks of rules-oriented religion, but *fundamentalist* is too restrictive a term. I will use *evangelical* (see Preface). The critical factor that causes the problems we will examine is the rule-based approach to the Christian life.

If you have struggled with the conflict between wholeness and "holiness," this book will help you realize that you are not alone in your struggle. This was one of my emphases in *The Dangers of Growing Up in a Christian Home* (Nashville: Thomas Nelson, 1986), and people from all across the country have written and phoned me to express their appreciation for the book because it helped them realize their problems were not unique. There is healing power in realizing that others share our struggles and we are not alone.

Although this is not a complete self-help book, the material will help you in self-understanding, provide a look at dysfunctional evangelical practices, and present ideas for pursuing wholeness while striving also for proper holiness.

2

ADULT CHILDREN
OF EVANGELICAL
CHRISTIANS

I can't believe she did this to me! Not only did she see this other guy, but she also lied about it, too!" Gene shouted the words as he and his wife sat in my office during our first session. The anger poured out as he described her offense against their marital relationship. "I have a hard enough time trusting her, and I didn't need this," he went on. I could see that he intended to say what was on his mind and was totally uninterested in anything I might say. "She has lied before, too—about money and other stuff. I've caught her in so many lies, and now this. She says nothing happened with this guy—How am I to know? She's lied about so many things before—How can I believe her now? Especially now!"

I observed as Gene exploded before me. He was small and wiry, in his late twenties, with a moderately thin beard. His sandy hair was combed back. He fidgeted in his faded work jeans. I was intrigued by the intensity of his anger that spoke of underlying hurt although it was not stated in his words. As he continued, I began to formulate several ideas about his background experiences.

Adult Children of Alcoholics

"I have always had a hard time trusting her," he continued. "When we were first married, I couldn't let her go into the grocery store alone, and I certainly don't want her to go to bars. I know what happens there. I need to know where she is, and it has been hard enough trusting her with all those other lies, and now this." His speech began to slow. He sighed and turned his gaze out of the window. "I just don't know what to do."

Sensing his fear of abandonment but also of closeness, I said, "I wonder whether you have experienced a lot of hurt in your life and have a hard time believing that anyone could love you just for yourself. Many people who have feelings like yours have grown up in homes where they did not feel safe. One or both parents were drinkers, and it was not safe to talk, think, or feel. They never knew what was going to happen." I said this intentionally to take the focus off the situation with his wife and to suggest that the real problem was bigger.

"Yeah, you got that one," he replied with a grimace. "My old man was always drunk, and you never knew what was going to happen. I was the youngest, and I was always having to stop fights between my mom and dad. I had to step in to protect her. Life was a mess, and growing up was all bad. No good at all."

He had experienced jealousy, fear of closeness, and fear of being abandoned. He responded with intense anger when he felt threatened. Unhappiness, frustration with life, and thoughts of suicide came out later in our discussion. Many of Gene's problems could be traced to the unstable environment his parents had provided, and his symptoms are typical. He fit the Adult Children of Alcoholics (ACA) pattern, and his present adult life was in trouble, which is also typical of many ACAs.

Adult Children of Evangelicals

Cathy was a trim, fashionably dressed woman in her late twenties with carefully styled auburn hair. Her general demeanor was quiet and demure, but lacked the self-confidence that her beauty should have provided. "I really don't feel like being a mother—or a wife, either, for that matter. Sometimes I feel guilty for not doing a better job with my kids. I can't stand my husband, but I don't know why. Sometimes I get so wild inside, I don't know if I can take it. Some days I feel like I might just let go and do something really crazy. I get so sick of trying to please everybody else. I have never done anything *I* wanted to do!" she finally asserted.

"Who are the people you have to please?" I queried.

"Oh, it seems like everybody. Every Sunday we have to go to my parents' house after church on Sunday to have coffee. My brothers don't go, hardly ever, and my folks think that is okay. But I have to go every Sunday. I don't understand it. And we have to do the same for my husband's folks, too. Except he really likes it and I don't."

Since she was less verbal than Gene, it took more time to understand her situation, but I surmised she had grown up in a Christian environment and was a sensitive person by nature. Her further comments revealed periodic depressive moods and suicidal thoughts that never reached fruition but certainly caused distress.

"Dad was hardly ever around," she added as I asked about her family. "He worked a lot, especially after he bought the store, and when he was home, he hid behind the newspaper. I never had much of a relationship with him. I never saw much affection between my folks, either. My mom raised us the most, and my brothers always teased me. They used to really get after me, and I remember this one time, especially." She slowed as she reached this point, and I could see that she was choking back her emotion, and I knew the next statement would be important.

"It was in the evening, about bedtime. My brothers teased me cruelly and had me so upset that I was crying and couldn't go to sleep, so I went to tell my mom, and I was crying when I talked to her. All she said was, 'You don't have to be so upset.' And that was it!"

"You mean she didn't ask about what was happening or anything like that?" I asked.

"No, she didn't. And I decided right then that it didn't do any good to talk to her. So I never went to her again about things." Cathy didn't feel safe in her home and could not count on her mom or dad to protect her. This fact assumed greater importance when I learned later that she had been sexually abused as a child but never told her parents. Now as an adult, she is struggling with depression, unhappiness, anger, hurt from her past, and guilt about wanting to please herself instead of others. Though her parents were Christians and not alcoholics, this did not mean she led a trouble-free life. In fact, many of her emotions were similar to Gene's. She was an Adult Child of Evangelicals (ACE).

Alcoholic and Christian Homes

Now what do their two stories have in common? And what does this have to do with growing up "holy" vs. wholly? A Christian home certainly is better than a home with a violent alcoholic. A Christian home is generally superior to one under the influence of non-Christian or alcoholic parents. But in working with clients who have grown up in Christian homes and churches, I have come to realize that many of these homes have emotional atmospheres quite similar to alcoholic ones. The most consistent trait is the lack of emotional safety for the family members. Gene never knew what to expect when his dad was drinking or when he would have to break up a fight between his parents. This tension created an atmosphere of uncertainty that forced Gene to grow up on his own, feeling insecure and unloved.

Cathy felt just as vulnerable in her Christian home, though it had nothing to do with drinking. Her mother consistently did not take her seriously when she needed protection and support, nor did she give much personal attention to Cathy. Her dad was an uninvolved father who spent his time working or reading the newspaper instead of reading to her, playing games, or enjoying her company. She could remember only one time that he gave her a hug, and that was when he learned that she was pregnant for the first time. Even that hug was suspect because she had a feeling the hug was for her child instead of her.

No one in Cathy's home took a personal interest in her or supported her as she struggled with her feelings. She felt unsafe and alone. The fact that her parents were active members in the local conservative church and were serious Christians had no effect on the way they treated her.

Many such stories could be told, but the point is that Christian homes are not always the safest place when one is growing up in our society. Youngsters have to master so many developmental tasks on the path to adulthood and must overcome so many obstacles along the way, that the task of growing up can be difficult under the best circumstances. When parents have their own dysfunctions in operation, the problems of growing up are intensified. The youngsters who grow up in alcoholic homes or dysfunctional Christian environments often are not whole persons, although the ones from the Christian homes may see themselves as "holy."

Obvious dysfunctions, such as alcoholism, drug abuse, and sexual abuse, are easily defined and tangible, while the subtle dysfunctions that can exist within the Christian family are much more difficult to see and understand because they are less obvious.

The Critical Difference

Being a parent is a difficult task for Christians and non-Christians alike, especially if one wants to be a quality parent and takes parenthood seriously. Although one has to be trained to drive a car, be a plumber, or work at almost any occupation, a person can become a parent with no training at all. Parents must make many decisions regarding their children, and many, Christian and non-Christian alike, approach this responsibility with a certain fear—fear that they must control their children to keep them from turning into criminals or from making horrendously bad decisions for themselves. This fear results in overprotectiveness and rigid control. We will examine several reasons for this control in chapter 5.

Ironically, these parents do not have evil intentions; they usually want to do their best for the children. But their own dysfunctions are such a part of themselves that it is easy to do what comes naturally, even though it causes problems for their children.

Christian parents who have a compulsive need to control their children have a resource that is unavailable to non-Christian parents. They often resort to God and Scripture to reinforce their personal efforts at control. For example, many Christian parents, my mother included, have used the expression, "What would Jesus say if He saw you do that?" This obviously is intended to produce guilt and shame in the child to gain compliance with the parent's wishes. Christian parents who begin to appropriate God as the authority for their need to control their children set the stage for serious problems.

The result is a Christian version of the dysfunctional home which often establishes negative survival patterns in children and sets them on the way to becoming ACEs — people who have grown up in Christian homes that distort the true meaning of Christianity, God, and of life itself. Adult life for these ACEs often features emotional and spiritual conflict, depression, anxiety, suicidal thoughts, and an uncertainty about the cause of the discomfort. When new converts adopt a rule-based evangelical version of Christianity, they also run a high risk of raising their children in the fear-grounded mode, rigidly applying Christian rules to personal development.

For non-Christian parents (alcoholic and nonalcoholic alike), God and His Word do not figure consciously into their thinking in raising children. They do not refer to God as an authority for their discipline in either a positive or a negative fashion. Their growing children may be spared dysfunctional Christian teaching, but they are also deprived of the positive Christian truths as foundations for their lives.

ACE Characteristics

The characteristics that I have seen in people from dysfunctional Christian homes that produce ACEs are a unique syndrome or collection of behaviors, attitudes, beliefs, and feelings. The following traits are typical of ACEs who experience conflict as adults.

The self tends to:

- be shy and nonassertive in personality
- be very sensitive to being hurt and rejected
- feel not good enough to be loved
- feel self-hatred or dislike
- have a sense of being stifled
- have a strong feeling of having never been loved
- distrust one's thinking and judgment

In relationships an ACE:

- feels that one has to be "good" or "perfect" in order to be loved
- is afraid to speak up and question others, especially parents, ministers, or other authority figures
- fears that pleasing oneself instead of others is wrong and has difficulty saying no — puts others first
- experiences confusing conflicts with family members and feels obligated to please them — especially parents
- fears expressing emotions, especially anger
- has difficulty trusting others

ACE's moods are characterized by:

- frequent sadness, depression, anxiety, and perhaps emptiness
- inner feelings of frustration, anger, and dissatisfaction

Spiritual state is characterized by:

- failure to feel better in spite of spiritual effort, prayer, and Bible study
- feeling more afraid of God then loved by Him
- pervasive sense of guilt, even about small, unimportant things
- difficulty enjoying life because it is somehow unspiritual to enjoy it
- trying to follow a list of rules

Although some people who have grown up in the Christian environment have many of the same emotional struggles as people from dysfunctional secular homes, they do have the extra dimension that the Christian belief system has brought into their sense of self and values. This adds an extra twist to their personal struggles because Christian values and teaching deal with such critical issues as self-worth, spiritual truth, fear of sin and eternal punishment, the soul, and ultimate worth. Therefore, the persons who have grown up in a dysfunctional Christian environment have not only many of the same emotional complications as their non-Christian counterparts, they also have theological distortions and fears to sort out. Unfortunately, many people have been taught — in the name of God — not to question or challenge what they have learned, which is an added complication in the already difficult process of working toward wholeness.

Rules in Dysfunctional Homes

The dysfunctional home has been described from a variety of perspectives by various authors, and the alcoholic home in particular has been identified as one that has specific dysfunctional patterns. The ACA literature identifies three rules that children typically must master in order to survive such an atmosphere: Don't Talk, Don't Trust, and Don't Feel.[1] When children from these dysfunctional homes reach adulthood, they may appear successful. But inwardly they are unhappy, discontented, and often empty because their childhood survival strategies were poor preparation for adult life, especially when they attempt to establish intimate relationships with others. The rules they had to learn can nullify any attempt to achieve closeness. Those rules have to be undone for closeness to have a chance.

As I have worked with Christians, I have realized that there is an evangelical version of these ACA rules operative in Christian homes, even though no one is drinking or getting drunk. Many children of Christian homes have trouble talking, trusting, and feeling because, like Cathy, they do not feel safe enough to speak up or to trust someone. To complicate matters the Christian version adds an entirely new focus and perspective to these rules, and sets the stage for people to develop the ACE syndrome.

3

PERSONALITY
MAKES A DIFFERENCE

A s I listened to Treva, whom we met in chapter 1, I noticed several points about her personality. When we discussed her past experiences, she reported incidents that revealed a keen memory, an eye for detail, and a definite tendency to hang on to hurtful experiences. The pain she had experienced—not only in her church, but at her father's hand when he did not appreciate her, compliment her, and even worse, tried to run over her with the tractor—was as vivid in her mind as if it had happened last week. This told me she was a sensitive person who felt pain deeply, and due to her natural tendency to keep emotions to herself, she had internalized and stored up her pain instead of acting on it or working it out of her system.

Personal Vulnerability

To gain the love and approval she was not receiving from her family, Treva had chosen the route of trying to behave and to be perfect so others would not criticize her or reject her. She had chosen the option of living by the rules—"holiness" at the expense of wholeness—because her personality bent was more toward compliance with others' wishes than toward forging ahead with her own ideas. Even now she is reluctant to trust her own judgment with regard to wearing jewelry and similar issues that require independent choices. Her sensitive personality had made her vulnerable to the positive and negative experiences of her family and church life, and it played a significant role in her becoming an ACE.

When we were discussing her church life, she gave several clues about its theological emphasis as she fumed, "There was so much I couldn't do. . . ." Her church seemed more concerned with setting limits to make sure she was in compliance with its master-list of sins than in developing a confident young woman. This expanded the picture developing in my mind of her life in her restrictive church that discouraged personal questioning, favored plainness, and encouraged conformity. Her sense of self was not supported or built up, and conforming to the church's dress code was more important than any of her personal feelings.

In order to have an adequate overview of the ACE syndrome and understand how and why it develops, we need to have two basic principles firmly in place. The first factor is a person's basic personality style, and the second concerns the Biblical concept of grace and the distortions that we often see in its everyday application in the home and at church.

Personality Styles

Through the years of working with individuals and families, I have noticed that one person may develop internal conflicts and experience trouble growing up in a Christian home, while a brother or sister in the same home has no apparent struggle. As a psychologist I have observed that the person who has a sensitive nature and who takes hurts and criticism seriously is more likely to have problems and develop ACE symptoms, or at least the sensitive person seems more likely to come for treatment. More specifically, one's personality type influences how a person responds to parental and church pressures.

It will help our study of the ACE concept if we have a system that helps us understand the reasons particular people behave as they do. The Personal Profile System is one that I have found particularly useful because it uses everyday language and is easy to understand.

The Personal Profile System

The Personal Profile System (PPS), though developed by a psychologist, was not intended as a scientific personality test to reach into the recesses of a person's mind.[1] It is based on a theoretical model that is not an extensively researched personality theory. The PPS was only designed as a method of describing everyday behavior (or behavioral tendencies), using uncomplicated language that the average person could understand. This system highlights the individual differences, identifies personal strengths, is easy to administer and score, and helps people understand one another.

The PPS questionnaire booklet contains twenty-four groups of descriptive words. To complete the profile, a person reads each set of four words and checks the one in each listing that is "most like me" and the word that is "least like me." There are no right or wrong answers, and the results are plotted on several graphs similar to figure 1. If a score is

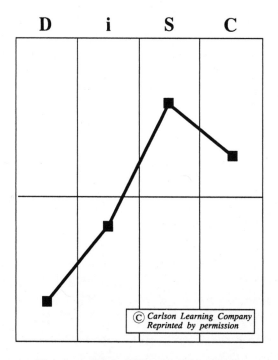

Fig. 1: A High "S" and "C" Profile

above the halfway point, or midline, that personality tends toward that particular behavior. If a score is below the midline, then the person is less likely to use that behavior.

When two scores are high simultaneously, they tend to modify each other. Detailed paragraphs in the PPS booklet explain the essential elements of various personality styles regarding needs, individual strengths, goals, typical responses under pressure, and so on.

The version of PPS called the Biblical Personal Profile yields results in terms of Bible characters.[2] Persons who complete the profile can learn whether they have personalities like David, Peter, Joshua, Moses, Sarah, Michal, Lydia, and so on. The workbooks make it a useful study course for church programs in personal development and strategies for meeting others' needs. For more information regarding the Biblical applications, refer to Appendix B.

For our purposes, I simply want to provide you with useful handles to help in understanding human behavior. As you read you will notice the traits I observed in Treva and you will find yourself in the descriptions.

In our society people are often divided into two broad categories, chiefs and Indians, leaders and followers, or those who make it happen and those who watch it happen. The PPS organizes people along these same lines and then divides each category into two subcategories: active and less active.

The groups differ in their approaches to life. The active people make it happen and act *toward* life. Since they usually have definite ideas about the desired results, they try to make things go their way. The less active people prefer to adapt or to adjust to situations rather than try to change things. They are concerned with how and why, and usually prefer to keep things as they are rather than push for change. They are the ones who watch it happen.

The active category consists of the "Dominance" and "influencing" behavioral tendencies, while "Steadiness" and "Compliance" are in the less active category. These are the four behavioral tendencies in the DiSC system. They are usually identified by their first letters, such as, "the 'D' tendency is to take charge," and so on. By way of explanation, when the PPS was first developed, the "i" was lowercased because of a printer's error. The profile's developers decided it added a certain distinction to the system and have kept the "i" as an unusual trademark.

DiSC System

To gain a general understanding of the DiSC System, we will look at each of the four dimensions and then examine specific highlights in each category.[3] People in the "D" dimension are characterized by dominance that appears as a thread through everything they do. When involved in a project, they want to be in charge because they have a clear picture of what should be accomplished and tend to push people into action leading to that goal. They shrug off questions about the right way to do things but pay close attention to suggestions that will speed up the project. They also have an inner confidence that they can make things work, and they are usually skilled at overcoming opposition. Business environments provide the opportunity for "D's" to exercise their abilities and make things happen.

Current businesspeople in the U.S. with the "D" style include Lee Iacocca, Donald Trump, and Ted Turner. In the Bible these characteristics may be seen in Joshua, Nehemiah, Paul, and Sarah.

People with the influencing or "i" tendencies also exhibit dominance in their behavior, but with more sensitivity than "D's." The "i" people need social approval, so they are careful of others' feelings, using verbal persuasion to influence others toward their point of view; a person's feelings have higher priority than actually completing the task. They tend to be impulsive, talkative, and emotional. Their style, characterized by verbal efforts to influence, often leads to occupations such as sales that require talking. Ronald Reagan and Hubert Humphrey are good examples in politics. Bible characters include Peter, King Saul, Rebekah, Abigail, and Barnabas.

People with the "S" characteristics are generally steady, dependable plodders who want to keep things the same. They would rather adapt than take charge of situations. Since they are interested in how and why things are done, they resist being pushed into action before they understand the reasons. At work they are usually reliable, productive workers. Steady dependability is their primary behavioral characteristic. They are not flamboyant and flashy, but they are the ones who get the job done.

Gerald Ford and George Bush are examples in politics, while Abraham, Jacob, Isaac, Hannah, and Dorcas are Bible characters with "S" characteristics.

People with the compliance or "C" tendencies also tend to go along with things (but only to a certain point). They ask *why* more than individuals with the other behavioral styles. Since they are most comfortable going by the book, they ask questions to learn what the rules are. Being quite sensitive they tend to be perfectionists to avoid doing anything that would bring criticism. They do not like surprises, so they want to keep up with what is happening around them. Although they like to hear that they are doing things correctly, they are often skeptical of compliments. Of the four behavioral categories, the "C's" are the most complicated and complex. They are calculating, analytical persons, and prefer to comply with their own standards. Jimmy Carter is a high "C," and Bible characters include Moses, Esther, and Luke.

As we look at Bible characters that illustrate these personality types, keep in mind that this model of human behavior has been developed in our twentieth-century culture and is being applied to people in Bible times who spoke a different language and had a different social system. Since we cannot personally evaluate these Bible characters, our conclusions may not be totally accurate. In spite of this, the system can be very useful in making Bible characters more human and understandable as we observe how God was able to use persons with widely varying personality traits, strengths, and weaknesses. We can feel encouraged as we observe characters with personalities similar to ours. Because women were valued differently in the Hebrew culture and did not play visible roles in their society, only a few women appear in this discussion.

High "D" Personality Traits

The Apostle Paul showed high "D" characteristics with a mixture of "C" traits. He seems to have been a confident, dominant person who also exhibited the "C" tendency to be precise and attentive to detail in seeing that people were living correctly. These traits served him well in his role as missionary and church planter, establishing new congregations in the face of fierce opposition and personal danger. His attention to detail and his confidence in pointing out errors to new congregations are evident throughout his epistles.

The "D" traits are also visible before his conversion. He was a leader among the Pharisees and had a high opinion of himself. In fact, he considered himself to be the Pharisee of the Pharisees, and even after his conversion, some people considered him arrogant. Paul was comfortable making changes, as can be seen by his aggressiveness in establishing new churches and pointing out their errors.

Nehemiah's life illustrates the goal-oriented nature of "D" personalities as he builds the wall around Jerusalem. His skill in organizing people and overcoming opposition to the construction plans is evident throughout the book that bears his name.

"D" personalities are unafraid of conflict, while "S" and "C" persons usually try to avoid it. Since making changes can result in resistance and conflict, the "D" personality is well equipped for this task, which is one of their valuable contributions. Nehemiah demonstrated these traits when he realized that the rich businessmen were taking such advantage of their fellow citizens that many families had to "sell their children or mortgage their fields" to survive. He took charge of the situation in an unflinching "D" fashion and confronted the exploiters.

> I was very angry when I heard this; so after thinking about it I spoke out against these rich government officials.
>
> "What is this you are doing?" I demanded. "How dare you demand a mortgage as a condition for helping another Israelite?"
>
> Then I called a public trial to deal with them.
>
> At the trial I shouted at them, "The rest of us are doing all we can to *help* our Jewish brothers who have returned from exile as slaves in distant lands, but you are forcing them right back into slavery again. . . .
>
> "What you are doing is very evil." (Nehemiah 5:2–9, TLB)

With the strength of his "D" personality, he backed the businessmen into a corner, and they promised that they would change their practices.

When some of the men married foreign wives who had such an influence on the family that the children could not speak the father's language, Nehemiah's anger again was stirred. "So I argued with these parents and cursed them and punched a few of them and knocked them around and pulled out their hair; and they vowed before God that they would not let their children intermarry with non-Jews" (Nehemiah 13:25, TLB). The books of Nehemiah and Joshua are very enlightening and interesting accounts of strong and confident "D" personalities at work.

Each personality dimension has a fear factor which is very important to understand because it plays a vital role in human behavior. Whenever the fear point is triggered in a person, hostility is aroused because that is the natural, human reaction when one feels threatened. However, each of the four behavioral styles has a different response to fear. When "D's" feel taken advantage of, the reaction is to go on the offensive. It is an I'll-get-you-before-you-get-me attitude. This is especially true if the "D" person is not a Christian under the Holy Spirit's controlling influence. Such a reaction is evident in Paul's earlier life (he was still Saul at this time). When he believed the Christians were becoming a threat to the Pharisees' traditions, he made specific arrangements to have them killed. Now don't get me wrong. I am not saying that "D's" become killers when frustrated, but they do become angry when their goals are blocked. On the positive side, once Paul became a committed Christian, he used his dominance and determination to deal with shipwrecks, physical abuse, and all sorts of problems as he worked to spread the gospel. "D's" have the ability to accomplish tasks and achieve results.

"D" personalities look for direct answers because they want to know what is going on and get to the heart of the matter. They become impatient when people spend time on details, which explains why "D's" often have trouble slowing down, while the "C" people are asking questions about the right ways to do things and want to discuss the situation in detail.

Sarah's life is an excellent example of a Spirit-controlled "D" woman. She used her determination in a positive way and was surprisingly patient with her husband, Abraham, who was an "S" type and had trouble facing conflict and making decisions, and often dragged his feet.

Some of her struggles remind me of a related problem that I have observed. "D" women often have trouble fitting into the typical evangelical church culture. I know of a woman who had learned to bend her "D" into an "i" style so she appears more social and friendly than goal-oriented and take-charge. In the church women are often expected to be "S" persons who are "submissive" to their husbands, and although they are expected to be loyal workers, they are not expected to direct programs (with the possible exception of such acceptable alternatives as children's Sunday school, junior church, or the nursery). When they do attempt to use their "D" confidence to accomplish tasks, they are often seen as "pushy" or "bossy."

At home the conflict can be even greater as opposites do sometimes attract each other, and "S" and "C" men marry "D" women. This creates a tremendous problem for those who adhere to the traditional interpretation of Ephesians 5:22 that wives should submit to their husbands. Submission is unnatural to the "D" personality, man or woman, and taking strong charge of things is unnatural for the "S" and "C" personalities in either sex. Consequently, we have a conflict when the "S" husband feels he should somehow overcome his natural tendencies in order to "be the head" of his "D" wife. If the wife, with great personal effort, manages to suppress her "D" tendencies and tries to fit the typical evangelical stereotype of an "S" wife, she may develop serious problems she does not understand, including depression and anger. She will be especially puzzled if she believes she is following scriptural guidelines, such as those in Ephesians, and so should have peace in her heart. The "S" and "C" husband will also feel stressed, because he will try to act in ways that do not suit him. The resulting marital conflict can be confusing and difficult to resolve, unless the partners learn to accept themselves and their natural personality styles as God-given and acceptable. Often just realizing the truth about their opposite personality styles will explain and relieve the tension so that an acceptable arrangement can be worked out regarding family issues, allowing each to contribute his or her strengths in a complementary fashion.

Too often the "D" woman concludes that there is something wrong with her since so many other women are content to assume task-oriented, helping roles as opposed to managing a job or a project at church. This is compounded when you realize that "S" and "C" types outnumber "D's" anyway, so a "D" woman is unlikely to find many similar women in her local church. Also, in our society, the "D" behavior of taking charge and getting it done (the macho type who climbs to the top) is encouraged in men, while the "S" and "C" men are seen by some as weak and wimpish. This is unfortunate, especially when it takes place in the church and when the traditional teachings put pressure on people rather than encouraging them to be their natural selves.

With these thoughts in mind, look again at Sarah. Her humanity as a "D" woman appeared when she became impatient waiting for God's promise of a child. In typical "D" style she decided to get the ball rolling. If she wasn't going to have a child, at least someone would, "So Sarai took her maid, an Egyptian girl named Hagar, and gave her to Abram to be his second wife. 'Since the LORD has given me no children,' Sarai said, 'you may sleep with my servant girl, and her children shall be mine'" (Genesis 16:2–3, TLB). Hagar triggered Sarai's fear of being taken advantage of when she became "proud and arrogant toward her mistress Sarai," probably because she was pregnant and Sarah was not. Sarah responded by blaming Abram, an "S" person who did not like conflict. He gave her permission "'to punish the girl as you see fit.'" Sarah beat her and Hagar ran from home (Genesis 16:6, TLB).

High "i" Personality Traits

Peter's life illustrates many high "i" characteristics. His emotionality and quickness to speak up are evident throughout the Gospels. Remember how he was often the first to answer when Christ asked a question, and almost as often seemed to put his foot in his mouth? Or how he impulsively jumped out of the boat and tried to walk on the water toward Jesus? He acted on the basis of his emotions rather than on logic or realistic appraisal of a situation. The "i" personality tends to act first and think later. After Pentecost God used Peter's quickness to positive advantage because Peter was able to take immediate advantage of unexpected opportunities for impromptu preaching. When the crowds were amazed to hear the apostles speaking in a variety of languages at Pentecost and some thought they were drunk, it was Peter who seized the moment and "shouted to the crowd, 'Listen, all of you, visitors and residents of Jerusalem alike! Some of you are saying these men are drunk!

It isn't true! It's much too early for that! No! What you see this morning was predicted by the prophet Joel'" (Acts 2:14–16, TLB). And he continued with a resounding sermon that resulted in three thousand people becoming Christians.

Another incident occurred when Peter and John entered the temple and ran into the lame beggar. After Peter had healed him, a crowd gathered to check out the excitement. Acts 3:12 clearly shows Peter's ability to use his quick verbal skills to take advantage of the situation. "Peter saw his opportunity and addressed the crowd, 'Men of Israel,' he said, 'what is so surprising about this?'" He delivered a stirring sermon on the spot.

Aaron in the Old Testament is a high "i" person, and God recognized his speaking ability. When God tried to recruit Moses to lead the Israelites out of Egypt, Moses was very reluctant to take on the job, which was consistent with his cautious "C" personality. After many reassurances God decided that he would have to bring in some help to complement Moses' technical abilities and low verbal skills. "Then the LORD became angry. 'All right,' he said, 'your brother Aaron is a good speaker. . . . So I will tell you what to tell him, and I will help both of you to speak well, and I will tell you what to do. He will be your spokesman to the people. And you will be as God to him, telling him what to say'" (Exodus 4:14–16, TLB). God knew that Moses would follow instructions because that was his strength, and Aaron could say what he was told to say because that was his gift.

The "i" people are fun to have around because they usually have a sense of humor, love people, are naturally optimistic, and help keep things from becoming dull. They love to be around people more than the other personality styles do, and if given a choice, they will choose social involvement over solitude. Their strengths are verbal abilities and social skills. A friend of mine, who is a typical high "i," enjoys people wherever he meets them. His "D" wife, who is goal-oriented and prefers to do her job without extra personal involvement, described her frequent frustration. "Whenever we even stop for gas at one of these places that also is a convenience store, I wait in the car while he goes inside to pay. Time passes, he doesn't come back, and I wonder what he's doing. I look around, and sure enough, there's Bill inside the store with a couple of people around him, people he doesn't even know, and they are all talking away. It's like he's always looking for a party."

They also tend to be disorganized and have trouble keeping track of details. They lose things, keep a sloppy room, and often show up late for events, usually because they became sidetracked talking to somebody. This can be especially annoying to an "S" or a "C" who is on time and doesn't understand why other people can't be as well.

For an "i," losing social approval is the motivating fear. Peter's fear of losing social approval is illustrated by his reaction to the two young girls in the courtyard who identified him as one of Jesus' men. He was concerned for what these servants thought, and the pressure mounted when a small crowd later echoed their observations about his identity. He used his verbal ability to talk his way out of the situation. "Peter began to curse and swear. 'I don't even know the man,' he said" (Matthew 26:74, TLB). This was a poor, impulsive act, especially considering that Peter had made a public pronouncement that he was ready to die with Jesus, but under pressure he actually backed down in front of two servant girls and a couple of strangers. Being concerned about social approval, he simply dug a deeper hole. Jesus exhibited His sensitivity to Peter's need by not confronting him directly about the denial. Instead He validated his faith in Him by commissioning him to ministry in front of the other disciples (cf. John 21:15–19).

Barnabas illustrates the optimism and social orientation of the high "i." When he and Paul had to make a decision about John Mark joining them on a second missionary trip, Paul was definite in saying no. He had been burned once by John Mark and did not want to take another chance. Barnabas, on the other hand, was interested in the young man and was more optimistic about people than Paul; he wanted John Mark to accompany them. He and Paul finally resolved their disagreement by parting ways, as John Mark traveled with Barnabas (Acts 15:36–41). While the "C" people usually can see what is wrong with a project even before it is started, the "i" person usually sees all of the reasons for going ahead with the project.

High "S" Personality Traits

Abraham's life illustrates many high "S" traits, although a serious Hebrew student may point out that the culture of Abraham's time encouraged such traits. In other words, families tended to stay together and maintain a security orientation. Nevertheless, we can learn from his life.

Abraham was a steady, home-loving person who had to think about things before he acted. When God asked him to move to Canaan, he only went part way, taking his father and Lot along, which illustrates his need for security and the importance that his family played for him. In spite of the difficulties he experienced, he remained loyal to God and open to His leading.

This patient persistence is also evident in Jacob's life when he was working for Laban to earn Rachel for his wife. When Laban tricked him by giving him Leah instead, he "raged at Laban" but agreed to work another seven years for Rachel (Genesis 29:25–28, TLB). A "D" person would not have agreed to work for seven years in the first place, and an "i" person would have tried to negotiate a better deal.

High "S" people have a great need for security, both physical and emotional, and losing it is their greatest fear. When "S" people feel threatened, they begin to withdraw into themselves, rather like a turtle when it senses danger. This does provide a certain protection, but it causes other problems because "S's" tend to avoid conflict so they will not risk their security. This means they tend to keep their opinions to themselves when something they do not like happens. They fear that a confrontation with someone may upset their security, and, as a result, they often keep too many of their feelings to themselves and build up internal frustration. Since part of forgiving and getting over hurts requires expression of feelings, "S's" tend to simmer longer inside because they don't like the conflict involved in telling someone about their hurt and anger.

When Abraham and his family moved to Egypt, he feared that Pharaoh would kill him in order to have Sarah, his attractive wife. To avoid the hassle and to save his life, he told Sarah to say that she was his sister. When his men began to have fights with Lot's men, Abraham went to Lot to talk it over. "'This fighting between our men has got to stop,' he said. 'We can't afford to let a rift develop between our clans. Close relatives such as we are must present a united front! I'll tell you what we'll do. Take your choice of any section of the land you want, and we will separate'" (Genesis 13:5–9, TLB).

His comments reveal his dislike for conflict and his commitment toward his family. Abraham resolved the conflict by letting Lot take his pick of the land, while he took the section that was left. This is a typical "S" response, holding back one's own desires while encouraging others to do what they want.

Since they fear losing their security, they like to keep things the same and not change any sooner than they have to, since change can jeopardize security. This is also part of their strength because it allows them to hang in there and keep plodding through thick and thin. True to this pattern, Abraham was slow to change, and this was his strength as he was a steady plodder who continued to move in the direction God wanted him to go.

High "C" Personality Traits

"C" people are perfectionists and set high standards for themselves and for others, but especially for themselves. When they do not meet their own standards or when an expectation is not met, they take it as a personal failure and become self-critical. Frequent letdowns can lead to discouragement or even depression. Remember how Jonah expected God to destroy Nineveh and was disappointed when God changed his mind? He sat outside the city and felt sorry for himself, wishing he could die (Jonah 4).

High "C" people are sensitive and intuitive, which means they quickly sense any rejection coming from other people and can see what is wrong with a situation or plan. They have a natural eye for detail and ask lots of questions, so they tend to irritate the "D" and "i" types who want to get on with the program. Moses is an excellent example of the high "C" personality. In Exodus 3 and 4, we see the encounter at the burning bush when God introduces Moses to the idea of going to Pharaoh on behalf of the Israelites. These verses contain an incredible amount of detail as God outlines His project to Moses to meet the "C" need for specific information. Notice how Moses kept backpedaling and asking questions that reflected his self-doubts. He was cautious about taking on such a challenge. Compare his cautious response to that of Peter who, as an "i," was ready to go even when he did not have the details. Or the way Joshua, a high "D", took over after Moses died and led the Israelites into Canaan.

When God finally saw that Moses was going to have trouble doing it on his own, he brought Aaron, Moses' brother, into the picture. "Is not Aaron the Levite your brother? I know that he can speak well. . . . So he shall be your spokesman to the people. And he himself shall be as a mouth for you, and you shall be to him as God" (Exodus 4:14, 16). Moses' personality style helped him handle God's assignment to be the writer and keeper of the Ten Commandments because by nature high "C's" are rule-oriented and like to do things correctly. God knew what he was doing when he picked Moses for the job of laying the legal and social foundations for the developing nation. He needed a person who was conscientious, loved detail, and followed directions without changing them to suit his own purposes.

Can you imagine an impulsive high "i" who needs social approval trying to set up a new government? In fact, this did happen while Moses was on the mountain meeting with God. Aaron was left to watch the people, and they talked him into making a golden calf and having a party (see Exodus 32).

High "C" people fear criticism, and this makes them cautious in personal relationships and reluctant to speak up because they typically do not like to draw attention to themselves. Since they can be easily hurt, they tend to maintain a certain distance from others. This sensitivity makes them extra vulnerable to comments, opinions, and criticisms from parents and church leaders. Since they want to be loved and cared about, their natural tendency is to try to perform and behave so perfectly that no criticism can be made. This attempted solution involves an unreachable goal, which brings additional frustration. In this way a negative cycle can start and continue.

High "C" persons are often subject to mood changes. Since they are acutely aware of how well they perform, and their performance affects how they feel about themselves, their high standards cause them to experience a drop in self-esteem when their standards are not met. When they begin a project, they can usually see the obstacles to be overcome, something that can be more discouraging than helpful. These "C" personalities are more prone to discouragement and depression than the other personality styles.

Comparing Personality Types

Now that we have reviewed the DiSC highlights, let's study the four behavioral dimensions in more detail. Table 1 displays the DiSC characteristics, comparing the personality dimensions according to twelve categories.[4]

To appreciate the rich differences between personality styles, read from left to right, starting with the category printed in italics. As you read the descriptions, you will begin to appreciate the complementary nature of the dimensions when they are combined into a patchwork of individual human qualities. In fact, some churches use the DiSC system to identify personal gifts within the church for ministry.

The Basis of Vulnerability

These brief descriptions indicate the differences between the active personalities who live in outward style and the less active ones who are oriented toward their inner worlds. The active people have an external focus and minimize attention to their own feelings, while the less active people have an internal focus and spend considerable time looking at their feelings. This has implications for the vulnerability of each type to situations and feedback from those around them. All children need security and consistency, but the high "S" and "C" types will be especially affected by emotionally unsafe situations. It is in their natures to take things seriously, feel things deeply, and to hang onto hurts longer than a "D" or an "i." They are more prone to struggle within themselves. The "S" and "C" people display a definite sensitivity that makes them vulnerable to hurt, a sensitivity made more acute by their natural inclination to keep emotions to themselves, letting them build up. Because they do

Table 1: DiSC Personality Characteristics

	Personality Types			
Categories	**"D"**	**"i"**	**"S"**	**"C"**
Greatest strength	Change-oriented	People-oriented	Loyal	Quality control
Other strengths	Takes charge Action-oriented Challenges Initiates Takes shortcuts Self-confident	Positive Enthusiastic Helpful Involved Persuasive Emotional	Worker Listener Patient Stable Slow to change Team person	Intuitive Detailed Controlled High standards Accurate Sensitive
Communication	Direct	Optimistic	Listener	Diplomatic
Decisions based on	Very few facts	Whether it sounds good	Trust in others	Information
Likes to be	Directly assertive	Socially outgoing	Predictably secure	Precisely correct
Prefers	To be in control	Involvement with people	Predictable structure	Procedures and order
Socially is	Blunt	Talkative, agreeable	Quiet	Distant
Desires an environment that has	Challenging activities	Unstructured activities	Kept status quo unless given reasons for change	No sudden or abrupt changes
Judges others by	Results	Flexibility	Consistency	Accuracy
Fears	Being taken advantage of	Loss of social approval	Loss of security	Criticism of one's performance
Greatest need	Personal attention Direct answers Step-by-step approach	Fun activities Social recognition Freedom from details	Security Agreeable environment	Exact expectations No surprises Personal support
Key word	Change	Social	Secure	Correct

not like the discomfort of negative emotions, either in themselves or others, they may try to avoid conflict as Abraham did or to perform perfectly within the rules as Moses or Esther.

On the other hand, "D" people speak their minds readily, as is evident in Paul, Nehemiah, and Sarah, so their frustrations are not going to build up internally. They take an active approach to life and keep moving, while the "S's" and "C's" hold back and wait for trouble to pass. The "i" types tend to handle things more on a surface level, without taking things too seriously. Although the "i" approach may appear frivolous to the serious-minded "S's" and "C's," this is their normal style and works well for them. Consequently, they tend to have fewer struggles.

The practical truths of these personal differences are evident to those who do counseling. The high "D" and "i" persons rarely come unless a spouse or some special life circumstances force them to come. Even then it is with reluctance because they typically believe that they do not need any help. An exception may occur when a "D" or "i" has strong "S" and "C" traits, also.

A "D" husband had been trying to be more accepting toward his "S" wife who had left him because she was sick of his domineering style and was hurt by his involvement with another woman. Although she had moved back into the house, she was having a hard time being affectionate and committed because, true to her "S" style, her trust did not return immediately. "I've about had it!" he exclaimed with consternation and anger in his voice during his one and only visit to see me. "I have said I'm sorry and haven't been with any other women for four years. I don't see why she can't forget it and go on from today. She has to make up her mind—either she wants me or she doesn't. What else is there to decide?" His attitude and perceptions were coming from a totally different direction from hers. He had no struggle and could not understand why her struggle continued.

So we see there are normal, natural differences among people, and certain personality styles are more apt to develop internal conflicts. This is not to say that someone who is a "D" or an "i" will not experience conflict. But both types take a more active approach in dealing with their conflicts and continue toward their goals in spite of the resistance. Their conflicts are usually external, whereas the "S" and "C" people have the turmoil inside. The importance of this difference will become clearer as we continue looking at the ACE issue, because the "S" and "C" persons are most likely to develop the typical ACE conflicts.

Returning to Treva's story (chapter 1), we can see that she exhibits many of the "C" characteristics in that she has an inborn sensitivity to the influences she has encountered in her life. The fact that her Christian father did not like women and thought they should be subservient to men left a lasting, painful impression on her. "He never did like me, and I never felt that he loved me." But did she fight back, express herself, or rebel against such treatment? No, she did not. She kept it all inside along with her resentment of the other teachings she heard at church about wearing her hair plain, brown stockings, and so on. Although she questioned what she observed and experienced, she kept all these thoughts in her heart because it would have been risky to raise any disagreement. If she had been born with a "D" or strong-willed personality, she would have fought back and given her father fits.

One high "D" woman who had grown up with the rules and restrictions of her Christian parents took a different approach. When her father told her to wash off her lipstick before she went to junior high school, she returned to the bathroom and left for school with a freshly scrubbed face. Since her personality did not feel the guilt or the fear of stepping over the rules as an "S" or "C" youngster would, she simply carried her makeup to school with her schoolbooks and added eye shadow to the lipstick after she was away from the house. With humor in her voice and a twinkle in her eye, she told me, "Whenever there was a rule, I figured it was there to be broken!" And she did, figuring that whatever consequences came, the fun she had was worth it. Since she kept the conflict from settling inside of her, she never had the doubts and struggles that Treva experienced.

In summary, remember that personality does make a difference in how people respond to life's experiences, and the sensitive "S" and "C" persons are more vulnerable to the dysfunctions described here than the "D" and "i" personalities.

4

TRAITS OF HEALTHY FAMILIES

There is an additional perspective that will aid in our study of dysfunctional Christian families and ACEs. Understanding the healthy family traits provides a backdrop for grasping the destructive dysfunctional family practices that we will examine later.

Delores Curran has done an excellent job of identifying fifteen basic traits that characterize a healthy, functional family. I have grouped her fifteen traits into three categories to make them easier to understand and apply.

The first category consists of basic values or beliefs that set the inner tone for the family. The second category describes the characteristics of interpersonal family relationships, and the last group explores broader family culture. Read through these traits, and you will realize that, in contrast to the skewed focus of the dysfunctional family, healthy families have a focus that emphasizes positive values, individual worth, and sharing.

Basic beliefs (spiritual values):

- provide a shared religious core
- teach a sense of right and wrong
- value service to others
- admit to problems and seek help for them

Interpersonal relationships:

- promote a sense of trust
- affirm and support all members
- foster communication and listening
- teach respect for others
- respect the privacy of one another

General family culture:

- balances interaction among members
- exhibits a sense of shared responsibility
- displays a sense of play and humor
- fosters family table time and conversation
- has a strong sense of family rituals and traditions[1]

Basic Beliefs

Shared Religious Core

A shared religious core is highly significant. It ranked tenth out of fifty-six possible family traits in Curran's survey, suggesting that religion is more valued in our culture than many people think. Other studies have found a correlation "between religion and success and happiness in all phases of individual life, not just family life. It's easy to see that a shared religious core can provide a base of common values and a sense of purpose in today's family."[2] Although Curran's survey suggests that any religious system helps strengthen the family, I believe true Christian concepts that emphasize individual worth in a spirit of acceptance and grace, along with faith in God, will provide the best foundation for the home. You can easily see how this contrasts with the home that uses scriptural principles to shame children into compliance.

The importance of having a shared faith underscores the need to have a balanced approach to Christian beliefs and practices in the home. The shared faith becomes the spring from which the essential family values flow, and family members can rally around their common faith in God as stresses and difficulties enter their lives. They can find mutual acceptance and support from one another as their faith provides a common resource of strength outside themselves.

Right and Wrong

Teaching a sense of right and wrong is a priority in healthy families. Of course, in Christian families, these principles are scriptural ones that can be used in everyday decision making. Honesty, respect for people and property, taking care of one's physical and mental health are aspects of personal decisions that need to be guided by values. Since the family serves as a teaching laboratory for growing children, if they do not learn these positive values at home, they are not going to be responsible members of society or the Christian community.

A local youth pastor recently told my wife and me over lunch about a session he had with his twelve-year-old son. "When I learned that he had a girlfriend, I decided it was time he and I had a talk." We expected him to relate a traditional birds-and-bees sort of experience, but Rick had a broader picture in mind. "I sat him down and told him that as a boy he has certain responsibilities if he is going to have a girlfriend." His instructions to his son were that he must respect a girl's feelings, treat her with consideration, show his caring perhaps by presenting a gift, and so on. Rick was actively teaching the basic concepts of relationship to his son. Having two daughters, I silently wondered whether some father out there was teaching his son his responsibilities toward my daughters?

Telling the truth, treating others fairly, and being conscientious in work are part of the concept of right and wrong children need to learn. These values provide an inner base of principles to guide them as they become responsible adults, and they can also be a part of their faith development. Paul Tournier writes regarding children, "To allow them to grow up in complete liberty and in ignorance of the moral and spiritual exigencies of life would, in fact, be to deprive them of the opportunity of the rebellion, or at least the crisis of adolescence, through which they must pass before finding a more personal faith."[3] Of course, it is important that parents agree on these principles and exhibit these values in their own lives to build a solid base of unity and consistency. Parental disagreement often brings tension and confusion; Mom may be teaching honesty while the children observe Dad lying to the neighbor or his boss.

Service to Others

The value of service to others is emphasized in a healthy family. Service has a place in most religions and certainly is part of Christianity. Essentially this means that people and meaningful relationships are more important than money and possessions. This attitude enables one to enjoy what one has and be content with one's life without going crazy trying to have the best and latest of everything. Families that can achieve such a state are able to empathize with others and get involved when people are hurting, without being critical or denying the reality of their pain. These families do not just talk about the needs around them, they do something about them. They put their talk into action in such areas as community and church groups, volunteer organizations, and scouting. They enjoy being hospitable and generous with their homes and their time and have a general openness toward people.

This trait characterized my mother as I was growing up. Our family farm was less than two miles from the little country church we attended, and my mother was always on the list to have missionaries, visiting evangelists, and neighbors over for Sunday dinner or to stay a few nights if necessary. A regular parade of people came through our house from all over the United States and many foreign countries. If the neighbor down the road needed a ride into town, my mother was ready to give it. If someone was sick, she would make pies and take them to the family.

Parents who value their families will even turn down promotions or more money if the move would damage the family. A number of years ago, the church I was attending asked a minister in another state to be our senior pastor. After thoughtful deliberation he turned down the offer, even though it would have been a positive move for him. One of his reasons was his respect for his daughter who wanted to finish her senior high school year with her friends. This minister exhibited the healthy trait of defining success in terms of quality family life rather than possessions, status symbols, and career moves.

Admitting to Problems and
Seeking Help for Them

Admitting to problems and seeking help for them is a trait of healthy families. One might think that healthy families do not have troubles, but they do just like anyone else, except they have a different way of looking at and dealing with them. Curran has noted that the healthy family "expects problems and considers them to be a normal part of family life."[4] This is basically a matter of honesty, a concept typically absent in the dysfunctional Christian home.

In his epistle, James writes, "When all kinds of trials and temptations crowd into your lives, my brothers, don't resent them as intruders, but welcome them as friends! Realize that they come to test your faith and to produce in you the quality of endurance" (1:2–3, PHILLIPS). I have often thought that people who can capture this attitude and live it will certainly have an easier time dealing with life's normal wear and tear. Incorporating this spiritual concept into the family's fabric of values will strengthen all family members.

In addition to expecting problems as a part of life, healthy families develop problem-solving techniques to meet the problems they encounter. They keep an open mind toward the situation and do not immediately give up in despair as they weigh a variety of options and determine what can be learned. As they struggle they support one another, knowing that in the last analysis a great deal of strength comes from family members being available to each other. An important key is the freedom to thoroughly discuss the issues, to air feelings about the problem they are facing. This openness can lead to new perceptions and ideas that individuals alone may not see.

Healthy Christian families are able to gain strength for present difficulties by looking back and seeing how past problems that seemed insurmountable were indeed handled. I keep a journal sporadically, and I am more apt to write in it when I am discouraged. So, reading through past pages, I realize what was troubling me and mentally picture how the problem was resolved. I often smile because in retrospect it was not such a big deal after all. Even when the situation confronting me today *really is* a big deal, I remind myself that today's big deal will look small in the future. God helped us work out the past situation, so He will also help with this one.

Interpersonal Relationships

Developing a Sense of Trust

Developing a sense of trust is one of the most vital and important aspects of a healthy family. Believing that others are dependable and trustworthy is the foundation upon which relationships are built. Here is the crux from which our lives develop in a healthy or unhealthy direction.

The psychologist Erik Erikson described the eight stages of psychosocial development. Though he wrote in the fifties, his work has held up through the years. He sees trust vs. mistrust as the primary stage of development during the first year of life. If we develop trust in those around us, we are able to move on to the next stage of growth, but if we learn mistrust, that will color our lives in all that follows.

"The infant's first social achievement then," Erikson says, "is his willingness to let the mother out of sight without undue anxiety or rage, because she has become an inner certainty as well as an outer predictability."[5] The infant realizes there is an outer consistency and predictability that coincide with his inner perception of reality, bringing a sense of sameness and consistency. Not only does the infant develop trust in others to meet his needs and a sense that others can trust him without being on guard (trustworthiness in self), he also begins to trust his own body and his capabilities to handle his urges.

Let me add that this idea of trust is not limited to one's early experiences in the family, as crucial as that is. Trust is a continuous thread that permeates the healthy family atmosphere, starting with the parents who are able to be open with one another as they remain committed and faithful to each other in all areas of their lives. Mom knows that when Dad leaves to go hunting that he actually is going hunting, and Dad knows she is having lunch with her friend. Their bond of trust and mutual support grows through the years.

The element of trust relates to the way members of healthy families keep their word. If Dad promises to take his son fishing but forgets to follow through or postpones the expedition at the last minute for shaky reasons, he is creating a relationship of mistrust. As parents follow through with their promises, they build a foundation of trust that what they say is reliable. This continues the initial pattern of meeting needs that Erikson identified as so important. Trust helps youngsters learn to delay gratification rather than instantly grabbing what they want. They know that their needs will be met and have no fear of being neglected or left out.

Trust is also evident in the family atmosphere. Sensitive feelings are not used as the point of jokes, and family members do not tell family secrets to outsiders. In a recent church discussion group, one mother described her family as a teasing family and noted that one of her daughters was quite sensitive and had difficulty handling the teasing. "We always tease in our family," she said with a certain pride, "and we usually do it until Shelley starts to cry, and then we stop and tell her that it is just our way and that is how we show that we love each other." As we made our responses, I asked, "Why not show her you love her by *not* teasing her!" Shelley could not trust because her feelings were not valued. Obviously, trust is closely related to the basic need for security.

Affirmation and Support

Affirmation and support for one another characterize the healthy family. This trait clearly builds on the foundation of trust and touches on the important need for significance. Everyone needs to feel worthwhile and loved, and since the family is the basic group that provides this foundation for growing lives, affirmation needs to be a definite part of the family system. The family is the primary source of our self-worth.

Affirming the people in a family involves saying positive things. "In the healthy family, the individual is affirmed for who he or she is and not for what he or she looks like, has, or does."[6] Individuals are accepted for who they are and do not have to work to earn love and approval. Such affirmation provides a sense of security and well-being in which family members know they can count on other family members to value and believe in them and encourage them in their endeavors. The healthy family functions as a place of refuge from the stresses of the world where loving and caring often are tied to performance. Home is a refueling stop for those who stop in for loving affirmation before returning to the fray of everyday living.

In Michigan we have cold winters and lots of snow, which makes winter driving hazardous. The highway department scatters tons of salt on the roads to melt the snow and ice. The salting does clear the roads, but it can turn the most expensive car into a rust bucket. The people who are extra fussy about their cars often buy a "winter beater" to drive in the salty slush while their well-polished car rests safe and dry in the garage. When spring comes the winter beaters can be seen sitting rather forlornly in suburban driveways, covered with salt residue, rusty holes scattered throughout the car's sheet metal. Sadly, they resemble family members who get no affirmation or support. The affirming and supporting family treats every member as proud car owners treat the cars they protect and pamper. They value them, treasure them, keep them clean, protect them from corrosion, and wash and polish them with loving care.

Support involves standing behind others, even when we do not agree with their point of view or particular actions. Because we value family members as individuals with unique differences, we can believe in them for better and for worse, even when we are not in agreement with them. Believing in them, we can support them as they work out their own ideas about themselves and life. Caring parents support their children in pursuing their interests even when it requires extra effort; the kids encourage their mother if she decides to go back to work or school to improve her skills. Their support can mean helping with the household chores, emptying the dishwasher, or making encouraging comments.

So many who seek my assistance need this support which has not been given. One Christian woman who is going through an unexpected and unwanted divorce said in agony, "I know divorce is wrong, and now my family will have nothing to do with me. My sister and I used to be real close, and she has not called me since last Christmas. I am not asking her to agree with me, but to just like me and believe in me. Is that asking too much?" In some families it is asking too much, but a healthy family is able to provide unconditional support to its members. They believe in the members of the family because they are all worthwhile. Support does not depend on believing the same way the others do. In giving such unconditional support, one can be a vehicle of God's grace within the family.

Communication and Listening

Communicating and listening are closely aligned with support. In fact, they are two methods of showing support for others. *Communication* is a common word that we often hear, but what is it? Communication is more than talking about facts and events; it includes expressing how one *feels* about the facts. Members of healthy families talk about the things they feel, their thoughts, and their inner emotions. This means they talk about themselves and get to know one another's dreams, hurts, fears, happiness, and so on. It is worth the effort to talk about what one feels, instead of trying to hold in emotions.

Before I had children of my own, I was playing on a softball team with other counselors and mental health professionals. The wife of a fellow psychologist watched the game as she supervised their two-year-old son. Somehow a conflict started between the little fellow and his mother. Understanding the principle of communication, the mother firmly insisted, "Now tell me. What are you angry about? I want to know what you are feeling. It is okay to be angry and talk about it." She was encouraging him to tell her what he was truly feeling — to communicate so she could hear him and understand.

The other side of communication is listening. People may talk in a family, but if no one listens to what is said, the words are lost and there is no benefit. To listen means to take seriously what is being said, even when one disagrees with the point of view. It is often easy to think that listening implies condoning what is being said. If what another person is talking about is wrong by our standards, we fear that listening will suggest our approval. But this does not need to be so.

It is particularly important for parents to listen to their children and ask questions that encourage them to talk about themselves, their ideas, and activities. Listening communicates caring and love to a child. In a healthy family, the father is willing to listen to his son, even when the football game is on TV or he is reading the paper. Taking time from one's own activity and interest communicates love and value.

Kirstin, a woman in her thirties who came for counseling, was beginning to deal with the painful realities of her childhood, and she described the rejection she experienced whenever her father refused to listen to her. "No matter what he was doing, he never took time to listen. I used to watch and try to figure out when he might have time for me, but he never did. And sometimes Mom would shove me away and say, 'Dad is busy. Leave him alone!'" The scars she bears will always be there as she attempts to reduce the pain of the wounds. But think of how meaningful it would have been if her dad *had* taken time to listen and affirm her when she talked to him! He could have had a powerful, positive influence on her life.

This give-and-take in family discussions has several benefits. Growing youngsters can practice identifying and expressing their feelings, which not only increases their self-confidence, but builds inner strength as they learn to think through situations and reach their own decisions. Learning to process emotions is a very important skill that will serve them well throughout their entire lives. Through these discussions, family members learn to respect one another's sensitivities and to take other viewpoints into consideration. They learn to respect individual differences and see the benefits of differing perspectives.

Respect for Others

Respect for others relates to the unique value of each individual. It has been touched upon in the discussion of affirmation. Differences are accepted and "individuality is prized in the healthy family"[7] because family members are expected to be unique people with their own particular interests. When I was growing up, my older brother was always fooling with electronic gadgets, radio transmitters, tape recorders, and the like, while I was the cowboy with boots and a spirited mare. My parents did not discourage our individual interests, and I, in turn, encourage my own daughters to do the same. Amanda is organized, saves things, and enjoys sports, especially gymnastics; Molly is the artist who enjoys drawing, flamingos, talking on the phone with friends, and sports.

Healthy families have positive outlooks on each member's uniqueness. Some families target a child from an early age with a negative label until it becomes part of the child's identity. I recall meeting a family where the youngest daughter was introduced as, "Susie—she's our mistake!" She must have been living with that negative label for years. A healthy family would not do that.

Individual opinions and attitudes are respected as part of individual differences. Everyone is not expected to enjoy camping, tennis, tomatoes, Bach, reading, sports, and so on. Each individual is encouraged and allowed to pursue individual interests. When some families go camping, for example, the one daughter may find a comfortable spot and read, while her sister hikes, Mom plays tennis, and Dad tries his luck at fishing. Individual interests are pursued and valued, but the family is able to spend their time together in support of one another. Individuals are not mocked or chastised for being different from everyone else.

This respect for individuals carries over into other areas. Family members respect people outside of the family and the property of others. One of my pet peeves is people throwing trash out of car windows, littering cans on the beach, and emptying ashtrays in parking lots. I wonder why their families haven't taught them respect for others and for the environment? Who do they think is going to clean up that mess?

Respect for Privacy

Respect for the privacy of others is a hallmark of the healthy family. Privacy means more than not snooping; it means allowing family members to be their own persons with individual tastes, preferences, and ways of behaving. Some practitioners use the term *boundaries* to describe the respecting of individuality. Some children are dominant by nature, while some are social and others are quiet and enjoy being by themselves. Such differences need to be respected. It is important to have one's private side in addition to one's role and function as a family member.

Families who accomplish this are able to look positively at the teenage years—as well as other developmental stages in their children—and appreciate the new events and experiences children bring as they grow older. "Parents from healthy families tend to look forward to the going-away years as part of the flow of family life, not so much a getting-rid-of-them sort of relief (although that is part of it), but more the won't-it-be-satisfying-to-know-them-as-adults kind of anticipation."[8]

As children mature and assume more responsibility, healthy parents move from a position of making all the rules to negotiating with their children and mutually working out rules. This transition from total parental authority to a mutual working together is a necessary part of normal family development.

Parents who recognize this and are comfortable with less authority as their children become teenagers are able to provide healthy home environments and to avoid many hassles common to dysfunctional families. The wise parent will pick battles carefully with teens and not make an issue of unimportant things. Things like hairstyles, clothing fads, and cluttered rooms are typical of adolescents and their developing need to demonstrate their independence. Wise parents overlook such things rather than put their relationship on the line over a passing issue. Privacy extends to children's diaries, letters, and personal effects. Privacy is respected because each person has worth and the right to his or her individual ideas. In the healthy family, children's feelings count. Parents do not snoop in their children's rooms or search their dresser drawers for information about their activities. Time alone is also permitted, and a closed door is respected. Parents knock if a child's door is closed and never just march in. Such a courtesy communicates the respect we are talking about here.

General Family Culture

Balance of Interaction

The family has a balance of interaction. The traits in this category relate to the general family atmosphere and ways of doing things. There is a sense of tradition, togetherness, equality, and balance in what takes place. The focus is on meeting everyone's needs and one's willingness to sacrifice, if necessary, when a person needs extra support during trouble.

In the healthy family, "there is a balance of time spent with individuals so that they can learn to know, appreciate, and love one another.

It's awfully hard to love someone you don't know. . . ."9 Healthy families use deliberate efforts to make sure that activities and work—the most likely culprits—do not take up so much time that they do not see each other. It is easy for some families to become so involved in good activities, including church, that they do not have sufficient time together.

In healthy families there are strong relations between the parents who appreciate and support each other without domination or belittling. The parents do not allow family members to develop sides or coalitions within the family. Some families divide up according to sex: The girls are Mom's and the boys are Dad's. Sometimes the children organize against the parents and may even organize against each other. These patterns may also occur when a married person has not detached from parents and turns to them for advice and support.

Sense of Shared Responsibility

A sense of shared responsibility can be a difficult task for many parents, particularly those who receive a great deal of satisfaction in doing things for their children. It is easy for such parents to do too much in an attempt to be over-loving and to save their children from pain. Sometimes this includes bailing children out so they do not have to face the consequences of their actions. Although there are times when it is appropriate for Jimmy's mother to take his lunch to school if he forgets it, a regular pattern of this does not teach Jimmy to be responsible for his own affairs. In the healthy family, parents teach responsibility to the children as they become older. They "support their children without removing obstacles from their lives that foster growth."10

Being responsible means more than doing chores or learning to have an orderly room. Responsibility includes values such as helping others, putting forth effort to develop harmony, anticipating the consequences of actions, and learning to think for oneself. Parents in healthy families know that they need to teach their children how to make decisions and analyze situations because they as parents are unable to guide them all their lives. If the youngsters can accept the responsibility of thinking clearly and learning how to make decisions based on their principles, then they are prepared to deal with their future even though they do not know what they will face.

Sense of Play and Humor

A sense of play and humor has a large role for the healthy family which realizes that play is as important as work and makes sure that time is found for enjoyable activity together. Some families believe that work must be completed first, but those that hold to this often do not have time for play because the work is always there. Healthy families make sure they plan a picnic, a trip to the beach, fishing, or to the stock car races. This fortunate type of family feels no guilt at letting the work slide while they have fun. Members are able to give themselves permission to sit back and enjoy one another and whatever activity they choose. They are able to have fun without spending lots of money and have a sense of humor as they laugh and play together. Humor is used constructively as people learn to laugh with each other and not at each other. Hurtful teasing is discouraged in families that respect each other.

When families have fun together, the members associate those pleasant times with positive feelings and memories, rather than the bad feelings developed in those whose families argue and fight whenever they are together. Bring up the idea of a family gathering, and the person from the healthy family is enthusiastic.

I grew up with three brothers on a farm, and one of the activities we started as kids has continued with us into adulthood. My dad bought an eight-millimeter movie camera when I was about twelve, and my oldest brother, Dale, who always liked electronic gadgets, had the idea of making home movies. Over the years, we acted out a number of stories on silent film. One involved the doghouse catching on fire and the efforts of firemen to extinguish the blaze. Another featured our windmill as a launching platform for our space rocket. And we also made a Western starring my friend and me along with our horses. Even as adults we have a great time when we crank out the old films. Now that video is available, we have made several movies incorporating our children into the cast.

Table Time and Conversation

Healthy families foster table time and conversation. This is usually the time when everyone is together and can put communication and listening into practice. The children can report on the day's activities and parents can discuss theirs. Parents have a chance to listen to their children, gain insight into their thinking, and encourage them in their efforts. An atmosphere of openness at the table helps set the tone for the family in all its activities. This is obviously a healthier situation than the one where discussion is discouraged or where mealtimes are characterized by arguing and fighting.

It is becoming harder to arrange time for leisurely meals with everyone present. More parents are working, the kids are busy with school activities, and schedules are more complicated to coordinate. It is harder to find a time when all family members are home together. The availability of fast food and the tendency to eat quickly and rush ahead are hard to resist. The healthy family guards against this trend and will also turn off the TV at mealtime so it does not interfere with family conversation.

Rituals and Traditions

Rituals and traditions develop naturally and easily in families that have a shared sense of belonging and history. The home is not simply a place to eat and sleep but should provide a larger sense of kinship and support as a basis for one's indentity. Family members from such a home value its legends and colorful characters. Family stories are passed from one generation to the next and provide a sense of continuity. My wife's family cherishes the story of how her great-grandfather lost his fishing business in the Netherlands when the government built new dykes and reclaimed a portion of the land from the sea. He came to Michigan and had to take a factory job to support his family. My family tells stories about how hard it was to communicate with great-grandma who became deaf at eighteen after she had scarlet fever. My folks tell how they feared for my safety because I climbed on everything, so they removed the lower section of the ladder on our windmill, and how my two younger brothers and a friend hauled an abandoned manure spreader to the high school driveway one Halloween night. Such stories become part of the family's history and sense of identity, making it unique and different from other families.

Most families have one person who takes the lead in promoting the family get-togethers. Some families like to gather at the old home place where they grew up. Others may have to use newer family homes as their focal point, but special traditions are begun and continued no matter where the family meets.

My wife brought a birthday tradition from her family that we have continued with our children. Whoever has the birthday chooses the restaurant for a special dinner, which is held in addition to cake, ice cream, gifts, and a party with grandma and grandpa. Delores Curran suggests several little ceremonies and customs that can become traditions:

- Wednesday is leftover night
- Youngest child always blows out the candles
- Leave notes on the refrigerator
- Dad gives kids "dutch rubs" on the heads when he says goodnight
- Mom hides the family valentines[11]

I am sure you can identify a number of traditions in your own family that have special meaning to you.

Summary

It is easy to see how a home atmosphere which includes a number of these qualities we have examined (no home is likely to have them all) will provide an environment of emotional warm sunshine that encourages family members to grow. Children who are affirmed, listened to, respected, valued, and protected are going to feel safe and free to express themselves as they develop. Their basic needs for significance and security are met through their homes, and they will have built solid foundations of self-worth that will carry them throughout their lives. Keep these thoughts about the healthy family in the back of your mind as we now consider the dysfunctional family.

PART TWO

THE FOUNDATION FOR "HOLY" vs. WHOLLY

5

CONTROL OR GRACE

D uring my middle twenties as I was working with Youth for Christ (YFC) in Detroit and my inner world was beginning to crumble, I somehow learned about Francis Schaeffer. A local person who had audio-tapes of his talks loaned me several, and I began listening to them in an attempt to gain insight into my struggles. One evening I took my tape recorder to the YFC office and listened to "Practicing the Reality of the Objective Existence of God." As I listened I tried to personalize what he was saying, to heed his encouragement to take what I believed and decide systematically, point-by-point whether my faith was something I could act upon as true. He gave as an example actually believing and practicing the fact that one's sins are forgiven.

The Unlovable Self

To apply Schaeffer's strategy to my own life and struggles, I started with the most basic point: Does God exist? Yes, I could believe and practice that. The next basic truth that came to mind was God's love for the world, and more specifically, for me. Pondering this, I was suddenly stunned to realize that I was unable to move past point two. I could believe God exists, but I could see no way to practice or feel God's love for me. In numb fear I slowly knelt beside a chair in the YFC office and admitted to God the dread truth that had just become apparent to me. I could believe that I was afraid of God—no problem. But the matter of His love was another story.

This reality has haunted me for years, and it has been difficult to shake. In fact, as I review my life, I realize the first time I really *felt* loved by another person was when I met my future wife. Slowly, through the years, I have begun to accept that the people who really loved me could care about me just for myself, without my having to do something special to earn it. But understanding and dealing with God's love has been a different matter.

Through my years of doing therapy, I have listened to many struggling Christians who feel guilty and unlovable, convinced that they must do something to bring self-worth into their lives and earn love. In fact, regardless of a person's other emotional or behavioral symptoms, the feeling of unlovableness is almost always there.

This is puzzling because as Christians we learn that we are created in God's own image, that Christ loved us so much He was willing to die for us, and that as believers we are the children of God. If we truly believe this, why do so many Christians feel unlovable? The Bible talks about God's grace, God's unconditional acceptance of us in our sinfulness, yet the feelings of unlovableness continue for many of us. Where is grace when we need it? This absence of grace is conspicuous in the lives of many ACEs I counsel.

My own life has followed a similar path. The Biblical concept of grace is one I have heard about from my earliest years, when my family and I regularly attended the rural holiness church two miles from our Indiana farm, but grace itself was something I did not feel or understand. Our church's emphasis was on fear. The hellfire sermons made God's wrath and anger real and believable—but grace? That was a different matter; it was familiar in name only. David Seamands makes a keen observation on this phenomenon which is the second factor in understanding ACEs.

> Many years ago I was driven to the conclusion that the two major causes of emotional problems among evangelical Christians are these: the failure to understand, receive, and live out God's unconditional grace and forgiveness; and the failure to give out that unconditional love, forgiveness, and grace to other people. . . . We read, we hear, we

believe a good theology of grace. But that's not how we live. We believe grace in our heads but not in our gut-level feelings or in our relationships. . . . But it's all on a head level. The good news of the Gospel of grace has not penetrated the level of our emotions.[1]

Why is this so? Why is the gut-level experience of grace missing when it is such a central element of the Bible's message? What is happening in the church or within Christians to keep grace from coming through? If grace is not experienced, what is taking its place? Questions such as these have puzzled me for years in regard to other people and my own life.

It is a fact that many churches promote dislike of self as a desirable spiritual trait, suggesting that to think of oneself as a worthwhile person is sinful and self-centered. Such thinking has been enshrined for centuries in Christian literature.

Carter and Narramore touch on this as they discuss the integration of psychology and Scripture, and point to the distinction between Biblical *fact* and Biblical *interpretation*. They assert that large portions of the evangelical church have been influenced by the Keswick Movement, which taught a morbid form of self-denial and debasement as part of a deeper spiritual life. They observe that such teaching can stir neurotic feelings of guilt and self-devaluation and offer this quote from Hession as an example of this negative teaching.

Those who have been in tropical lands tell us that there is a big difference between a snake and a worm when you attempt to strike at them. The snake rears itself up and hisses and tries to strike back—a true picture of self. But a worm offers no resistance; it allows you to do what you like with it, kick it or squash it under your heel—a picture of true brokenness. Jesus was willing to become just that for us—a worm and no man. And he died so, because that is what he saw us to be, worms having forfeited all rights by our sin, except to deserve hell. And he now calls us to take our rightful place as worms for him and with him.[2]

Can we seriously believe that Jesus became "a worm and no man" for us and that we are supposed to "take our rightful place as worms for him and with him"? When Philippians 2:5–7 states that Christ chose to take the form of a servant even though He was God, this is not wormlike action. The very notion is degrading and hardly fits the larger Christian message.

This problem of negative Christian teaching about the self is also tackled by Robert H. Schuller, who touches on this worm theology being promoted by Hession.

> One reason many Christians have behaved so badly in the past two thousand years is because we have been taught from infancy to adulthood "how sinful" and "how worthless" we are. The self-image will always incarnate itself in action. A negative diagnosis will become a self-fulfilling prophecy. The most difficult task for the church to learn is how to deal honestly with the subject of "negativity," "sin," and "evil" without doing the cause of redemption more harm than good.[3]

Schuller is convinced that the major component of our sinful nature is a negative sense of self-esteem that results in lack of trust and shame.[4] From his perspective, this deep feeling of unlovableness is a part of our sinful human condition, and the church too often promotes this feeling of shame by its manner of teaching applied Christianity.

Control or Redemption?

C. FitzSimons Allison is another Christian writer whose observations illuminate this subject. He also believes that the church often misrepresents grace, and he provides a sensible framework for understanding the relation of grace and self.

Allison acknowledges that the role of Christianity in society has been that of catalyst for social change and positive improvements, but he also notes a more significant negative side.

> However, the vast preponderance of the Christian role was seen to be, overwhelmingly, that of control rather than redemption. . . . A religion of nagging—of exhorting and rebuking, of law and control, of condemnation and fussing-at—is a big part of the picture presented as Christianity, not merely by popular distortions but within the very citadels of scholarly learning. . . . Christianity tends in each epoch to be "domesticated" and acclimated to the contemporary culture, subsumed under the establishment's need for controls, and seduced by the powers of civilization to be its servant.[5]

The phrase that captured my attention and placed the issue of grace in perspective is that "the vast preponderance of the Christian role was seen to be, overwhelmingly, that of control rather than redemption." In psychological terms, he believes Christianity has served primarily as superego, not only for individuals, but for society as well, while keeping the real power of grace hidden behind the control system.

Seeing the two truths of redemption (or grace) and control posed as opposites or choices within the context of Christianity explained what had happened in my life and in the lives of other countless Christians I had observed. My parents and my church had emphasized control, not grace, in their relationships with me as I was growing up. As I examined the use of fear, guilt, and shame which I had experienced, it all began to fit together in new ways. My primary spiritual experiences growing up were exercises in control with little exposure to grace. In fact, my mother's well-intentioned efforts to make sure that I grew up as a Christian ultimately caused me a great deal of trouble. She regularly used shame to control my behavior and even called upon Jesus to make me feel guilty. One of her favorite phrases was, "What would Jesus say if He saw you do that?" Or she would intone with her best guilt-inducing voice,"Aren't you ashamed? Aren't you just so ashamed?" She was more concerned with controlling me than encouraging me. My duty was to live up to her expectations, not my own.

As I was working out my own feelings, I realized that these early experiences had planted deep and fearful feelings toward Jesus, who was used to shatter my self-worth; the same Jesus who had died to save me was called on to put me to shame. And I was supposed to feel close to Him? If I could not feel that my mother cared for me just for myself, how could I possibly feel that God cared?

With Allison's comments in mind, I began to observe the Christian practices around me and the struggles that were brought to my office by frustrated Christians. My observations confirmed the truth of Seamands' statement that Christians do not live out grace at the gut level, Allison's belief that control is emphasized more than redemption, and Schuller's belief that shame and unworthiness are included at the base of our low self-esteem.

Many of the Christians with whom I work have spent years denying emotions, hiding their true feelings, and trying to control what they sense as their inner badness so it will not pop out unexpectedly and cause others, and God, to reject them. This inner feeling of badness surfaces in various forms and with various names. "If people really knew me, they wouldn't like me." "I have to keep these walls up so people don't see who I really am." "What I have done is too bad for God to forgive." "I'm just so bad inside. I must have deserved what my father did to me. Why else would someone who loved me do that to me?" And unfortunately the church helps to perpetuate this destructive thinking.

A Moral or Relationship Problem

There is a related emphasis of evangelical thinking regarding the Fall that serves as the lynchpin on the side of control instead of grace. Christians generally believe Adam's sin created a moral problem (meaning human nature is partly bad or self-centered) as well as a relationship problem (meaning human beings are out of relationship with God, themselves, and others). The practical implications of emphasizing one over the other of these points are significant in terms of everyday Christian practice.

There is no doubt that people commit evil actions, but what is the answer to the human dilemma? Do we emphasize an inherently bad inner self that is immoral and "wormlike" and tell people how bad they are, as Schuller describes? Or do we emphasize healing the broken relationships with God, self, and other people?

If we emphasize the moral problem, we will want to use control to contain the evil, which places Christianity in the control position Allison has described. On the other hand, if we believe people's self-centeredness is increased *as the result* of a relationship problem, then we will see grace as the remedy for healing the relationship.

The moral emphasis often comes up in sermons when the minister wants to drive home the point that evil is rampant in humanity. "We are born in sin," the pastor insists. "It is born right in us. The other day my three-year-old son lied and said he had not hit his sister when I saw him do it. Nobody had to teach him to lie. It is in him. And at the age of three, his sinful nature is showing itself."

Parents who hear this teaching emphasis and accept it are going to view their children with the same type of attitude. They are going to emphasize control to stop the emergence of this inevitable evil that lurks inside their children. They will approach their children out of this fear and try to extinguish any signs of budding "sinful" behavior. This explains why many parents will go to any lengths using fear, guilt, shame, and manipulation with Scripture to keep their children in line. By this standard of thinking, self-esteem and personal security are expendable commodities that pale by comparison with the potential evil that children may commit. Containing the immoral potential is the only acceptable spiritual goal, and there is little room or need for grace.

The relationship view provides an entirely different perspective. Adam was built with a perfect design to live in a perfect world in relationship with God. Through his sin, this perfect relationship was broken and was unrepairable by Adam. This also resulted in personal shame and fearfulness for Adam and Eve (Genesis 2:25; 3:7–10). The broken relationship between God and people is the theme of all Scripture. The Bible is the story of God reaching out to people as He attempts to restore the broken relationship.

Because people are not in right relationship with God, they are not in a correct relationship with themselves or other people, either. This causes them to mistreat others since the primary relationship issues concern relationships to God, self, and others. An examination of the Ten Commandments reveals that they are all relationship issues, first with God, and second with others. Jesus also emphasized this point when He cited the greatest commandment which involves relationships with God, ourselves, and others: "'You shall love the Lord your God with all your heart, with all your soul, and with all your mind.' This is the first and great commandment. And the second is like it: 'You shall love your neighbor as yourself.' On these two commandments hang all the Law and the Prophets" (Matthew 22:37–40).

Grace heals the broken relationships with God and declares that we are whole and acceptable people. This fact, when experienced at a gut level, builds an inner self-worth and helps us want to love others because we are loved and declared acceptable in spite of our imperfections. When we are in correct relationship with God through grace, He is able to work with us on our self-centeredness which leads us toward wholeness, as we will discuss in part 5. To help you understand the contrast between the control emphasis and grace, you may want to read Appendix C, an excellent treatise on grace, before continuing.

Sin: The Master-List

The Christian focus on control instead of grace sets the stage for pathological actions. Personal openness and growth are actively discouraged in a controlling, shaming atmosphere. Compliance and submission are rewarded rather than creative ideas and personal development.

On the political level, this concept produces totalitarian governments that jail independent thinkers who do not comply with the leaders' pronouncements. Those in control have a list of rules that spell out acceptable behavior. Within this framework behavior is not determined to be acceptable by its own merit, but by the degree with which it complies with the stated goals of the leaders. Not obeying the delineated rules can result in extremely negative consequences. Should a similar pattern be followed in the Christian community?

The church in general has emphasized control of conduct more than redemption. Allison cites the traditional devotional materials that have been written since the middle of the seventeenth century as evidence that most of them emphasize a version of Christianity similar to that of Jeremy Taylor, a popular devotional writer of the era. "Christianity was for Jeremy Taylor a promise of pardon, acceptance, and forgiveness *on condition that* the person fulfill the demands of the law," writes Allison, ". . . this misrepresentation of Christianity has rarely been criticized since then." Such evidence leads Allison to the view that Christianity has been misrepresented as "a religion of control and condemnation."[6]

Now I am not suggesting that control is all bad. Obviously we need to have control in our personal lives and in our society in order to live normal, healthy, peaceful lives. But the lack of balance in certain segments of Christianity has pushed grace aside, and this imbalance has had destructive results.

When control is the primary Christian emphasis, the following scenario is likely: The unacceptable behaviors are defined, a motivational
system of fear and guilt is established to ensure compliance, appropriate
rewards and punishments are set up as reinforcers, and this entire structure is justified by Scripture.

Sin, unacceptable behavior in the evangelical church, is generally
defined in two ways. First, there is a specific master-list of sins, but
there is also a second "list" of vague and implied sins, generally including anything that is "selfish." The second category seems to be a catch-
all for anything not specifically on the master-list. The behaviors to
avoid are usually related to sin being operationally defined as moral
badness. I'm referring to the everyday definition and not the official
theological statements in the major confessions.

The master-list plays a crucial role in the control system and causes
all sorts of confusion for Christians who are told that they are saved by
grace through faith but then must, for some reason, keep the rules to
maintain their standing with God. Allison cites one reason for this conflicting theological practice.

> Indeed, Roman Catholicism in the sixteenth century and most of An-
> glicanism and English-speaking Protestantism in the seventeenth cen-
> tury made a tragic mistake, with sinister pastoral results, by essentially
> defining sin as being only conscious and deliberate, in spite of the
> Biblical, patristic, and medieval traditions to the contrary. This pushed
> the root problems of the human heart underground and left the confes-
> sional and pulpit dealing with the symptoms of sins, theologically iso-
> lated from their deeper, demonic, and often unconscious roots. The
> expectation, that a man's will can be changed by exhortations to con-
> trol, was the essence of Pelagius's heresy, yet it has become a com-
> monplace of traditional and establishment Christianity.[7]

Even though I grew up in northern Indiana thousands of miles from
seventeenth-century Protestantism, I can see the truth of Allison's observation in my holiness church's theology. There the master-list included
smoking or chewing tobacco, drinking alcohol, dancing, bowling, movies, cards, and, of course, such things as lying, stealing, and not going to
church. Other sins included wearing jewelry, open-toed shoes, and short
hair for women, flashy clothes, and so on. Television was just starting to

get off the ground, and it was often referred to as a tool of hell. The emphasis was very much on specific behaviors to avoid.

Although master-lists have many points in common, they vary according to denomination and geographic location. A Lutheran fellow from St. Louis moved to a conservative Dutch area in west Michigan. Accustomed to mowing his yard on Sunday, he innocently broke the Sunday morning silence with his noisy lawnmower. After stern looks and remarks from his neighbors, he gradually began to see the differences between their styles of Sunday observance and realized he was violating the community's master-list. He stopped mowing on Sunday.

After considerable debate, two Christian Dutch families, who had cottages adjacent to each other on a lake, resolved the problem of what each family could do on Sunday. One family decided they could sit in their lawn chairs if they only faced the lake but did not go into the water. The other family decided they could also sit outside, but they had to have their backs to the water.

In some families the definition of sin becomes so narrow that one's personal nature is stifled, and a sense of guilt is strengthened as unrealistic goals are set for "holy" living. A woman, who had grown up as a minister's daughter, told me that as part of her early Christian training her godly grandmother had repeatedly drilled into her the verse in James, "Therefore, to him who knows to do good and does not do it, to him it is sin" (4:17). This verse had a deep effect and influenced her life from the time she was a youngster. For example, there were occasions when walking through the house she was tempted to simply ignore some lint on the carpet. As she approached the lint, however, this admonition entered her mind and threw her into conflict. She knew picking up the lint would be the right thing to do, and, therefore, to just walk past without picking it up would be sin. However, as she searched her heart, she did not feel like picking it up, and this trivial matter became a choice between obedience and sin—a heavy and unnecessary choice for a young child. Another woman in her thirties told me that she still feels guilty using scissors on Sunday mornings, even to trim a loose thread from her daughter's dress. Until recently, if she had to use scissors on Sunday, she selected a pair with plastic-wrapped handles as insulation for her hand from the lightning she expected. Although she knew rationally that this was not necessary, she did it anyway.

It is tempting to narrate the humorous things Christians sometimes do as they attempt to keep within the bounds of the list but still do what they really want to do. Is it okay to get the Sunday paper if it is delivered Saturday before midnight? Should we put the TV antenna in the attic so others do not know we have it? May we eat out on Sunday if it is far enough away from home so no acquaintances can see us and be offended as the weaker brothers?

In churches like the one in which I grew up, a person could lose salvation by not attending to the rules. Obviously, making a wrong move could mean eternal damnation, something no sensible-minded person would want to risk. I have friends from other churches that believe in eternal security who worry that they may not have been saved in the first place, so their security is no more certain than that of their Arminian friends.

Consequences of Christianity as Control

This emphasis on control can have devastating effects on those who have become Christians as adults and are entering the church community for the first time. They come into the church on the refreshing wings of grace only to be hit with the master-list of things they must do or not do. Many first-generation Christians who have run into this have developed a bewildering sense of frustration in their new Christian lives, and a negative process then begins to develop.

This process can have one of several outcomes. First, there are some individuals who become very good at following the list of proscribed behaviors. They become the expert, professional Christians who have all of the answers, say all of the right things, and begin to feel critical toward those who are less successful in keeping within the rules. They typically are not very forgiving toward others who obviously (at least in their view) have the greater sin.

A young, college-age Christian couple who had been dating for several months contacted me after reading my earlier book. According to the DiSC criteria, the young man was a definite "C" who had very high ideals and standards, and the young woman seemed to be a more easy-going "S" with some mild "D" traits. Tentatively and with some apprehension and nervousness, they began relating their story to me. Both had been raised in Christian homes, although she had grown up in a military family that had moved around the world. Her view of life was larger than her boyfriend's, and her personal experiences had been much broader since he had grown up in a small community. Everything in their relationship seemed fine except for one problem that they had not been able to overcome.

With some encouragement, they uncomfortably admitted what that problem was (actually, it was his problem, although it affected her). He had grown up so controlled in his behavior and attitudes that he committed almost no "sins" on the master-list and so thought of himself as a "holy" person. He had no sense of either sin or forgiveness in his life. The issue that caused endless conflict was the fact that she had been sexually involved with a high school boyfriend, but had sought and received God's forgiveness and had abstained from further promiscuous activity. Her prior experience interfered with his goal to enter married life with a virgin girl and his dream of sharing all new experiences together for the first time. He could forget about her actions for a short time, but when it entered his mind, he became depressed and mildly distraught. He had learned to be such a "holy" Christian by meticulously following the rules that he never developed a sense of personal grace for himself or for others at a gut level. He prided himself on his spiritual achievements and looked with disdain on those whose lives were less than perfect.

Another problem can develop for those who are unable to master the list. "S" and "C" types of personality are especially vulnerable to the consequences of failure to keep the rules and live up to the stated expectations. They are apt to feel guilt and shame for being such sinful people and unworthy Christians. The way they deal with these heavy, negative feelings is to try harder to keep the rules and therefore "be good." But no one is perfect, so the try-harder routine results in failure, which leads to more guilt and low self-esteem. This cycle of failure resembles the circular trap characteristic of other compulsive disorders involving food, drugs, alcohol, etc.

I met Smitty, who was a cement finisher, while working on construction jobs during the summers to pay my way through college. As the summer progressed, I frequently helped Smitty pour concrete, and I began to learn more about him as I listened during breaks and lunch. He was in his mid-thirties, married, and had two children. By my "holiness" standards, he was basically a moral fellow. He did not get drunk, run around on his wife, or anything like that. At the worst he would make some suggestive remarks about women who passed by, and he sometimes ordered a little more concrete than the job actually required so he could take the leftover quantity home for another job he was doing on his own time.

He knew I planned to work with Youth for Christ after college, and we had some discussions about Christianity, but they had little impact on him. A year or so later when I was with YFC in Detroit, Smitty's son was killed in a tragic car accident. Smitty was plunged into turmoil. He became concerned about salvation, and he feared for his son's eternal destiny since he had not been a professing Christian. I had a friend who worked for the same construction company, and he influenced Smitty to attend the rural church where I had grown up. As a result of his son's death and the witness of my friend, Smitty went forward one Sunday and gave his heart to the Lord.

My mother, who had been present at the service, wrote to me about Smitty's conversion. However, she added an ominous comment, "Now that Smitty is a Christian, the next thing we have to do is get him to quit chewing tobacco!" Her remark sent a cold feeling through me. I had worked with Smitty, and I knew how stressed he became when we were on a big pour. As the cement truck rumbled up, he would carefully pack his cheek and spit with obvious satisfaction as he troweled. Tobacco chewing was a ritual to him, and the nicotine calmed his nerves as he worked feverishly to stay ahead of the drying concrete.

Subsequent letters from my mom described the continuing efforts to persuade Smitty to part with his tobacco. Sometimes they used outright verbal pressure; and they even suggested that he substitute gum for his tobacco. But Smitty said, "It just isn't the same!" Even though there seemed to be a little bit of sympathy for his struggle, the seriousness of his sin outweighed any inclination for empathy the church folks might have had. Finally, my mother wrote that victory had been achieved; Smitty had given up tobacco. *At what price,* I wondered silently. Not long afterward, my mother reported that Smitty had slacked off in attendance and eventually stopped coming altogether.

The little rural church had mounted a campaign to control Smitty's behavior, to bring him in line so he could lead a "holy" life by its standards. In the process it overlooked the basic concept of grace that God loved Smitty for Smitty, and he didn't have to prove anything or earn continued grace by performing to the control tune. Grace would have freed him by affirming him, and God could have spoken to him about the tobacco if it were a major problem. The church lost Smitty through its own efforts to control and make him "holy."

If people have definite needs for security and significance (love), but are born with shameful feelings of inferiority, how can they develop a sense of being loved? How can they learn to trust others? What effect do family and church experiences have on development? We will look at these issues and examine how emphasis on control can lead to an unhealthy focus for families and become part of the foundation for ACEs.

6

MAKING RULES
FOR LIVING

The story of Cathy illustrates the making of personal rules (see chapter 2). When her brothers' teasing distressed her so she could not sleep, her mother simply told her that she did not have to be so upset. Technically this was correct, but it was not what Cathy needed to hear at that moment and certainly not without sympathy or explanation. Her next statement has definite significance. "I decided right then and there that it didn't do any good to talk to her. So I never went to her again about things!"

Out of this painful experience of not being supported by her mother, Cathy made an assessment of the situation and decided that the pain of not being listened to was worse than imposing silence upon herself. Without consciously realizing it, she was making a basic decision about how her needs could be met, how much she could trust others, and where she could turn for protection. This rule became a principle that guided her life from that point onward.

Cathy is not alone. Many of us who have grown up as ACEs have developed similar rules based on our own individual experiences. However, such inner rules are not the exclusive possession of ACEs, but are a part of human nature everywhere.

Personal Rules

Rules for living exist on many levels, and there are many ways to refer to them. Terms like *basic beliefs, unifying principles, perceptions,* or *values* have all been used to mean the same thing. Basic beliefs are concepts we use, consciously or unconsciously, to make decisions for living. They include our highest principles, both spoken and hidden. Inner rules help us organize the separate parts of ourselves into a meaningful system. These basic beliefs can bring unity and integration to our lives, but if the beliefs are distorted or in conflict, they can lead to dysfunction. The nature and quality of our lives flow out of these basic belief systems.

Even one's most personal rules and perceptions operate on two levels. The external level consists of our conscious, everyday attitudes that we could recite as our philosophy of life. They help us in decision making and we base our conscious behavior on them. We are all familiar with common external rules, such as pay yourself first, work smarter, not harder, never put money into stocks that you need to feed your wife and babies, be on time, do your best, to have a friend, be a friend, and so on. On the same level, my wife has decided that if you wait you can always buy what you want on sale.

Inner rules are much more deeply personal and profound because they concern one's deepest needs. These beliefs have the most pronounced effect on one's behavior, even though an individual may be unable to articulate them. If we really want to know a person, he or she must be known at this level. The principles that make up the real person exist here. These deep inner beliefs determine whether a person tries to get others before he himself is taken, tries to avoid conflict at any price, or expects to be blamed if anything goes wrong. Here, too, is the destructive, inhibiting belief I see in so many individuals, "If people really knew me, they wouldn't like me."

Positive inner beliefs can be powerful sources of energy and commitment for living. Norman Vincent Peale, Robert H. Schuller, and Denis Waitley are three contemporary individuals who inspire positive inner principles that can help pull people through difficult times and guide their lives. They encourage such positive belief statements as: "I am a worthwhile, lovable person." "If I can picture it in my mind, I can do it." "If God is for us, who can be against us?"

Society's Rules

Many of the assumptions about life and ourselves are shared by people in general, and these shared beliefs bring stability and order to society. In our country the Constitution and Bill of Rights contain the basic beliefs and assumptions that govern political life. Concepts such as freedom of speech, the presumption of innocence until guilt is proven, due process under the law, the right to privacy, and the like are grounded in those fundamental documents. There is also general agreement about basic honesty and personal responsibility which operate to motivate most people to be at work on time, to drive safely, to pay bills promptly, to send children to school, to pay their taxes, and behave as responsible citizens.

Much of our shared social belief is stored in proverbs and common sayings that have been handed from one generation to the next. "A penny saved is a penny earned." "Don't cry over spilled milk." "What goes around comes around." "If at first you don't succeed, try, try again." "What a man sows, that will he also reap." "If you want a friend, be a friend." New principles or assumptions are being developed in our current social climate that drinking and driving are an unacceptable combination and nonsmokers should not be forced to breathe smoke against their wishes. I am sure you can think of other principles being wrestled with to increase social responsibility.

Family Rules

Every family has a particular belief system with rules to guide domestic behavior and decisions. These basic beliefs set the tone for the families' activities and interests and determine the emotional atmospheres. These rules can be either healthy or dysfunctional. Healthy rules such as "Everyone's feelings are important," "Each person is valued," "Discussing problems is important," "Each person's boundaries are to be respected," and "Playing is as important as working," provide a positive environment for each family member. Dysfunctional rules include "Do what you are told and don't give your opinion," "Always keep Dad happy no matter what," "Don't count on others to come through for you," and "If you want to be loved, act right." The dysfunctional types of rules provide destructive, emotionally unsafe atmospheres.

Family rules usually operate on two levels — the rules that are openly stated and the ones that are actually practiced. These two should be one and the same, but too often parents will say one thing and do another. For example, Dad may say, "All of my kids are important," but never spend time with his children. This confusing parental discrepancy can cause serious trouble for growing children. The dysfunctional family styles will be discussed later in more detail.

ACEs and Their Rules

As important as beliefs and principles are for the stability of society and of families, personal beliefs are the ones that truly affect our behavior in the most significant areas of our lives. Our personal beliefs provide the foundation from which we can make decisions about our lives and situations that we face. As we have seen, Cathy adopted a rule that led her to withdraw from her mother. Such personal rules can be positive or negative in their effect upon us. One person who had grown up in a dysfunctional home with an unreliable parent who consistently let her down recently told me, "I have learned through my experiences that good things never last for me." Since this had become one of her basic beliefs about life, she grew nervous when things were going well for her. She continually worried about when the good would end.

On the other hand, some individuals act on positive, energizing principles: "I want to do the best job I can in anything." Whenever the person who believes this faces a task that requires a decision about the degree of quality needed to accomplish the task, the outcome is obvious. Likewise, the person who believes, "I am a friendly and likeable person" will attract friends.

Beliefs Determine Actions

We are working here to build a framework to understand the ACEs, and it is essential that we see the crucial relationship between one's beliefs and one's behavior.[1] It is a fact that people generally do what makes sense to them; their actions are consistent with their beliefs.

I knew a young Caucasian who was dealing with a variety of personal conflicts and was convinced that his eyes had an Oriental slant. This troubled him, and he was self-conscious about what he called his "Chinese eyes." In a social situation, even going to the mall, he was very sensitive about people looking at him. His inner belief that influenced his behavior was, "I have Chinese eyes that make me look so different that other people are going to notice me."

On one occasion, when he attended a formal dinner as part of a wedding rehearsal, he kept his ears tuned for any remarks that might refer to "Chinese eyes." Halfway through the meal he was sure he heard such a comment, and this was all he could think about for the rest of the evening. His behavior (scanning to see if anyone was talking about him) was determined by his belief ("I have an unusual appearance"). By carefully listening for such a remark, he fulfilled his own prophecy and "heard" someone mention his eyes.

Sarah and Devon, a young couple in their early twenties, had been married for about three years. When they came to see me, their marriage was in shambles. In fact, coming to see me was a last-ditch effort recommended by Devon's divorce lawyer.

Devon and Sarah had dated since their junior year in high school and married when they were twenty years old. Because he was rather skinny and marginally attractive in his teens, he was shy with girls, socially reticent, and lived a rather narrow life. Sarah was an attractive girl who had dated a number of fellows before she and Devon became serious, so she had a broader social experience. The problem that had brought their marriage to the brink was what Devon called Sarah's silent treatments. These silences had actually started before their marriage. If she became upset about something, she never yelled, screamed, or argued. Instead, she simply became silent, holding her frustrated feelings inside. She continued in silence until Devon approached her and apologized (even if he had done nothing wrong). This pattern continued through their courtship and into the marriage. Each time Devon felt a small piece of his love dying because he had to pursue her in order to end the conflict.

His own frustration gradually began to mount, and his love for her was being slowly eaten away. Finally, he decided that he was going to wait out the next silent treatment to see how long it would take for her to approach him.

In the past, silent times had lasted no more than two days, but as he waited, a week went by, then two. He kept his thoughts to himself and began to wonder if she wanted a divorce because she was making no moves toward him. When he noticed that she had removed her rings and put them in the dresser drawer, he began to think that she was ready to get out of the marriage. Still he continued to keep his own silence rather than pursue her.

After a month Sarah had become concerned because he had not come to her or responded to her removing her rings — something she did to trigger his attention. One day she approached him and began to talk about their relationship. "Maybe we should get a divorce," she said. Devon, who suspected that this was what she wanted, was quick to agree. His instant agreement shocked Sarah, who had only suggested divorce to capture his attention and draw him back. To complicate things Devon had become interested in a younger girl at work during these silent treatments.

It struck me as I listened that they had been going through this same cycle for four or five years. "At any time," I asked Devon, "did you ever ask why she was so quiet and why you always had to be the one to end the silent treatment?" He answered "No," and his answer clearly illustrates the connection between his beliefs and his actions.

When he and Sarah were first dating, he made a mild criticism of her. In the course of their conversation, Sarah suggested that he should date other people to gain a broader perspective of girls and relationships. Devon was rather insecure at the time and possessive of Sarah, so when she said this, it really frightened him. He was already fearful of losing her, and now when he made a criticism to which Sarah was sensitive, she suggested that they break up. This incident made such an impression on him that he never again brought up anything he thought might upset her.

Devon certainly did not like silent treatments, but he wasn't going to say anything because he always remembered what had happened earlier. "If I do anything to make her angry, she'll drop me," was Devon's belief based on that one incident. His keeping quiet was determined by his belief about Sarah and their relationship. He did what made sense in the circumstances as he saw them.

These inner personal beliefs are important because they determine our behavior and influence our perceptions of the world, the people around us, and God. To understand the ACEs, one must understand the importance of these inner rules because they play such an important part in their struggles. Once we understand how these rules work, we can grasp the essence of the ACE conflicts.

Two Kinds of Sense

Sometimes people's actions are hard to understand because they appear foolish, impractical, and even stupid. What kind of inner rules do those people have if their actions truly make sense to them? Our newspapers carry frequent stories that illustrate this point. Recently, a young father, accompanied by his family, drove to the foundry where he was employed. As he left his wife alone in the car, he told her he was taking the two children inside the foundry to show them where he worked. Twenty minutes later, he returned to the car without the children. He had placed them in the foundry's ladle which was used to heat molten steel and had turned on the heat, killing the children.

This story is an extreme example of the point we are examining here, but it is typical of incidents we read about every day in our newspapers. Other examples that are less extreme are no less puzzling. What about the young housewife who leaves a note for her husband saying she has had enough. She has decided to leave her two children, her house, and family and go to Las Vegas. "How can she do that?" people wonder. "She was such a good Christian!" Others have seen the minister run off with the church secretary. Recently TV ministers have been caught indulging in the very sins they had so vehemently condemned.

In looking at these types of situations which do not make sense, we need to realize that there are two kinds of "sense," logical sense and psychological sense.[2]

Logical sense is what is reasonable according to most people's standards. Rational, logically thinking people do not put their children in a foundry furnace, shoot their neighbors with automatic weapons, or abandon their families. Logic tells them life is more rewarding when they are kind to their neighbors, go to work and pay their bills, and stop at traffic lights.

On the other hand, psychological sense works according to different rules. If something in a person's behavior does not make logical sense, it most likely will make "psychological" sense. Psychological sense means looking at a situation through a person's point of view and personal inner rules. *If actions make sense according to the person's own point of view and is consistent with his/her own inner rules, then we are looking at psychological sense, not logical sense.* And since many people make decisions based on their emotions rather than rational reality, a great deal of human behavior must be analyzed at this level if we are going to understand it.

The fellow who burned his children in the foundry was mentally ill, so his inner rules were distorted. He had heard voices that told him to kill the children, so it made "psychological sense" to obey the voices. The mother who ran away from home had grown up with strict parents who had kept her under tight rein. Marrying at seventeen years of age to get away from home, she had never developed herself as her own person in order to do what she really wanted. Finally, the inner pressure of doing what she was supposed to do instead of what she wanted became too much, and she gave in to the inner urge to just get out of the situation. Devon, in the situation described with Sarah, never discussed his concerns about their relationship because he feared that he would lose her.

Just because something makes psychological sense does not mean it is right or justifiable. It only means that according to the person who commits the action, it somehow seemed the reasonable thing to do. This leads us to another important point that also is a foundational concept for the ACE rules: *Distorted perceptions and rules have as much influence on our behavior as true ones.*

If we believe something to be true, we act as though it is true, whether or not it is. We have seen that Devon acted as he did because of what he believed about Sarah. Sarah herself has said that his perceptions were wrong. It was all in his mind. In reality she was trying to get him to tell her about his feelings, to respond. Devon's distorted belief influenced his behavior as much as if it were true.

If we believe someone is rejecting us, we will feel rejected and act accordingly. If we believe that people are unfriendly, we respond to them as unfriendly people. If we believe we are late in arriving for an appointment, we hurry. If we are unaware that we are late, we will not be concerned about the time. When our beliefs and perceptions seem true and accurate to us, we act on them, whether or not they are in fact true.

7

THE FAMILY FOCUS

R osie was the ninth and last child in a Christian family. Her birth seems to have taken place in spite of medical recommendations to her mother that she not have any more children. This fact, along with many other experiences, troubled Rosie's sensitive nature deeply. Although her father was a respectable member of the church, he had many bad habits that played havoc with the family. Feeling safe was not a common feeling for Rosie in growing up. Because her father was unreliable in paying his bills, the gas company often came and turned off the heat. Bill collectors were regular visitors, and she watched as her Christian father attempted to deceive them. He also had a severe temper. Some said he secretly drank beer out in the barn, and he beat the horses mercilessly for minor infractions. Although he never abused Rosie, she witnessed severe punishment meted out to her siblings, and her sensitive nature experienced the blows as sharply as if they had been delivered to her own body. This had a profound effect on Rosie because she did not feel physically or emotionally safe in her home, and her childhood pain followed her into adulthood.

Basic Needs

In addition to the physical needs for food and shelter, there are two basic emotional needs that must be adequately met if one is to function as a healthy adult, and Rosie's experiences illustrate what can happen when they are not. Security and significance are so crucial in terms of personal development that if they are not met the result can be personal difficulties in adult life. Understanding these needs is critical to gaining a perspective on the ACE problem because many of these people have not had these needs properly met.

These needs are critical because the most influential inner principles a person develops are directly related to how these basic needs were met during childhood. These inner rules play a governing role in the attitudes and behavior affecting every area of one's life.

Need for Security

The need for security includes a feeling of safety and belonging, which comes from being loved. If one is truly loved, one is safe. A professor of mine put it this way, "If I am truly loved by someone, I am as safe as I would be if I had total control over that person." We are born into the world totally helpless and dependent on the people who receive us into their lives. As we experience them, we begin to develop a perception of what the world and the people in it are like. To trust or not to trust is a basic lesson that we learn as infants. This trust is related to how much we can count on others to meet our needs. If we are treated kindly, carefully, and consistently, we begin to feel safe and confident that someone will take care of us. Does someone come when the infant cries? Are wet diapers replaced with comfortable, dry ones? Does the growing child feel safe, emotionally and physically, with the parents?

A safe home helps the child develop confident inner convictions: "I can trust others to care for me. People are good to me. I can let others know what I need and they will respond. I am safe with other people." On the other hand, the child who does not feel secure begins to develop inner rules that help cope with the resulting uncertainty. "The world is not safe. People reject me. If I want to feel safe, I cannot rely on other people. I must hide the fact that I need anything and depend only on myself." Such rules, designed to find some type of security, take root as the person begins the struggle to survive. Too often, children who do not learn to trust during their early development experience havoc in later years.

During Rosie's early elementary school years, she had to hike alone for a mile or so on deserted roads to reach home after school. Often to save time she took a shortcut cut through the dark woods, but it was frightening for her. Since she was growing up during the war years and heard stories about the bombing raids in England and Germany, whenever she heard the drone of an airplane overhead as she was walking home, she feared it might begin dropping bombs on her community. With these fears compounded by her father's unreliability and her sensitive personality, she was ill-prepared at thirteen for her mother's sudden death. She was plunged into deep, heavy grief, but no one, not her father or her Sunday school teacher or her favorite teacher at school, ever expressed an interest in how she was feeling about her mother's death. To make things worse, one of her older brothers who promised to help her and be there when she needed him never followed through. Is it any wonder that she developed fearful, defensive inner rules? To survive in this Christian home, she had to focus on developing her own method of achieving safety since it was not available in her relationships with other people, especially her family members.

She learned her inner rules so well that now, as an adult, it is difficult for her to be close to people because her experience taught her to be cautious and constantly on guard against the threat of rejection. In reality she is a delightful person with an engaging sense of humor and an inner sparkle, but she herself has a hard time believing it and continually stifles her personality, believing that will make it easier for others to accept her. Unfortunately, her quiet husband encourages her to stifle her sense of humor. He is an adult child of alcoholics and becomes uncomfortable when she jokes, even if with the waitress when they eat out. His reaction to her personality and her own stifling of herself to please him adds to her lack of safety and her conviction that others will not like her.

Sense of Significance

The sense of significance is also a basic need. The terms *self-worth, self-concept, self-image,* and *self-esteem* are currently in frequent use, and all deal with the concept of personal significance. The critical thread that runs through each of these is the sense of personal value that, as a person, one has inner worth. Such a sense of intrinsic worth forms the basis for a good self-image.

The importance of positive self-esteem and self-image is emphasized in many writings from a secular point of view, but it is also a valid Christian concept. David Seamands insists that a proper self-love is essential in the Christian life, contrary to what many ACEs have learned.

> The truth is that self-belittling is not true Christian humility and runs counter to some very basic teachings of the Christian faith. The great commandment is that you love God with all your being. The second commandment is an extension of the first — that you love your neighbor as you love yourself. We do not have two commandments here, but three: to love God, to love yourself, and to love others. I put *self* second, because Jesus plainly made a proper self-love the basis of a proper love for neighbor. The term *self-love* has a wrong connotation for some people. Whether you call it self-esteem or self-worth, it is plainly the foundation of Christian love for others. And this is the opposite of what many Christians believe.[1]

Not only does Seamands demonstrate that positive self-worth is vital as a foundation for the Christian life, he also points out that the opposite trait, low self-esteem, can bring a host of other dangers into a Christian's life. Unfortunately, many people who have grown up as ACEs have been taught that the very form of inferiority he describes is spiritual and pleasing to God!

> Satan's greatest psychological weapon is a gut feeling of inferiority, inadequacy, and low self-worth. This feeling shackles many Christians, in spite of wonderful spiritual experiences, in spite of their faith and knowledge of God's Word. Although they understand their positions as sons and daughters of God, they are tied up in knots, bound by a terrible feeling of inferiority, and chained to a deep sense of worthlessness.[2]

Self-Image Guides Behavior

Self-image guides behavior because our inner rules and principles are developed out of our sense of worth. These inner rules guide our actions and are the foundation for our behavior. Since our self-image brings our behavior in line with our beliefs about ourselves, a sense of personal inferiority is especially damaging because we will conduct ourselves externally in a way that is consistent with our internal sense of inferiority, instead of actualizing and expressing our true personal qualities or abilities.[3]

Suppose a golfer who sees himself as a player who scores in the high 90s suddenly realizes that he is playing much better than usual, and if he continues at the same pace, his score will be in the high 70s. If his inner perception of himself is a 90s golfer, a low score inconsistent with his self-image will make him uneasy. His self-image thermostat kicks in to bring his behavior into line. Consequently, he begins to miss putts, land in sand traps, and slice the ball until his score returns to the 90s, consistent with his self-image.[4] The thermostat principle operates in all areas of life, and I have observed it in most of the people who come to me for therapy. People act in accordance with their image of themselves.

Patrick Carnes has developed a model for sexual addiction and adds his support to the chorus saying self-esteem is a critical underpinning for problems. His concept of being unlovable incorporates the emotional content of low self-worth. Carnes has identified several core beliefs that underlie sexual addiction, and these same beliefs or inner rules apply to most people who struggle with low-self-esteem.

- Belief 1 (self-image): I am basically a bad, unworthy person.
- Belief 2 (relationships): No one would love me as I am.
- Belief 3 (needs): My needs are never going to be met if I have to depend on others.[5]

Persons with these inner beliefs cannot trust others to meet their need for love and significance, so they must do something themselves to meet their needs. For those who decide that sex is their most important need and the only avenue available to bring good feelings into their lives, the addiction cycle develops as sex becomes the all-consuming focus of their lives. The same dynamics take place in people who pursue otherwise unattainable good feelings by way of alcohol, food, drugs, work, power, and so on. As one woman told me, "There are only two things that bring me good feelings — eating and shopping. I just love to eat and spend money."

A similar pattern can be seen in the lives of people who have grown up in dysfunctional Christian homes. Take, for example, those ACEs who have been hammered down at home and church, told that they are no good and that what they do is shameful. Not only do they have a low sense of worth (belief 1), they also have trouble trusting, and this interferes with their ability to relate to others (belief 2). Without the foundation of trust, it is impossible to have meaningful relationships in which they can be open and reveal their true inner selves. Even Christians then fall into the same negative pattern of thinking: "Since I am a bad person, I will not let others get to know me, and I will not trust others to care for me. I will hide my true, awful self. If they really knew me, they would not like me." Such people cannot rely on others to care for them (belief 3), so they must find some way to meet their legitimate, but unmet, need for significance and security.

A Christian with this self-image may choose a persistent, continuous effort to live a perfect Christian life by developing a rigid set of rules and meticulously following them in the hope of being loved for performing so well. Trying to develop a sense of "holiness" to counteract inner shame and unlovableness leads to a life of plodding Christian duty with little joy. This solution, however, does not really touch the true problem of inner shame and low self-esteem because the inner pain and loneliness is avoided. The inner feeling and belief of worthlessness colors relationships with others and God as one relates in a superficial, mechanical fashion.

Origins of Inner Beliefs

The importance of early childhood experiences within the family for personality development is a well-accepted fact in psychology and human development fields.

I have discussed the effect of parents' everyday behavior on their children and the concept of how family relationships parallel spiritual ones in *The Dangers of Growing Up in a Christian Home.* Beginning with our birth into this world, we have contact with people who are our primary caretakers and very important persons in our world. As infants we are totally helpless and completely dependent on others to care for us and meet our basic needs of food, hygiene, and love. These are the people with whom we have relationships, and from these relationships we begin to learn about ourselves. Do people accept us as we are? Is the world a safe place for us? Can we trust others to care for us when we need it? Are we significant? Are we loved unconditionally, or do we have to perform to be loved?

Early childhood experiences make deep impressions and color one's view of the world and oneself. Unless modified through therapy, a distorted childhood view usually remains with a person for life. This can be difficult for people, especially from Christian homes, to accept and understand.

Ingrid was in her fifties when she attended my ACE group. After a painful childhood, she had experienced a number of significant losses in her adult life. Since she had learned to bury her feelings as she was growing up, Ingrid had accumulated a lot of emotional pain that had never been released. As she became more aware of her early hurts, she felt embarrassed and impatient with herself. "I don't know why this still bothers me. It has been so long ago, and they say that time heals wounds. Well, it sure didn't do that for me. I should be over it, but it hurts like it happened last week. I didn't think past things like that could have such an effect." Her early experiences had shaped her perception of herself and of others as she developed her rules for living.

Healthy Family Focus

Since a person's early childhood experiences have such a profound effect on later life, it is essential that we have an understanding of what constitutes a healthy family environment. Specific family rules flow inevitably from the family's primary focus. Once we understand a family's focus, we can look at the family environment and see whether or not it is a healthy one. The family focus is determined by the values and beliefs to which the family ascribes. This value-based focus is the basis for making decisions, spending time and money, and setting priorities.

As we have seen in chapter 4, when a family has a healthy focus, each member is valued as a unique, important individual with needs that should be met. Obviously, situations arise in which the extraordinary needs of one member must be met, and other family members accommodate their own needs to this. Such an occurrence does not necessarily make the family dysfunctional. If Dad unexpectedly loses his job, the family's focus changes as income drops, and everyone helps tighten the purse strings. Mom may have to take another job, and the kids have to pull extra duty with household chores and earn money for some of their activities. These family adjustments are discussed openly and handled within the family, and once Dad returns to work, the family shifts back into its normal way of functioning. All families are going to experience the normal adjustments of birth, marriage, illness, death, and unexpected events. Healthy families work at getting back on track to care for everyone in the family; dysfunctional families are consistently offtrack.

A psychologist friend in his thirties recently welcomed his first child. As he told me about his own changes, he was defining his family focus. "I was talking to my wife the other day about how things change. Before I was married, I had all of the vote. After I married I had half of the vote. Now with our son here, I don't have any vote. He has it all!" His focus changed as his life progressed from being single to becoming a husband and a parent. And as the son grows older, the focus will change again. The son will need him less and less, and become self-sufficient. The healthy family is able to shift when necessary to meet the changing needs of the family members.

Dysfunctional Family Focus

Focus in a dysfunctional family is pulled away from meeting everyone's needs and is usually directed toward a specific family member whose needs dominate the family structure. The rest of the family set their needs aside to meet this dominant need. This dysfunctional focus can occur because of some circumstances beyond the family's control. When one member has severe physical problems—Alzheimer's disease, cystic fibrosis, Down's syndrome, paralysis, blindness, and the like—that person's special needs take over the family focus.

One family has a teenage son confined to a wheelchair. To transport him outside the home, the family must buy a van specially equipped with a motorized lift. When they plan vacations, they must choose locations the boy can handle with his wheelchair. Around the house his needs must often come before those of other family members because he is incapable of total self-care. Having to care for this grown child certainly changes their family focus. They have to accommodate their life style to meet the special needs of this child who will never be independent.

But even these special conditions need not make homes dysfunctional. However, these conditions do change the focus, and if the family is not careful, dysfunction can develop unless the focus is broadened to include other family members.

Emotional problems can also result in a dysfunctional focus. When one parent enjoys control and wants everything to be his or her own way, the family focus does not include the opinions and ideas of each family member but concentrates instead on how to keep the mother or father pacified. Sometimes the husband insists on being in charge of everything, invoking Ephesians 5:22 to prove wives should be in submission to their husbands. One Christian husband insisted that his wife preview her grocery list with him item by item. He also insisted that the shade on their bedroom window be lowered only three-fourths of the way even at night when his wife was undressing.

A number of years ago I visited in a friend's home where the mother demanded that things go her way. Over the years the family members learned to avoid hassles and intense verbal scoldings by letting her do what she wanted. It was interesting to go to a restaurant and observe the family members shuffling around the table waiting for her to choose her seat first. They had learned that if anyone picked the seat Mom wanted, the meal would be eaten in a tense atmosphere with Mom casting piercing glances at the offenders. Once she had selected her seat, the rest of the family quickly found places around the table. Since she was a critical person, quick to let people know what she did not like, the family had to maintain a careful watch over everything they said to avoid being lashed by her sharp tongue. Keeping Mom happy was the focus of this dysfunctional family, not individual freedom of choice.

Family focus can also be determined by parents' beliefs. Often what the neighbors will think functions as a guiding principle. One client told me in disgust that what she heard all the time she was growing up was,

"'What will the neighbors think?' It didn't matter what I thought or felt was right. It was always the neighbors." In other families the focus may be good grades, making money, being the best, or perhaps being "holy."

In my family each of my parents had an individual focus, but they were complementary. My dad was a sensitive person, concerned about how other people saw him, and he always wanted to have his best foot forward. As we were growing up, his focus was the family image, which meant he didn't want us doing anything to attract critical attention to the family. My mother always wanted her four boys to be nice. "Let's all be nice," she'd say. As an adult I figured out this meant, "Be passive. Do what I want and don't make a fuss." What we boys thought or felt was not a priority. So her efforts complemented my dad's focus.

The focus in the family of Treva, who had to wear the funny brown stockings as a teenager, was to live an exemplary life by adhering to the "holiness" rules of Christian behavior. Treva had to put aside her true desires, such as playing in the band, wearing stylish clothes, and being a normal teenager, and pull her personal life toward complying with her parents' master-list of sins. She was never encouraged to develop her inner self.

The focus in Gene's family was determined by his father's drinking and unpredictable behavior. Since Gene never knew when his dad might go into a drunken rage and start a fight with his mother, this uncertainty captured Gene's attention. To survive in the insecure atmosphere, his focus was external, toward his dad, to the neglect of his internal emotional development. Gene had to push aside his own needs because it was not safe to express them or trust anyone to meet them.

Jerry was a committed Christian who saw himself as a caregiver to people in his church and community. He enjoyed helping others as an expression of his Christian life. His home life, however, ran into trouble as his wife became frustrated with the amount of time he spent away from home. Jerry justified it because the job required it. He had been a detective with the state police and was often called in for special investigations. Frequently he had to leave in the middle of meals, during family events, and the early morning hours. After he left police work, he took another job that also required extensive hours away from home. "I don't like holidays. There isn't much to do, and I don't always enjoy all of the people. I'd rather work." As he said this, I could see the pattern of being more comfortable with work than with more intimate relationships at home.

His family history indicates such a pattern. He had been taking care of himself since he was twelve and learned to keep his emotions under control, trust himself for survival, and work hard to earn enough money to live. His family had not been a nurturing one, and he had become a workaholic as an adult. On the surface his hard work had a positive look: he was responsible, earning a living, and doing constructive things, as opposed to Gene's dad who was roaring drunk at unpredictable times. Nevertheless, his work created a distorted focus for his family who spent many hours at home without him.

The focus in many Christian homes can be destructive in subtle, often undetectable ways because on the surface it has a positive appearance. Who can argue with parents who want their children to be well-mannered, polite, productive, joyful, and pleasing to the Lord? It sounds constructive to say, "Now tell her you are sorry you took her doll. You know Jesus wants us to share." It is easy for many well-meaning parents to emphasize control with their children, as they are teaching Christian principles, and actually stifle their children without being aware of it. It is easy to focus on having the family be exemplary, or even perfect, Christians—to be "holy" while the concept of wholeness as individuals is overlooked.

As you can see, any number of factors from personal emotional problems to physical illness to sincere Christian ideals can serve as the organizing point around which the focus is concentrated. Some dysfunctional practices are so obviously destructive that we wonder why it took so long for people to recognize and accept the fact of child and sexual abuse, which are direct assaults on children's needs for significance and security. Other practices, especially within the evangelical community, are often seen as good Christian training, and their dysfunctional sides are overlooked because the destructiveness is so subtle. In fact, the subtle dysfunctions can be just as destructive as the major, obvious ones.

The point to remember is that dysfunctional families consistently have an unhealthy focus that concentrates on meeting one person's needs at the expense of the other family members. As a result, the individuals with the unmet needs often develop disabling perceptions and inner rules about the world and how to cope in it.

Pulling together several threads, we can see that in a dysfunctional Christian family the parents often emphasize control more than acceptance or grace. This control emphasis can be conducted in the name of God, which makes its destructiveness very subtle. In the name of living up to Christian ideals, control or conformity is valued more highly than individual development, and in the process individual need for significance and security is ignored. The "S" and "C" children are most vulnerable to this type of family environment because they are especially sensitive to acceptance or rejection. The "D" and "i" types may have trouble as well, but as we have seen, they do not internalize it as intensely. Their struggle will take a different form as they attempt to work it out themselves. As dysfunctional family practices and personality styles converge, the stage is set for youngsters to develop inner perceptions and personal rules that lead them into the ACE pattern.

8

SURVIVING IN A DYSFUNCTIONAL FAMILY

S*urviving* may sound a little extreme, but if one is lost in the desert, the basic need is for water in order to survive the heat. The emotional need for security and significance is equivalent to the physical need for water, but emotional needs are often overlooked because they seldom result in physical death. A physically starving person looks emaciated and appears to be ill, but a person with unmet emotional needs can look physically healthy. When emotional needs are unmet, emotional survival becomes a serious problem.

What do children do as they grow up in dysfunctional homes starving for significance and security? They may be fed and grow physically, but what happens to their emotional needs? If they do not feel safe, whom can they trust? What perceptions and inner rules do they develop about life and themselves? What can they do to survive emotionally?

Remember what Gene said about his home? "My old man was always drunk, and you never knew what was going to happen. I was the youngest, and I was always stopping fights between my mom and dad. I had to step in to protect her. Life was a mess, and growing up was all bad. No good at all."

What a way to live as a youngster! To survive in this home of inconsistency, unpredictability, and insecurity, Gene had to do something to meet his need for security and significance. He could not trust his father to take care of him or count on him for anything. Such uncertainty leads to fear and pain. Gene had no idea when the next blow-up would come or the next big fight between his parents would require him to step in. To obtain some security for himself, he did what many ACAs do; he tried to control situations to reduce the possibility of surprise and hurt. If things were under his control, then nothing threatening could happen, and he could feel safe. He could not count on others to provide safety for him.

He also learned that it was dangerous to have feelings in his chaotic, fighting family. "I've been through so much hurt in my life. My family, other kids picking on me, and now this. If my wife wants to leave me, she'd better just do it and get it over with. I can't take any more."

Even though he had grown up physically, Gene's emotional needs of significance and security had been unmet during his early years. He could not feel safe with his father or within his own home because his father's unpredictable rages kept the atmosphere tense and ready to explode. To survive in this dysfunctional alcoholic home, he developed his own inner rules.

First of all, he decided not to trust. No one was there to meet his needs, so if he trusted people he would only be hurt and let down. Second, he decided it was dangerous to feel, so he did his best to bury his pain and put it out of reach. Third, he didn't talk about personal feelings because no one was interested, and everyone ignored the drinking issue. Then he developed a personal rule that eventually had a profound effect on his adult life, "I will control situations and people close to me so I can feel safe."

These inner rules helped him survive in his alcoholic home, and it is easy to see how he could come to these conclusions. But his pattern for survival became his way of living and continued into his adult life, even when his dad was no longer around. He brought it with him into his marriage.

Following his inner rules, he could only trust his wife when he could literally see her. It made perfect sense to him to accompany her to the grocery, the mall, or wherever she went. He wanted to control what was going on to reduce the possibility of being hurt. It made sense to him to question her thoroughly after she had gone out by herself. He wanted to know the people she was with, where they had gone, to whom had they talked, and if there were any guys there. Not knowing answers to these questions drove him up the wall. His wife became sick of it, but he interpreted any reluctance on her part to answer as proof she was trying to hide something. Finally, just to shut him up, she'd give him an answer that seemed to be what he wanted, even though it was not true. When he realized she had lied, this reinforced not only his belief that she could not be trusted but also his childhood rule of not trusting. Then in sad and ironic imitation of his father, he developed a drinking problem that made it easier for his temper to flare and explode.

Alcoholic and Christian Homes Compared

The lack of safety is easily understood in an alcoholic home, and it is easy to see why family members don't talk, don't trust, and don't feel. Alcohol changes one's behavior and attitudes. It promotes inconsistency, broken promises, and isolation. What is not so obvious is that many Christian homes are just as unsafe, dysfunctional, and emotionally dangerous. This may seem like a blasphemous statement because we usually value a Christian home and consider it the ideal place for children to grow up—a place where they can learn about God from their mother's knee, learn about Jesus at Sunday school, and share family devotions as they live with godly parents who instruct them in the ways of the Lord. Unfortunately, this picture is often not true in the real world. Those of us in the counseling professions have seen too many damaged individuals from "Christian" homes to believe that this idyllic picture is true of all Christian homes. In fact, there are qualities in many Christian homes that can make them as dysfunctional, but more dangerous, than alcoholic homes.

Cathy, whose story we read in the second chapter, did not feel safe in her home any more than Gene did, but for different reasons. Her experiences with her absent father, her indifferent mother, and teasing brothers caused her to developed her own set of rules to survive in her home. As we worked out the issues in her family, I asked her to write out the personal rules by which she had learned to live.

1. Don't allow yourself to get emotionally close to anyone because you will end up getting hurt. Don't trust.

2. If you have an opinion on something, keep it to yourself because nobody really cares what you think.

3. Avoid friction with people such as parents. Just agree with
   them or be quiet.

4. Do and say whatever is necessary to keep people happy;
   and so you don't hurt anybody, do and say the same things
   they do.

5. Always try to do what will make your parents approve and
   respect you.

6. You can't count on your parents for support because they
   can be warm or cold, and you never know which it will be.

7. Spending money and eating will always make you feel better.

8. Try to be perfect. Try to make perfect decisions.

9. You can't really trust God because He is going to hurt you
   in some way, by either sending a catastrophe or not giving
   you what you want.

These rules share a common foundation of defensiveness or fearfulness. The goal is to avoid or to ward off danger from the outside world.
Cathy was guarding against the experience of not being loved and accepted by her parents. She was attempting to survive in a family where
her emotional needs were unmet. She was trying to find some sem-
blance of acceptance in a family that overlooked her emotional needs as
much as Gene's family did. How can this happen in a Christian home
where the love of God is supposed to be demonstrated and members
have value and worth?

Unfortunately, many evangelical Christian homes do not provide an
environment that meets a child's basic emotional needs for security and
significance. The atmosphere is determined by the master-list of rules,
and fear of breaking those rules, or bearing the guilt if one even thinks

about breaking them, hangs heavy. This is particularly oppressive for sensitive "S" and "C" personalities, who think when they hear a rule that they had better remember it so as not to get into trouble! An "i" person scarcely remembers it, and one "D" person told me, "Whenever I was told a rule, I saw that it needed to be broken!"

Not only do many evangelical homes and churches interfere with children's emotional needs, they systematically teach them that these needs are wrong and should not be met. As if this were not bad enough, it is done in the name of God and tied to the destiny of one's soul, making a heavy-duty issue. This added spiritual dimension can make the dysfunctional Christian home even more deadly than the secular dysfunctional one.

Personal Focus for Survival

The rules Gene and Cathy established for personal emotional survival were thoroughly defensive. In a healthy family environment where children are secure and have significance, there is no need to be constantly on the alert for emotional dangers. The security of being loved and valued allows them to relax and let their attention flow in many directions. They are comfortable expressing their opinions, feelings, and even negative emotions because they know their parents still accept them. They do not have to edit their thoughts or, as Cathy learned, "Do and say whatever is necessary to keep people happy." Emotionally secure children are comfortable with their parents' reactions, even when they become angry because the healthy underlying relationship is always intact and is not broken every time an upsetting incident arises. In such an environment, children are able to grow emotionally because they are able to bring their emotional needs into the open for discussion and resolution. The emotional focus can be shifted to fit various situations and needs. In homes that lack such safety, the personal focus is always defensive and external as survival becomes the immediate goal.

In terms of emotional development, this means that the focus is outward, away from the individual, and this interferes with personal growth. Gene's attention was consistently focused on his father to see what his mood was and if he was threatening his mother.

Cathy watched for signs of disapproval from her mother and tried to copy others' actions and words, hoping that by saying what others wanted to hear she could be accepted. The idea of expressing her own opinions and feelings was not even considered. The focus was outside of herself and away from her internal state; her own feelings did not count. This defensive stance throughout her childhood stifled her inner self. It was not free to roam and grow as it could have in an accepting, affirming, safe environment.

No wonder she exclaims, "I feel confused, like I hardly know who I am. I don't feel like a wife and mother. I don't know what I really want. I really feel like a little girl, but I can't feel that way. I just want my daddy to hug me and kiss me. Take care of me. But I can't be that. I have two kids of my own to take care of. I can't expect someone to come and take care of me!" The price of her external focus has been the stifling and undernourishment of her inner little girl.

After Bea had been coming for several sessions, I began to see certain patterns emerging in the basic beliefs that guided her decisions and her life. During her preschool years, her Christian father developed a brain tumor, but since he had his own unique set of inner rules, he did not want anyone to know it for fear that it would bring problems into his life and jeopardize his job. It made sense to him to tell only his wife and pledge her to secrecy. When Bea was eight years old, her father died. The day after the funeral, the thought struck her, "Beginning with today, I am going to be alone in living my life and making decisions." Her mother was still alive, but apparently she had insufficient attachment to her mother to fill the gap created by her father's death.

As she described her past experiences, I could see how the loss of her father and the limited attachment to her mother had shaped her inner rules. Her older sister remembers being physically abused by their father who became violent as the tumor progressed. He knocked her around and pushed her down the stairs. Bea remembers none of this, and in fact she has no childhood memories before the age of eight when her father died. Her mother maintains that "Dad really was a good man," and she never saw any violence in him. Bea does remember being mercilessly teased by two neighbor girls, and no one, not even the girls' parents who attended the same church, intervened on her behalf. She lived a life of submission to others' taunts, and the pattern continued in junior high and into her adult life. Although her parents were Christians and she found Christ in a meaningful way during her early twenties, her internal struggles continued. She used drugs to cope with her pain, even after she became a Christian.

As we continued together exploring her life, two of her inner rules became obvious. The first was to avoid pain at all costs. This was the rule that kept her from remembering eight years of her life. She repressed feelings that were painful. Next, when she discussed painful experiences that she could remember, she only talked about them, she did not express the emotion that accompanied the action because her rule was to avoid pain.

She had also chosen to live with as little risk as possible (her second rule), and during counseling she began to realize that she had withdrawn into a small, safe circle as a child and had continued this pattern into adulthood. "I have chosen safe people for friends, and I can see I would have had a better life if I had spoken up to the girls in junior high that were picking on me. It was easier to ignore them than to fight back, and when I did finally take a stand, they left me alone. Now, most of my friends are rather safe. I want to start picking people as friends that are more challenging and exciting." Coming to therapy was part of her decision to expand her life, and she hoped eventually to recover her lost childhood memory.

"Do you really want to make some changes," I asked. "Are you prepared to tinker with your basic beliefs? You can't avoid pain and also remember what you have repressed. If you want to have a more fully developed life, you will have to take risks." She could see my point but admitted it would be difficult to modify her basic rules. She had developed rules in order to survive at home and was now the victim of her own success. She had avoided the pain so well that she did not feel or remember it. She realized she had managed to reduce her personal risks to the point that her life had become truly dull, even by her own standards. I knew that beneath these rules lay a sense of personal shame, low self-esteem, and lack of trust in others, but at this point in therapy these concepts were apparent only to me. I knew she could understand them eventually as we worked out the details in her life.

Bea had developed her rules to survive in her parents' Christian home, but they were an inadequate foundation for her adult life. The rules provided an avenue for safety when she was a child, but these same principles interfered with her adult relationships and personal growth because she always tried to choose the safe, painless route whenever she was faced with a decision.

Control vs. Grace

When we look specifically at families in the evangelical community, we often see an external focus that is uniquely Christian. The focus is on correct behavior at the expense of children's emotions. I realize that Christian families are not the only ones who emphasize correct behavior, but there is a unique quality here simply because it *is* Christian. This emphasis includes powerful spiritual truths, but these truths can either be helpful or they can have definite negative effects. Christian parents can invoke God and spiritual truths in their desire to control their children, a weapon unavailable to non-Christian parents.

The dysfunctional Christian family emphasizes only control at the expense of grace or redemption in the family system. This emphasis on control leads to an oppressive atmosphere that stifles freedom and openness. The parents in the name of God introduce rigid goals to obtain the desired result in their children. The goal to encourage children to live godly lives is laudable, but the method can be emotionally devastating.

Often there is an unhealthy connection made between control and redemption: in order to receive grace (i.e., unconditional acceptance), one has to earn it by exercising personal control and exhibiting correct behavior. Being loved and accepted becomes conditional. One is loved if one behaves. Love is withheld if behavior is unacceptable.

Hank, who is a friend of mine, related a personal experience that illustrates this point. His parents were serious Christians who were obviously high "C" types, quite concerned about doing things properly. This was their emphasis as they raised him, the oldest son. When Hank graduated from the eighth grade, it was a highlight experience for him. As part of the graduation celebration, his church youth group planned a party at Chicken Charlie's restaurant. After the nervous tension of the graduation program, Hank and his friends suddenly realized they were very hungry. When they arrived at Chicken Charlie's, Hank ordered a

T-bone steak with a baked potato and thoroughly enjoyed the food and the fun.

After the new graduate returned home, Hank began to talk excitedly about the evening. There was pain and frustration evident in Hank's voice as he recalled his experience thirty years ago in his parents' kitchen. "My dad's only response was to scold me for getting the T-bone dinner. 'Don't you think that was a heavy meal to have at ten in the evening? Now if that had been six or so, that would be different. It isn't good for you to have such heavy food in your stomach before you go to bed.' His negative response took the shine right off my good feelings. Why couldn't he have said, 'Hank, I can see you are all excited about graduation, and if a T-bone sounds good to you, just go for it!'?" Hank, as a trained theologian and psychologist, understands the principles of control vs. grace. "My parents were quite concerned about raising me correctly, and they did everything by the book. But in doing it, they didn't really relate to what I was feeling. Now what is such a big deal about a T-bone steak at ten in the evening?" In their effort to be correct, they missed him at the emotional level.

In Hank's family and in many others like it, the emphasis is on behaving and living by control under the threat of losing love. The children's focus becomes externalized because they do not feel the consistent safety that builds internal trust, security, and significance. Feeling unsafe, they must concentrate on behaving, which means they must overlook and suppress their true feelings in order to earn love and acceptance. To the extent they do this, they lose sight of their true, inner selves and are unable to grow as they should.

Though many might like to deny this, it must be added that many Christian homes are secretly alcoholic, and the children living in these homes receive a double dose—all of the destructive traits of the alcoholic home mixed with the Christian dysfunctional traits. The result is even more inner conflict that must be resolved and handled.

"Holy" vs. Wholly and the Evangelical Rules

This brings us to the conclusion of part two which has examined the foundational concepts for "holy" vs. wholly and the evangelical version of the alcoholic rules. As you read through the next chapters, you will see a pattern appear in the rules as each one has two parts. The first one identifies either an activity or personal attribute that is forbidden. Personal activity on this side of the rule is typically considered to be unspiritual and displeasing to God. The second part of the rule contains the prescribed activity or personal attribute that is acceptable if one wants to live up to the "holy" standards. Although adhering to the second part of the rule may lead to "holiness," it also leads one into the ACE syndrome.

PART THREE

THE EVANGELICAL RULES

9

RULE 1:
DON'T TALK – DO SAY

V era was a petite woman in her late thirties who was having trouble in her marriage and felt intense dislike for herself. She usually felt responsible for the problems in her marriage, and this seemed to suit her husband who encouraged her self-blame. Vera's mother had been a heavy drinker during her childhood and acquaintances considered her to be an alcoholic. When Vera described a recent conflict with her mother, I asked, "Did you say anything to her about the problem?"

"No. No one said anything about it. Mom did the same thing when I was a kid – she didn't talk about things. My dad never said anything either. I figured if it were okay to say something, someone would have. No one talked about what Mom did or said. She complained all the time, and it was everyone else's fault." She sighed as she recalled her painful memories. Her next comments provided another glimpse of how the alcoholic rule of don't talk operates in families.

"One time we were visiting at my aunt's house. They lived next door to a bar that they owned, and one day my aunt was walking back to the house from the bar when she was drunk. She fell in the gravel driveway and her husband left her there. No one said anything. My sister was with me, and we watched, scared, but acted like nothing happened. The next day no one said anything, but her leg was all cut up. It was plain to see."

Vera's experiences clearly illustrate the denial that exists in families of alcoholics. The obvious truths and experiences are ignored as everyone acts as though these unusual activities are really ordinary and undeserving of discussion. Children learn not to talk because no one else does, and they also learn to keep their thoughts and observations to themselves. For one thing, no one is really interested, and second, what good would it do to remind a drunken father that he was contradicting his previous permission for you to visit a friend's house? "Keep your mouth shut and avoid the hassle" the child begins to learn as he struggles to survive. The don't talk rule is certainly present in the alcoholic home, but it is also present in the evangelical home.

Don't Talk Rule in the Evangelical Home

"You know how hard I have worked at becoming my own person, and the trouble I had with my mom. She'd never listen to what I had to say or accept what I wanted. I had an experience the other day I could hardly believe. Boy, was I mad!" Dixie exclaimed as she slammed her fist down on the arm of the couch in my office. She was an ACE and had been coming to me for therapy. Her mother presented herself in a very spiritual way and could quote a Bible verse to suit her own intentions for almost any occasion. It had been a difficult struggle for Dixie to sort through the emotional tangles that developed in her family. On this day Dixie was referring to an encounter between her eighteen-month-old daughter, Angie, and her mother's version of *don't talk—do say*.

"My babysitter canceled at the last minute, so I asked my mom if she could watch Angie for me. She was glad to do it, so I drove to her house and took Angie inside with all of her stuff including her car seat because she likes to 'go away.' I tell you, the situation was like reliving my past. Angie said, 'Go away!' And my mother started right in while I was still standing, 'You don't want to go away, Angie. You really don't want to do that. Now tell Grandma you really want to stay here at her house and look at the toys! Come on—tell Grandma!' Standing there watching my mom with this little kid just blew my mind. She did the very same thing when I was a kid, too! She didn't care what Angie wanted, in fact, she didn't even listen. What's more, she insisted that Angie tell Grandma what Grandma wanted to hear!"

"That's true," I replied. "And what makes it even more difficult, here is this good Christian woman basically teaching you and now Angie to be dishonest. To please your mother, you had to be systematically dishonest." This is the don't talk — do say rule in operation.

Jim's experience is similar because he had to be dishonest to keep his parents' approval. He is a high "C" person with definite perfectionist traits. He had grown up in a Christian home where his dad sat quietly and regularly in the living room chair emotionally uninvolved with either Jim or his sister. As Jim was working on his anger toward his parents in therapy, I asked him to write out his honest feelings toward them as an exercise in becoming more aware of and accepting of his feelings. One section of Jim's writing dealt with how he felt about being unable to express his true thoughts in the family.

> It seems unfair to me that when I was younger I would need to lie to you when I would go to a movie with sex or swearing in it. I wouldn't dare tell you I was exploring the world, for I knew you would judge me. We would have no discussion exploring the issue. You would have simply said it was wrong. No room for learning, no room for exploring, no room for errors, and no room for my questions. It angers me that I experienced this guilt and all this control at your hands, without being able to express myself. Rules. We had to follow the rules!

Jim felt forced to be dishonest in order to maintain his safety or security in his family. This started the split that took place within him as he attempted to divorce himself from his true thoughts and feelings that were unacceptable at home and at church.

Denial in the Christian home usually revolves around other issues and needs than drinking. This denial is a subtle rejection of the self that pervades the family atmosphere, and it usually is done in such a way that it does not appear damaging because it is presented in the name of God as a spiritual quality. Such spiritualized denial is an attitude that pervades all the evangelical rules of behavior in the home.

Dawn is a college junior who has grown up in a minister's home. As she began to look at her life and tried to understand some of her confusing emotions, she described the influence of her family this way:

The biggest inhibition I got from my parents was that they treated me as a child. Perhaps they even see me as a child. I was not able to make my own decisions; they were made for me. It seemed that what I had to say was not important. Usually what I had to say was funny and did not need to be taken seriously. My opinions and desires do not seem to matter. What my parents said was final. Being treated as such, I find it hard to believe in myself and see myself as worthwhile. Lack of communication of beliefs and feelings led me to become a closed person. I have trouble expressing myself and letting my emotions show. I have trouble trusting in people because nobody trusted in me. This reflects in my spiritual life. How can I trust God? Another inhibition was that Christianity was always assumed, especially when you're the minister's daughter. Nobody permitted us to question our beliefs; nobody even questioned whether we believed. We were taught all about God and His laws, but we were never given the heart knowledge. My parents did not express much open love to their children, and that is what I wanted.

Dawn shows accurate insight as she connects her family experiences to her difficulty in believing in herself. She also recognizes that the lessons she learned in her family interfere now with her communication with others. She had absorbed the don't talk—do say rule.

Dixie's mother directed little Angie not to give her true opinion. Angie wanted to "go away," but Grandma did not accept this request, and she was unwilling to consider it with Angie and insisted that the child deny her own wishes. This is often typical of Christian parents who are surprisingly more inclined to actively discourage their children's self-expression than alcoholic parents are. Even when youngsters express themselves acceptably, many Christian parents are not interested in what they have to say. To Christian parents who emphasize control in their familes, any form of disagreement with their views is considered unacceptable. "Children simply should keep their views to themselves and let the parents handle things." Many "S's" and "C's" who are quite sensitive and unlikely to fight back in the face of discouragement have said, "Me—say anything to my folks? You must be kidding! They never wanted to hear what I had to say, and if I ever did speak up, that was backtalk."

Bianca, an attractive college student in my class on personal growth, described her family's rules. "My father was very strict with discipline. My brother and I were not allowed to explain ourselves whenever we got in trouble. My father felt that any act of defense was also an act of 'talking back,' and we would be punished more." Her father was using the don't talk—do say rule as part of his control strategy. He did not emphasize acceptance and grace or redemption.

Christian parents who are especially concerned about maintaining control often quote the Apostle Paul's admonition, "Children obey your parents" (Ephesians 6:1), believing that Scripture gives more muscle to their demand that children keep their thoughts to themselves. It is a handy verse to use when the parents want to close a discussion and bring their chidren into compliance with their wishes. And it usually works on the sensitive ones who detect their parents' growing disfavor and learn to silence their thoughts. This starts a pattern of stifling one's thoughts (and feelings, as we shall see later) that can lead to inner conflicts and depression later in life.

Unfortunately, many parents misinterpret their children's silent compliance as contented acceptance, but as my father often used to say, "Just because you silence a person does not mean you have made a convert." Just because a child has been silenced does not mean he or she is contented or in agreement with what is happening. In fact, the sensitive children are the ones who withdraw the most readily and suffer the long-term damage that this withdrawal brings. They withdraw because their need for security is not being met.

When Dixie's mother insisted that Angie "tell Grandma you really want to stay home and play with the toys," she completed the second half of the don't talk—do say rule. After effectively telling Angie to deny her true wishes, she told Angie to say what Grandma wanted to hear. "Don't talk about your true opinions and thoughts, but do say what I want to hear"—that is the complete rule. How often do parents insist, "Now tell your sister you are sorry!" when the guilty child obviously is hurt, angry, and nowhere close to being sorry. Overlooking these signs of inner conflict, many well-intentioned parents push ahead to what they believe is the greater goal—teach Jimmy to apologize and to act as a Christian should. When Jimmy is pushed to say "I'm sorry" before he has been able to get rid of his hurt and his anger, he is being taught to deny his true feelings and to lie to keep his parents happy and receive their approval.

You can readily see that a steady diet of this in the home is going to result in Jimmy learning that his true opinions and feelings are either wrong or they do not count. To be loved he must do what his parents expect of him; to do otherwise would bring very serious consequences.

Dawn put it another way and, in doing so, put her finger on a common parental practice that causes trouble. "I felt what I had to say as a child was not important. This happened because people didn't listen to me." When parents do not listen to their children, they communicate the message that their children and their opinions do not count.

The don't talk—do say rule creates a false dichotomy—deny your true self but believe and say what others think you should say. Let others define for you what is true and right. An entire childhood of this produces a youngster whose focus is on doing what he must do for acceptance and approval while he systematically denies his true ideas and opinions. Jean, a minister's daughter, summed it up very well when she described her feelings about her spiritual life at church. "Most of my memories of church are negative. I grew up feeling as though it was wrong to question or doubt the church concerning anything. Somehow the church gave the impression that it had a direct line to God and that everyone should just accept its teachings as right."

Paying attention to her own ideas and expressing them would have brought the disapproval of adults down on her head, as happened to Angie. Jean had to disown or split away from herself and her true thoughts in order to be accepted. Her internal self has been ignored in an attempt to survive the dysfunctional home and church environment.

This dichotomy or split in personal development is another characteristic of the evangelical rules, as will become obvious as we proceed.

Don't Talk About Inconsistencies of Parents and Church

As we have seen, parental inconsistencies are not discussed in the alcoholic home. The same silence is enforced in the dysfunctional Christian home that lacks emotional safety. Although these confusing realities and contradictions are observed by everyone in the family, it is somehow understood that they are not discussed.

Cathy put it this way. "I never understood it. My dad was a big leader in the church, and everybody saw him as this wonderful Christian, but he was ripping off old ladies at his business during the week." Her father did not spend time with her, her mother was always angry, and the general family atmosphere was not secure. She did not dare say anything about the discrepancies she observed, any more than Vera dared to comment about her drunk aunt who had fallen in the gravel drive.

Jackie's observation is typical of many that I have heard. "People at church would never believe me if I told them what my dad was like at home. He has a good reputation at church and in the neighborhood. They wouldn't believe me if I told them he came into our bedroom at night and fondled my sister. They just wouldn't believe it." Jackie, of course, never said anything either and continued to act as though everything was fine at home.

Missy is a sensitive young woman who had grown up in a small community and had become increasingly confused and frustrated with the events in her family and church. Her sad countenance reflected the discouragement of her words.

My family doesn't make things any easier. We'll hear a sermon on obeying your parents and how the father should not provoke his kid to anger. The minute we get into the house, everybody's yelling at the other person. God is very seldom mentioned in my house. When the pastor visits our home, my dad will lie through his teeth about family relationships. I get so upset at him sometimes, and yet I can't tell him how I feel. I probably would hurt his feelings. I hate seeing my parents being hypocrites, too! The community is bad enough. I find myself getting so frustrated with it all, that I don't even want to go back to church.

My own growing up presented similar, though not identical, problems. My family attended a small, rural holiness church that preached salvation, sanctification, and lots of hellfire. The message of self-denial was emphasized repeatedly, and it seemed that God wanted a great deal from me. I was supposed to give up all notions of anything I wanted to do or be in order to serve Him. But there was no discussion about it. In fact, it was rather evident to me that no one really cared what I thought. I was just supposed to understand it all and live for God. As I observed people at church, it looked as though everyone else had it all figured out. At Wednesday night prayer meeting, people usually rose to their feet and gave glowing accounts of their personal faith. I didn't hear any talk about struggling. "It has been twenty years since I was saved," Amos would say. "I can still remember the spot right there at this altar where I met the Lord. My walk with Him grows better day by day, and I press toward the goal which is my high calling in Christ Jesus." I believed this is what I should say, too, and that my inner resistance to what I heard at church was definitely a sign of sin that, at worst, should be ignored, but, ideally, should be rooted out. After all, I was supposed to be a victorious Christian. I couldn't have doubts and ambivalence. I was supposed to say the right things—"Jesus never fails," "All is well with my soul," "Not my will, but thine be done," and so on. Home and church were not safe places to raise contrary questions, so I had to hide them deep within myself, hoping that God would not see them as I worked hard to say what I was supposed to say.

Those who grow up with this rule learn to be against themselves and their own opinions in favor of whatever the important people in their lives think. The effects of this teaching strike at the heart of healthy, personal development because developing one's own opinions and attitudes is essential to effective autonomy and living.

10

RULE 2:
DON'T TRUST – DO TRUST

C laudia Black illustrates the don't trust rule by describing Allen's experiences.

> Allen, age 32, told me of a time when he was 11 years old. He had returned home from school and found his mother intoxicated. As he came through the door, she started an argument with him. She began to scream and shout at him, and he began to scream and shout back. This was a typical after-school scene but, this time, Mom picked up a broom and began hitting him about the head and shoulders. While Mom was screamimg and hitting, Allen was ducking and hollering back at her. He ran to the phone and called his father. (Allen's father lived away from home.) Allen was surprised when his father answered, but he did at least answer! Imagine the scene of an 11-year-old Allen yelling into the phone explaining what was happening, ducking the broom, while his mom screamed at him and continued hitting him. . . . His father shouted back into the receiver, "Don't worry, she won't re-member it tomorrow." . . . Allen, like so many others, learned through similar experiences not to trust.[1]

For children who live in alcoholic homes where such events are a regular occurrence, it is easy to understand why it would be difficult to learn trust. The environment is unsafe and unpredictable. The adults who are supposed to be taking care of children's needs are preoccupied with the alcoholic and related situations, so they are not available or interested in what the children need. Children learn not to count on them to be there, because when they do, they are let down.

Since trust is the basic element in a working, healthy relationship, children of alcoholics have a strike against them as they grow up, unable to trust that others will nurture them and will be available when needed. Since they usually carry this lack of trust into their adult lives, their intimate adult relationships are often difficult.

Don't Trust Rule in the Evangelical Home

For a youngster in a Christian home, learning to trust in others can sometimes be just as difficult as in an alcoholic home. It is true that Allen's parents were unpredictable because his mother was a heavy drinker. However, just because Christian parents are sober does not guarantee that they are interested in their children's emotional needs or are open and available to them, even though they may be consistent. In fact, many Christians are quite consistent to the point of rigidity and inflexibility when it comes to rules and ideas about running the house. Although this makes them quite predictable, it also means that they consistently practice their dysfunctional behavior. When Christian parents do not meet their children's emotional needs, for whatever the reason, the net effect is similar to that of alcoholic parents.

Erving was a tall fellow in his early thirties. Because he was married and had two children, he had a fair amount of responsibility at home, but he was uncomfortable handling it. Coping with daily pressures was difficult for him, and he changed jobs frequently, usually because of job pressures. "If only I could win the lottery, then I wouldn't have to work," he told me. His expenses exceeded his income when he was unemployed; he feared that his savings would eventually be gone and that he would fulfill his negative destiny by killing himself rather than face moneyless humiliation.

Several elements in his childhood home contributed to Erving's difficulties as an adult. Erving's father was a pastor who was a definite, committed Christian. He spent long hours working with his parishioners, but he spent very little time with Erving as he was growing up. Such things as playing ball and fishing simply were not in the picture.

As we were discussing this during one of his therapy sessions, he lamented about a fellow from his church who had said he wanted to get together with Erving but failed to follow through. "Why do people treat me as though I am worth less than nothing? He said he'd call me. If not Monday, then count on Tuesday. I have not heard from him yet. He said he wanted to be my friend, but he couldn't even call to say he couldn't make it." His pain and frustration were evident as he spoke. Several clues to his deeper feelings emerged as he began talking about his father.

"My dad also never accepted my feelings and wants. Work was his primary thing. Whenever I would tell him something I thought or wanted, he would say, 'That is not you talking. I know you better than that. You are just talking nonsense.' Even now when I tell him how I really feel, that's his response. I can't get past that with him. He rejects what I tell him." Now as an adult, Erving has a difficult time developing relationships with others because he distrusts them, expecting them to reject him.

Allen had learned his mistrust in a chaotic, alcoholic home as he evaded his angry mother's broom. Erving learned his mistrust in a Christian home where there was no drinking, but neither was there interest in him as a person. Both men learned that they could not trust others to really be there and to care.

Melanie is a sensitive girl in her early twenties who has grown up in a Christian family, but has struggled with her faith, as well as with anger toward her father who is unable to work due to a physical disability. Her comments also illustrate the lack of trust that can develop in a Christian home. "All my family can do is fight and argue—just the opposite of what we should be doing. It's hard for me to perceive God as father because my dad doesn't know how to meet our needs. When I was younger, I used to dislike my dad a lot because he would always yell at us, especially at my brothers. I feel I can honestly say my dad has something to do with the way I relate to God now. I see God as a disappointment at times, and this really bothers me. I say to God, 'I trusted you but you've let me down.'"

An important point to be considered is that some Christian parents do become violent at home and provide a chaotic environment for their families. This need not be the result of drinking, for there are other serious emotional issues that can cause even sober Christian parents to become abusive to their children, physically and emotionally. One thing is certain: When children's needs are not met, they learn the don't trust rule that keeps them from relying on their parents, Christian or not.

Don't Trust Your Reasoning Ability

In the evangelical environment these rules take on their own particular flavor in contrast to the ACA model. The *don't trust — do trust* rule for an evangelical includes not trusting one's own opinions and ability to think or reason, but there is a contrasting emphasis that leads to internal splitting: Do trust *others* to tell you what to think and believe. This emphasis obviously pulls the focus toward the external at the expense of developing one's internal beliefs and values.

Basically, it amounts to not accepting responsibility to reason things out and work toward being one's own person. There are similarities with the don't-talk-but-do-as-I-say rule, but there are more profound implications. Not only are young people to be silent about their thoughts, they are not to trust their own abilities to think and reason, especially if thinking leads to inner questioning about their parents or God. Of course, if someone does begin to think as an individual, that must be kept inside. The first part of the rule amounts to this: Don't trust your ability to think; and the second part: Do trust us (parents and church leaders) to tell you what you should think.

None of this is intended to downgrade or discredit parental and church authority as teachers about God and truth. We all need instruction, but the way the teaching is done is critical. I am referring here to the common practice of discouraging independent thought and expecting people to simply accept what they are told, without questioning it, and to make it their own truth. In such a system, people simply become containers for knowledge without ever incorporating it into themselves. However, people need to process what they have been taught in order to integrate it into themselves in a meaningful manner. Evangelical parents who are emphasizing control are the ones most likely to offend in this category.

The idea that people should distrust their own abilities to think and reason, but accept what the church says, has had a profound effect on church history. This official attitude contributed to the Reformation. The church at that time kept the Scriptures out of the laypeople's hands, which forced them to depend on the church leaders to interpret God and theology. People could not study the Scripture themselves to determine the reality of God's truth for their lives.

Martin Luther, to the consternation of the church leaders, began to pay attention to his own inner thoughts and feelings, and as he read the Bible, he began to see discrepancies between the official church position and what the Bible said to him. Moving from the original position of not trusting his own ability to reason but trusting the church, Luther eventually moved toward personal integration by using his ability to think and reason as he studied the Bible and relied less on the formal church. Acting out of his honest, heartfelt convictions, he nailed his "Ninety-Five Theses" to the door and began the Protestant Reformation. The full impact of this particular rule is evident in his life and work.

"I have tried to kill myself three times. That's why I am here now. I have been here three weeks." Darcy was a sober, serious woman in her late twenties, and she spoke with little emotion as I sat with her in the psychiatric hospital. Because she was struggling with Christian issues, she had come to my special program in the hospital, and this was my first visit with her. I inquired about her past experiences, realizing that something must have troubled her deeply if she had actually attempted suicide.

"You must have really lost hope," I commented, hoping she would tell me more.

Even though we had just met, she was quite open. "I was raped when I was sixteen and lost the baby in a miscarriage. That is what started me drifting from God. I don't know why He didn't stop it from happening. Then, after I was married, I had several miscarriages, and when my son was born, he had a cleft palate. I don't know why so much happens to me. They say God doesn't give us more than we can bear. But it's more than I can take. I have been depressed for a long time. I just realized a while ago that I have a lot of anger toward God."

"What do you do with your anger? Are you comfortable expressing it or talking about it?"

She shook her head, slowly. "No, I have kept it all in, and I have a lot of bitterness. I grew up Catholic and was taught that God was Almighty. He knew what He was doing, and we were not supposed to question it. The nuns were pretty strict about that. We couldn't question them either. I have never understood how God could let all of this happen to me."

I had the rules about not talking and not trusting one's ability to think in mind when I said, "It sounds like you weren't allowed to say what you really thought, but instead you were supposed to say and believe what the nuns told you. You couldn't disagree with God, have your own opinion, or anything. You were supposed to say what God wanted to hear."

A small, knowing smile spread into her sober look as my words touched her inner, unspoken feelings. I could see in her eyes that her conflict was genuine and that she was experiencing an internal split by trying to follow the evangelical rules.

"I don't dare question God," Terri protested vehemently to me as we discussed her handicapped, terminally ill daughter. "God does everything for a reason, and He gave me my daughter the way she is. Since it is His will that I have her, I am supposed to accept it. If I complain about something in my life that God has put there, then I am sinning. And God may very well say, 'Well, if you don't like that, I'll give you something to really be upset about.' And I don't want that. I have enough to deal with now."

She was experiencing the split of trying to distrust and deny her own internal questions as she accepted what she believed was the truth of God's will in her life. The result was tremendous conflict that she was unwilling to face for fear of what God would do to her, so she lived in a trapped, emotionally divided state.

Betsy had grown up in a Christian home and learned all the right things. She has some "D" tendencies which the family did not understand or value, so, consequently, she was put down and made to feel different by other family members. Her independence was discouraged, as her family wanted her be more submissive. Members of her family broke promises frequently, and if her father said he would take her some-where on Saturday, Saturday often came and went with nothing taking place. Consequently, she developed the personal rule of taking the quick, easy way to get things done and avoid the pain of prolonged effort and possible disappointment. She also learned that she should stifle herself to keep others happy with her and to gain their acceptance.

She lived a life with little risk and primarily tried to please others more than herself. When her quiet, "S" husband suddenly decided he did not want to be responsible for his family and moved out of the house, it thrust Betsy into a panic. She had married young and had never held a full-time job or lived on her own. While the divorce was in process, she had to make decisions, obtain a job, and rely upon herself in ways she had never done before. The interesting thing was that she began to look brighter, was more energetic, and became more attractive as a person. When she and her husband eventually reconciled, she began to fall back into the duller, please-everyone pattern.

As we analyzed this one day, we began to look at the splitting that had taken place within herself and her family. She had developed a pattern of looking to others for approval and the correct way to do things. Spontaneously, she blurted, "You know, I was taught not to trust my own judgment when I was growing up. I looked to others for what I should do. But as I look back to when Doug and I were separated, I can look at what my opinions were compared to what other people said I should do, and I can see that my judgments were often better than what they said!" As we examined her life, she began to realize the need to reevaluate the don't trust—do trust rule.

Pete's experience illustrates the same point from a more positive angle. Pete was the son of a prominent minister who had a rather healthy home environment for his children. According to Pete, "I can honestly say that many of the evangelical rules were not applied in my home, except the questioning of faith. Doubt was kind of taboo. I remember having strong doubts in high school, and my parents really had no idea how to react. It was the same with my older siblings. I remember the anguish my parents felt as my brothers' and sisters' church attendance dwindled. I remember feeling particularly responsible for their guilt feelings and their fear for my salvation when I went through the same stage myself." Eventually, by facing his doubt and working through his honest feelings instead of staying with the emotional split, Pete came to a legitimate expression of his faith that was truly his own and not an extension of his parents' beliefs. If he had withdrawn into his doubts and tried to hide them from himself, his parents, and God, he would have had serious trouble later in life because they certainly would have resurfaced.

The reality of this rule is also evident in church life. When a local church was in the process of locating a new pastor, the search committee started a discussion on the qualifications they believed were appropriate for their new minister. A woman on the committee opposed this discussion and asserted, "It doesn't really matter what his education is or the types of books he reads. If he has the Holy Spirit in him, then whatever he says is from God, and I don't have to question it." She was putting aside the responsibility of using her own judgment and simplistically accepting whatever the minister has to say.

A very different attitude was taken by the people of Berea, and their stance is one that makes sense to me. After the local residents heard Paul and Silas preach, "They searched the Scriptures day by day to check up on Paul and Silas' statements to see if they were really so. As a result, many of them believed, including several prominent Greek women and many men also" (Acts 17:11–12, TLB). These people were willing to think for themselves, check out the Scripture to verify what they had heard, and this study led to their conversion.

Although most evangelicals would not knowingly associate with a cult, the ones who do not think for themselves are treading the same path as cult followers who unquestioningly accept their leader's control. A number of years ago Jim Jones made the news when he forced hundreds of his followers to commit suicide at his command. The members of his group had given up all right to think for themselves and simply believed whatever Jim told them. They were living out the internal split caused by the rule that says, "Don't trust your ability to think, but do trust ours."

Don't Trust Your Feelings

Emotions have been giving Christians fits for years because there seem to be so many we shouldn't have. At least that is the impression left by many evangelical teachings. Doubting one's feelings involves questioning their validity; i.e., are the feelings appropriate to the event? Even when one's feelings seem valid, the rule prescribes stuffing them because they are wrong. Distrust of one's feelings is similar to distrust of one's thoughts and judgments. As persons we recognize our emotions, but the rule leads us to believe they are not valid.

Becky's experience in her Christian home illustrates this. She had grown up with very little internal focus, even though she was an "S" person who needs security and usually pays attention to internal issues. Reflecting on her experiences at home, she stated:

> My Christian upbringing taught me to discredit my own feelings and care only for the feelings of others. As an "S" type person, this was not too hard for me to do because I want to avoid conflict in the first place. I do not like to tell people when I am upset because I feel they will think that my reasons for being upset are not valid. Furthermore, I fear that I will be criticizing the person if I tell her that I am upset with some things she did. I keep my emotions inside, thinking that if I do not acknowledge them they will go away.

Becky recognizes that her method of handling emotions does not work. "My emotions build up over a period of time, and then something sets me off, and I blurt out every transgression that has ever been done to me."

The dilemma causing her conflict grows out of trying to put others first, by denying and smothering her true feelings. For many Christians the problem takes on an added dimension when Scripture verses about turning the other cheek, suffering for Christ's sake, and thinking more of others than of ourselves are invoked. When the struggle takes place on a spiritual level, it can be deeply disturbing to those sensitive people who are naturally inclined to keep feelings inside and who believe it their Christian duty to always put others first. These scriptural concepts are indeed valid, and they must be applied to everyday living with balance and without emotional dishonesty. We often need to put others first, but one has to achieve a certain amount of personal growth and maturity to do this. A troublesome emotional split occurs when a person denies his or her true feelings and tries to cultivate those that others say are correct.

Dawn grew up in a minister's home, and she was trapped in the pattern of split thinking. Her family experiences were conditioned by the don't talk and don't trust rules, which had a deep emotional impact. Even though she was sure her parents loved her, she said, "I come from a family where we did not express our feelings, opinions, and ideas. It was almost like a dictatorship. Not being able to come to my parents and share my feelings and opinions, I have learned not to trust in myself and others." Showing some maturity and insight, she was also able to apply this to her spiritual life. "Not being able to communicate with myself and others, I find it very hard to trust and communicate with God." The don't trust—do trust rule has worked so well that it causes interference in several areas of her life.

Don't Trust Your Ability

The don't trust rule that undermines ability hits "D" people the hardest because by nature they are inclined to make things happen. They enjoy challenges. "The best way to make sure I do something is to tell me it can't be done. Then watch out, because I'll do it!" said one of my "D" clients. Such confidence can be a great strength, though it can be a weakness if not handled properly. "D" people often experience conflict in their spiritual lives because by nature they depend on themselves. To depend on God is contrary to their natural tendencies, whereas for "S's" and "C's," who by nature are doubtful about their abilities, it is much easier to rely on others and on God as well. Even so, this aspect of the don't trust—do trust rule can further weaken their shaky confidence and turn them more deeply inward.

Many people have absorbed a vague concept at church that suggests it is un-Christian to place a lot of confidence in one's own abilities. This relates to the notion that we are unworthy people and so should not have a high opinion of ourselves. That would be pride. The logic is that because we are, in fact, tainted, sinful people our efforts to accomplish goals will also be flawed if not self-serving.

Not long ago I learned of the paralyzing way in which a large, conservative denomination practiced this principle until recently. If a young man (in this church there are no women ministers) felt God was calling him to the ministry, he could not speak of it to anyone. He had to wait for one of the church leaders to approach him. Once this had been done, the door was open, and the young man could openly state his call to the ministry without fear of being seen as proud.

A friend who has a "D" personality struggled for years in the church with his strong tendency to take charge of things, until he learned more about his personality type and realized that wanting to achieve and accomplish things was natural for him. As a young person, he felt rebuffed by his church's teachings on meekness and self-denial, because he wanted to work at making things happen in his life, rather than waiting for God to do it for him. Although he now has begun to see the balance between doing as much as he can himself and including God in the process, his youthful struggle was painful. "I thought I was put together all wrong. It seemed like the way I was and what I wanted were so different from what God wanted."

As we have seen in our study of Biblical personalities, God can use this natural drive and ability to accomplish great tasks, as He did with Joshua, Nehemiah, and Paul, who were all "D's." In fact God uses the natural tendencies of all personality styles. Each can have confidence in his or her own abilities and methods, and we see in Scripture how God uses all sorts of people in His work.

In spite of Biblical examples, we are often expected to belittle our abilities. If someone asks "Can you do this? Are you good at taking care of this kind of project?", we are supposed to look shyly downward, especially if we believe that we can do a good job, and say, "Oh, I don't know. I try to do the best I can. I suppose I can give it a try." It doesn't seem to fit the stereotype of Christian humility to say with a smile, "Yes, I think I can handle it. It sounds like the type of thing I enjoy doing and am good at!"

Of course, it is important to be sensitive to God's timing and work in our lives, but it is sometimes too easy for people to believe that to put out very little effort and wait for God's efforts to come through is spiritual. Such an attitude is characterized by very little trust in one's own judgment and by the belief that our efforts will be ineffective. Those who avoid risks by passively waiting for God to make things happen often wait a lifetime for opportunities that never materialize because they did not seize existing chances or simply overlooked them.

Each variation of the don't trust—do trust rule can prepare the way for an inner split. The rule is to be negative toward one's own self and positive toward others and God, and that sounds very spiritual. But we run into trouble when we belittle our true abilities. The better approach is to develop a realistic view of ourselves, including our weaknesses and our strengths.

It is obvious that those individuals and churches and families who emphasize control rather than grace will use this rule because it keeps others dependent. This stifling of independent thought widens the emotional split, undercutting one's ability to become responsible for the demands of personal growth and healthy psychological autonomy. When this happens, the ACE syndrome develops.

11

RULE 3:
DON'T FEEL — DO FEEL

W hen Gene and his wife came to me for therapy, and as we
touched on his family, he had exclaimed, "My old man was
always drunk, and you never knew what was going to happen" (see
chapter 2). Gene's growing up in an alcoholic home fit Claudia Black's
description of how feelings fit into such a family.

> The alcoholic family's law of DON'T TALK and the premise DON'T
> TRUST teaches children it isn't safe to share feelings either. Children
> learn not to share their feelings and, inevitably, learn to deny feelings
> because they don't trust these feelings will be validated by family
> members, other relatives, or friends. They don't trust their feelings will
> receive the necessary nurturing. Children of alcoholics don't perceive
> others as resources, therefore, they live their lives alone. . . . They
> learn how to discount and repress feelings, and some learn simply not
> to feel.[1]

Don't Feel Rule in the Evangelical Home

Black's observations on the don't feel rule in the alcoholic home applies
equally well to many Christian homes. There is a tendency in many
evangelical environments to either discourage or prohibit the expression
of emotions in general. Such an atmosphere contributes to the internal
split so harmful to one's emotional well-being. There is usually a differ-

ence between what youngsters actually feel and what they are allowed to accept or show.

A quiet, young college student of mine, who had a "C" personality and came from a Christian home, told me that despite many positive elements in her home life, she experienced the impact of the don't feel rule.

> There was a negative connotation associated with the display of emotions in my family and, to some extent, in the church as well. We were always pressured in my family to be strong, and part of that involved not showing emotions because my parents were uncomfortable having us cry, and eventually we, as children, became uncomfortable expressing our feelings. This is true yet today for me.

Even today she is pulled in the two directions of the split. She has to present herself as strong in order to live up to their expectations, which means hiding or denying her emotions even though she knows she has inner emotions that could come out.

A young woman, who had read my first book, called from the West Coast to discuss her painful situation, her conflict with her husband, her guilt, and the critical advice from other Christians. Her comments sounded so familiar. "Mom and Dad were good parents, but they taught us to hide all emotions. It was silly to show emotion. I tried harder to behave than most of the kids. But my parents never responded by showing affection. Last summer, when I had my breakdown, Dad came and sat next to me. He put his arm around me. It was the first time he ever showed that he loved me."

Don't Feel Pain and Anger — Do Feel Forgiveness

Black's statement that children in alcoholic homes who "don't trust their feelings will receive the necessary nurturing" is true in many Christian homes when it comes to emotional pain and conflict. We have already seen this in Cathy's life when she went to her mother regarding her brothers' teasing and Mom didn't respond. She decided Mother was not a reliable resource, so she decided to stop going to Mom for help when she was hurting. This lack of nurturing seems incredible in light of the gospel's message of redemption and its emphasis on acceptance and grace. But where control is the emphasis, nurture is lost in the process, and children learn to hide their true feelings.

No one likes to experience pain, and we develop all sorts of mechanisms to avoid it if possible, but it is unfortunate when our families do not provide enough security to allow us to express our painful feelings. This is particularly true of pain and anger, for when these cannot be honestly expressed, the internal split develops.

We have all heard parents say to their crying children, and especially to their sons, "Now wipe away those tears! Big boys are tough. They don't cry like babies!"

See the split? "Don't feel your pain. . . . Do feel tough and act like I say you should!" If the child is sensitive and wants the parent's approval, the map to receiving it has been laid out, "Do it my way." Most children who honestly want to be loved will attempt to stop the crying, stuff the feelings, and act as though everything is fine.

The more critical areas include anger and emotional hurt, and they are so closely related. Hurt is a primary emotion that takes place prior to anger. In other words most anger is a reaction to being hurt. Many evangelicals have been taught to deny the reality of their hurt and anger and to feel lovingkindness instead.

A psychiatric nurse in the hospital where I conduct a Christian-oriented therapy program recently asked me for some material on forgiveness. Wanting to know more specifically what she needed, I asked her to explain her question a little further.

"Well, last night I was at a meeting at church. We were talking about forgiveness, and this one woman gave an example from her own life. She said she had been hurt by someone and found it hard to be forgiving toward that person. The other people in the room really got after her and told her that she couldn't do that — as a Christian she had to forgive the person."

This nurse disagreed with the group's reaction to the woman's self-disclosure because she had worked with enough struggling people to know that the group's advice was short-sighted. She wanted material that would help point out the error of their criticism.

I am sure the group members had good intentions, but they did not provide a safe atmosphere in which to discuss personal pain and struggles because they did not nurture or support the woman's painful emotions. Instead they chided her for having the very hurt that troubled her! They were saying "Don't feel that way, feel this way." To deny and put her true feelings aside and feel what they told her would mean experiencing the inner split we have been examining.

You may protest that the Bible says we are to forgive. It does, and forgiveness is a very necessary part of the Christian life. I think the problem comes with how we try to reach the point of forgiveness. Too often I see people trying to impose feelings of forgiveness over their hurt and anger, trying to deny that they are really angry as they struggle to generate warm feelings of forgiveness toward the person who has truly hurt them. The forgiveness does not feel genuine precisely because it is not genuine — it is a forced forgiveness that is not from the heart. For true forgiveness to take place, the heart must be emptied of the painful grievance and anger. Otherwise it is like painting over an un-treated rust spot on a car. After a time the untreated rust begins to spread, and eventually it breaks through the paint that covers it. The paint job only looked good temporarily because the untreated rust con-tinued to act like a growing cancer.

Paul Tournier has provided a useful insight on this subject.

> But I also think it is utopian to ask God to flood our hearts with fine feelings of forgiveness and love if we still have all our demands locked up inside our minds. . . . A committed Christian finds it more difficult than an unbeliever to express resentment and dislike. What will people think of him, professing as he does the religion of love? Then he makes an effort to forgive, and the need for an effort is the sign that he has not truly forgiven. . . . Premature forgiveness has a good chance of being false forgiveness. . . . True forgiveness is some-thing quite different. It is a grace, and not the result of an effort. It is a liberation, not a burden.[2]

If we handle our feelings appropriately, dealing honestly with our pain and anger, true forgiveness comes as a by-product and is a natural action as we put the offense against us to rest.

Parents often open and perpetuate this split without realizing it. "Jo-lene, now don't be angry at your sister. You love her. Let her use your toys and share your things." Maybe Jolene doesn't feel like sharing and is really angry about something. It would be better to let her talk about it and work out the anger instead of trying to make her deny its existence. I am not suggesting that we should not admonish or instruct our children about sharing and handling emotions; I am suggesting that the methods we use in teaching them can do more harm than good.

Though Jean had grown up in a minister's home, she had experienced a number of the conflicts we have discussed. When it came to feelings, she believed her parents missed the mark because they did not take her feelings seriously, and herein lay the problem. "Being the only girl in the family, I seemed to get teased the most. Since I am a high 'C' person and quite sensitive, this teasing used to really bother me, and sometimes I was hurt by what my brothers and even my father would say."

Having described this scenario, she explained how her parents applied the *don't feel—do feel* rule. "When I expressed my feelings, my parents would just laugh it off and tell me that I was being too sensitive. I think that my parents needed to realize that just because my brothers could take it, didn't mean that I was like them." Essentially, what her parents said was, "Don't feel hurt from the teasing. You only think you are hurt, and that is because you are too sensitive. Deny your hurt and be without hurt."

Anyone who is sensitive and has experienced hurt that is significant will immediately see the folly in this approach and how little it does to help. If Jean was hurt by the teasing, her hurt was real and should have been taken seriously. Diminishing the reality of her pain diminished her worth as a person because it treated her as if her pain did not matter. Obviously, if her father made the remark, she knew that to gain his approval she must be less sensitive and take the teasing. She must master the rule of not feeling what she is feeling to *earn* his approval, and, in doing so, increase the split between her true hurt and the happy face she must present at the supper table next time the teasing happens. It became an unwitting but obvious lesson in dishonesty at the pastor's kitchen table.

The rule about not feeling anger is especially troublesome for ACEs who believe they should not feel angry toward their parents, even if their parents have abused them as children. As we noted earlier, anger comes in reaction to hurt, and if a person has been hurt, you can be sure there is anger also. "But I can't be angry at them. It isn't right. I am not supposed to be angry. I am supposed to honor them and feel forgiving, but what I am feeling is not very honoring." Variations of these words are repeated many times by all sorts of Christians as they struggle with the pain of their childhoods.

This same reluctance to admit to anger also applies to people's feelings toward God. In a group therapy I was conducting for ACEs, Karla described her situation as having grown up in an evangelical church, but she was verbally and emotionally abused by her parents so badly that she had a nervous breakdown at twenty years of age. In fact, her early childhood treatment was so painful that she remembers very little of it, but its effects have followed her through her life, affecting her career and her self-confidence. Now in her late thirties, she has had to give up her profession because of her emotional condition. "I really find myself angry at God and disappointed. Where has He been while all of this was going on? Doesn't He care what happens to me? I have prayed, read the Bible, and done everything I can think of, but it hasn't made any difference."

"Have you always been comfortable being angry at God, or is that something that has come lately?" I asked.

"A year and a half ago or so when I was in the hospital, a woman from a church I attended came to see me a number of times, and she helped me see that it was okay to have angry feelings toward God, and that has really helped me. Before that I felt it was wrong."

Suddenly another woman in the group exclaimed, "I'd curl up in a corner if I were angry at God! I grew up in a private Catholic school, and we were taught that you don't go against the grain!"

The rule against being angry at God can bring complications to an already frustrating life situation when people do their best to live Christian lives and their suffering continues. They feel abandoned and ignored by God, which makes them angry, but they feel they must not be angry at God for fear He will abandon them even more. The message many ACEs have learned is, "Don't feel angry at God, but do feel grateful, happy, and rejoice anyway. After all, all things work together for good."

Josh was a handsome fellow in his early thirties who had just entered the hospital. He had a wife and two children at home, but things had not been going well for him. His expression was solemn and listless as he sat in my ACE group. "I have been depressed for five years," he said glumly. "Five years of trying all kinds of medication, and one guy even had me on a special diet that was supposed to cure everything. God wants His children to be happy, and I'm not happy." One could tell that by looking at him.

Listening carefully I could tell he had many high "C" characteristics and would probably be slow to express his feelings. I wanted to help him identify them and start bringing them into the open. I tried to say out loud what I figured he must be feeling based on the few comments he had made. "You must be really feeling frustrated. Here you believe God wants His children to be happy, and you have tried to do all of the right things. You pray as much as you can, read the Bible, and try to believe the promises. 'If you ask in my name, I will give it to you.' 'Knock and it will be opened to you.'" As I was speaking, tears welled up in his eyes, and I knew I was on the right track. "You have done all of this, and you're still depressed. Where is God? Doesn't He care? It isn't fair, and you feel like telling God what to do with it! You feel mad and cheated!"

"Bingo!" he said through his tears. "You really hit the nail on the head. That's exactly how I feel!"

Carrying the thought a little further toward some possible action, I inquired, "Have you ever told God how you feel—that you're really angry? Talking to God about how you honestly feel is another way of praying."

"No, I never have. I have never considered praying to be like that."

A few minutes earlier a woman in the group had explained that she and her young son had regular "bitch sessions" which consisted of sitting down together and discussing any complaints they had toward each other. I suggested to Josh that he might need to have a "bitch session" with God. "Tell Him what you feel. I think God can handle that, and, besides, if that is what you really feel, then you are being honest with God and that is as much as you can do. Job expressed his anger, and David shows his anger in the Psalms."

"I think I will try that," Josh returned. And he did it regularly over the next few weeks. "It really helps," he reported.

Josh had learned early to deny his anger and had become an expert at smothering his true feelings. Even after he began to admit his anger a little bit, he never thought about expressing it to God. It had never entered his mind. Once he was able to communicate his true feelings to God it made a difference.

Darcy's anger toward God took her in a different direction. As a teenager growing up in a Catholic home and schools, she learned about the almighty nature of God and was somewhat fearful of Him. In spite of this, she was a bit rebellious, and her outgoing nature led her into situations where she was drinking. When she was sixteen, she sponsored a party at her parents' home while they were out of town. As she was accustomed to doing, she had her share to drink and began necking with a neighbor boy who was also at her party. As the physical intensity increased between them, he ignored her wishes to stop and took her outside where he forcibly had sex with her.

This incident was devastating to her. She felt guilty for having the party behind her parents' backs and was afraid to tell them what had happened. She became pregnant as a result of this one sexual incident, and when she eventually had the child, it died. Emotional pain, guilt, and anger at God all began to accumulate in her life as time passed. "I started to be angry at God. Where was He when this happened to me? Because I was angry, I started to stay away from God and church. I really pulled away because I was so angry and guilty. I felt He was paying me back for what I had done."

She was unable to comply with the part of the rule that required her to have good feelings toward God, so she discovered another route — just pull away from God altogether so He does not see the anger, and she would not have to deal with Him regarding her feelings. In spite of this, she experienced a degree of internal split. She was trying to deny her anger, and ever since the rape experience, she had internalized her emotions, especially her anger. As a result she had become depressed and suicidal.

Don't Have Sexual Feelings — Do Have Neutral Feelings

Sexual feelings and the problems they generate are as old as the human race. They get quite a bit of attention in the Old Testament. For many Christians, especially young people, there is often more emphasis on not facing or having such feelings than on what to do with them or how to manage them. This only contributes to the split. Carol described how it was handled in her Catholic school when she was a teenager. "The nuns tried to tell us not to be sexual, even though I was. They brought in this scary movie to show us, and they gave us these chastity cords to wear which were supposed to remind us of what God wanted."

Joe described how his sexual feelings had to be stifled along with other emotions as he struggled to conform to the don't feel—do feel rule followed in his family.

> In my family, if any emotion or something came up, I had to put it away. My folks couldn't accept it. "Just laugh it off!" they told me when kids pushed me in school. So I had to put part of me away, having less of me to please others. Then the Bible came along and talked about denying myself. It all seemed to be the right thing to do. In our family we were not supposed to have any feelings. If they came up, attention was given to something else. I had to learn to hide them, which worked pretty well until adolescence and sexual feelings started. Then I hid them pretty well—so well that people wondered if I was normal or what.

Brian was pastor of a church in a rural area and was himself the son of a minister. Handling sexual feelings was a problem for him. He tried not to feel them, but as often happens when we actively resist an emotion, the feelings seemed even stronger. Brian had set the standard for himself of having sexual feelings only toward his wife, but as is the case with many men, he was attracted to other females who caught his eye. This was particularly true when he went to the beach, so he gave up going to the beach.

Like many other Christians, Brian had made what I believe is a misinterpretation of Jesus' statement regarding lust and adultery. "But I say to you that whoever looks at a woman to lust after her has already committed adultery with her in his heart" (Matthew 5:28). I have heard people use this verse to back up the don't-have-sexual-feelings rule, implying that sexual feelings are wrong and we definitely should not have them. To me it seems that Jesus is making the point that sin is universal, common to everyone. Therefore, we are all equally guilty before God, whether we have lusted after another person or actually committed adultery with our bodies. The complementary point is that Jesus is more concerned about *sinfulness*, which is a matter of the heart, than about sins as specific misdeeds.

Don't Feel Self-Worth—Do Feel Loathing and Shame

. Of all the areas impacted by the evangelical rules, this is one of the most critical because a person's self-concept is a foundation for the rest of his or her life. The person who feels like a loser lives out a loser's attitudes and is one. The person who feels like a likable, worthy person lives and acts like a worthy person.[3]

The worm theology we encountered earlier (see chapter 5) seems to have established itself in the evangelical churches, and many people believe it is wrong to feel good about themselves. I have known Christians who believed that the more they disliked themselves, the more they despised themselves, the more acceptable they were to God.

When I was in college, we had early morning prayer meetings, and there was one fellow in particular who followed this pattern in his prayer. He could pray steadily for ten or fifteen minutes on how bad, unworthy, and undeserving we were as Christians, and only then could he move on to other topics. I often listened with amazement at the many different ways he could think of to say we were no good. "Oh, God, our Father, we are just so undeserving in Thy sight. We don't deserve to approach Thy throne. Please look upon us with mercy. We deserve Thy wrath and judgment. We have all sinned and gone our own ways. Our righteousness is as filthy rags before Thee, and we are so unworthy in Thy sight. We are like worms in Thy sight." And on and on. This young man was emphasizing low self-worth as a meaningful spiritual exercise. He was living out the rule, don't feel good about yourself—do feel loathing and shame.

Jean grew up in a minister's home, and, with her "S" and "C" personality traits, she took seriously what she heard. "The most inhibiting factor in my family environment was the heavy emphasis on self-denial. I always felt it was wrong or un-Christian to feel good about myself. I was always warned about not being too proud. I think this really affected my self-image. Even now I have a hard time doing things just for me and to feel good about me. I have felt a lot of fear and guilt from my early church experience."

Terri heard a steady diet of similar admonitions from her Christian father, who apparently did not want her to develop a positive sense of herself. "Pride comes before a fall," he consistently warned. "Don't brag about your grades." As Terri summarized it, "The end goal was to do your best but not to feel good about it. You had to be humble and feel as nothing. You couldn't say you were good at something." The way her father encouraged negative feelings was vividly brought home to Terri again when she heard her father scold a three-year-old grandson, "What you did was wrong. You were naughty. Jesus doesn't love naughty boys!" Such a statement can only induce guilt, unworthiness, and shame.

Many sensitive ACEs experience conflict if they start to have good feelings about events in their lives, such as success in sports, good grades, a smooth-running car, nice clothes, neat-appearing house, or fun trips. They believe such good feelings should pale in comparison to spiritual experiences. I experienced this conflict when I was beginning to become aware of my true inner feelings during my twenties.

We had a speaker at one of our YFC rallies who had been a successful and well-known college athlete. As I listened to him, I was stricken with guilt and felt the pressure of the emotional split we have been looking at. He described the excitement he experienced playing in the Rose Bowl and the thrill of helping his team to victory. So far I was able to relate to what he was saying. "But the biggest thrill of all, even in comparison to playing in the Rose Bowl, was the day I met Jesus Christ as my Savior." He paused a second for his remarks to sink in, and then concluded, "That was the biggest thrill of all, and nothing can ever compare to that!"

I stood there in the rear of the Masonic Temple and reflected on my own life and compared it to his. Although I had never come close to playing in the Rose Bowl, I could imagine some of the excitement, but I was a long way from feeling that meeting Christ was the biggest thrill of my life. I had heard about Jesus for as long as I could remember. My contact with Him was largely negative, as my mother used Him to shame me, and it was to please Jesus that I had to behave and could not do many things that appeared to be fun and interesting. But the speaker was saying I should feel that meeting Christ was the most exciting event of my life. "Don't feel what you do feel, but feel instead that Christ is the greatest thing that has happened to you." If I was honest, I could not say that, so what to do with the truth of my inner feelings? I wondered whether something was wrong with me. Was I a bad, unworthy person for having good feelings about other things?

People want to feel good about themselves, and I believe this is one of our basic needs. People need love to give them significance and security.

So many Christians who come to me for therapy have a definite struggle with their inner sense of low self-worth. Many see that part of themselves as bad or unworthy or unlovable. It also can be shame, but it is a deep sense of not being worth much. To defend against the sense of shame and unlovableness, many people develop compulsive behaviors related to such things as sex, alcohol, drugs, food, power, and work. It pains me to see the church and Christian families promoting this sense of shame that fuels so many of the problems that contemporary Christians are experiencing.

Since emotions play such a significant role in human lives, this particular rule is quite deadly in its impact because it is definitely unwise to ignore a major component of the human personality. When we feel shame instead of self-worth, the entire fabric of our lives is negatively affected. When the New Testament good news of grace becomes a message of control and shame through this rule, we turn on ourselves to escape from God as Adam and Eve did in the Garden of Eden. We become ACEs who don't feel good about ourselves but do feel unlovable and shameful. As David Seamands has reminded us: "The truth is that self-belittling is not true Christian humility and runs counter to some very basic teachings of the Christian faith. "[4]

12

RULE 4:
DON'T WANT – DO WANT

I don't think I should have ever gotten married, considering how all things have turned out. All the problems I have had with Cal and Lester." Sally paused and tugged a tissue from the box beside her on the couch to wipe the tears. She had grown up in a minister's home, but in her own analysis, she doubted whether her father was actually a Christian. She was now experiencing conflict with her husband, and their teenage son suffered from an attention deficit disorder which made school difficult and complicated life at home as his impulsive movements and awkward coordination caused him to drop dishes and trip over lamp cords.

"You know, I think this is God's way of paying me back," she mused. "I should have stayed single. But I wanted to get married so bad. I wasn't much of a Christian back then, but I kinda felt God wanted me in Christian work. But I wanted to get married really bad. And when Cal came along, I figured this was my only chance. I guess I should have known better, but you know me— once I get an idea in my head. The trouble has continued with my kids. After a couple of miscarriages, I finally had Lester, but even now things aren't okay. He can be such an aggravation. Sometimes I don't think I can go on anymore. Things aren't working out in my life."

"But do you really think God is getting back at you?" I inquired.

"Oh, yeah. I think it is like in the Old Testament where people pestered God because they wanted certain things. God didn't like it, and He 'gave them their request, But sent leanness into their soul' (Psalm 106:15). That's how I feel. God gave me what I wanted, but all my problems are His way of punishing me for wanting it in the first place."

Her present agony was real, but so was her spiritual consternation, believing that God was displeased with her wanting. She not only had real conflicts to handle in her life, but also the guilt that her "wants" had been in disobedience to God's will for her. She believed she was now reaping the results of her own self-will.

Don't Want for Yourself — Do Want
What "God Wants"

With this rule we make our most significant departure from the ACA model which has three rules. This one comes up often enough in the evangelical setting that it warrants listing on its own behalf and supports the fact that under the evangelical umbrella, there is more insistence that people adhere to certain beliefs in order to live acceptable lives than in the ACA model of behavior.

This *don't want — do want* rule is a corollary to the implied definition of sin that says anything I want for me is probably wrong. In the evangelical community, self-denial is presented as the life God expects from Christians, reinforced by Jesus' statement, "If anyone desires to come after Me, let him deny himself, and take up his cross, and follow Me" (Matthew 16:24). Such an attitude brings uncertainty into Christians' lives as they suspect many of their motives and desires. "Am I acting out of selfishness?" "Should I be saying this or wanting this?" "Are my desires a sign of my sinful flesh?" "How well am I doing at denying myself?"

Mabel has a son in his early twenties, a daughter in her teens, and another son who is eleven. She and her husband grew up in the church, although his family was dysfunctional because there was heavy drinking and limited positive contact between him and his parents. He was a typical ACA with many of the attending characteristics. He himself was not an alcoholic, but he was a workaholic and spent most of his time away from home. This left Mabel to carry the major burden of the family operations alone.

His lack of attention began to wear on her to the point that she developed depressive symptoms and required hospitalization. Since then she has progressed in her Christian life to the point of being able to admit her intense anger against her husband. "He is just always gone. And the worst part is that he spends most of the time doing stuff for the church. Our church sponsors this mission outreach across town, and he drives the bus to pick up the kids for church. Lots of times he spends ten hours on Sunday driving, and now they are buying three new buses."

Trying to gain a clearer picture, I asked, "What is it that bothers you the most about this?"

She took a deep breath. "We live right next to a small lake, and my youngest son just begs his dad to take him fishing back there. We have lived there ten years, and he has taken him fishing one time. He spends an hour every Saturday morning with my son going out for breakfast, and that's it. But he can spend ten hours on Sunday driving for other people's kids."

"What does he say if you ask him about this?" I queried.

"He says I have my priorities all messed up. God is first, church is second, then his job, and then the family. He wants me to stay home and not work, and when I make any objection, he says I'm selfish. Do you think I'm asking too much?"

Mabel has discussed the problem with her minister and wishes he would encourage her husband to spend more time with the family, but the minister just sees the husband's side and says, "But he is working for the church and helping people out. At least he is not out drinking or anything like that."

Mabel is struggling because she wonders about the correctness of her desires and wants what's best for her family and herself. Although she tends to trust her own judgment, she continues to feel some guilt. Should she give up her own wants and go along with her husband's view that God wants her to become more involved in the church's outreach project and drop her complaints about his being too involved?

These two examples show how the emotional split occurs. Don't want for yourself because that is against what God wants, so give it up and don't have desires for yourself. Just want what God wants, or in Mabel's case, what her husband wants.

The rule of not wanting for oneself extends into many areas of life. Within the evangelical community, it often is tied in with the master-list of sins that defines what the "holy" Christian life should be. That list doesn't leave much room for personal wants. In this perspective the rule is: don't want anything for yourself; instead, want everything others and God want for you. If I want too much for myself, it is my inner sinful nature showing its ugly head, and I will lose favor with God. If I want to have any value, I achieve it by doing for others, putting them first, and denying myself any pleasures in life. If any trace of fun or good feelings begins to show, I must quickly douse them before they take control of my life and attitudes.

It seems that if a person is not careful, he or she can become hooked on a way that is unacceptable to God and ultimately destructive for himself. Of course, such a thing is entirely possible, but it is unlikely for sensitive people who are genuinely concerned about doing the right things and avoiding God's wrath. Such folks often go to extremes and deprive themselves of so much that they get off balance and strive to be "holy" at the expense of being whole persons.

Don't Want for Yourself—Do Want for Others

This notion of not wanting for ourselves can come upon us in subtle ways we do not easily recognize. Many times within the church community the people who are seen as spiritual heroes and selfless givers are actually co-dependent people who are meeting their own needs by rescuing others. This fourth evangelical rule so easily reinforces what appears to be a "holy" way of living that it can be very destructive in its true effect upon people because it keeps them from developing as whole individuals. Co-dependency can easily masquerade as "holiness" and is often applauded in the church community. Unfortunately, many sincere Christians are unaware of the real truth that is taking place in their lives and the emotional price they are paying for being dishonest with themselves.

Roger is a fellow in his late forties who went into the ministry after a successful career in real estate. His family of origin was dysfunctional, with a father who was unable to work due to emotional problems that developed during the Second World War and a mother who had a severe physical and mental handicap. His older brother was removed from the home, and Roger grew up trying to save the family and keep it together. His father spent most of his time sleeping. When he did try to do good things for Roger, they usually were less than successful in spite of the effort. For example, he signed Roger up for Cub Scouts, but he bought a uniform so oversized (presumably so Roger could grow into it and would not have to buy a new uniform every year or so) that Roger went to the Scout meetings looking absolutely ridiculous with the long pants rolled up so they wouldn't drag on the ground and the sleeves turned up on his arms. Roger was haunted by the fear that he was weak and ineffective like his dad, and this motivated him to work extra hard at what he did. He also developed a rescue pattern of behavior to gain the affirmation and nurture his parents never provided.

When he took his first position as a pastor of a small church, he worked long hours, hardly ever said no to requests for help, and volunteered as chaplain for the local ambulance. This led into more contact with rescue work with the ambulance crew. His entire life consisted of giving, and to make matters worse, his wife was a "C" personality who resisted spontaneity and was less affectionate than he. They had difficulty working out a system by which they could meet each others' emotional needs.

Roger's heavy schedule, along with the emotional strain of losses and deaths in the church and on the ambulance runs, took its toll, and he became anxious, worried about losing his children, experienced depression, and at times wondered whether he could handle all of his commitments. The inner vacuum suddenly exploded when a young, single woman in the ambulance department showed sincere interest in him and inquired about how he was doing. He spontaneously burst into tears and began to pour out a long list of pent-up emotions, as he felt cared for by this young woman. After this Roger experienced conflict and upheaval within himself and his family as he struggled with his feelings. Fortunately, he had enough insight and personal control to keep the relationship from becoming sexual, as he began therapy and struggled to straighten out his personal issues.

On the surface he appeared to be a hard-working pastor who was selflessly involved in the community and the lives of his parishioners. Actually he was not taking care of himself physically, was not taking time off for personal renewal, and spent little time with his family. By evangelical standards he was following a "holy" way of life, but he was not a whole person, as he lived by the don't want for yourself but do for others rule.

Jamie is an attractive, petite lady in her late thirties, but she presented herself as a depressed woman. As I inquired about her situation, the reasons for her depression became clearer.

"My husband is a minister, although he is not the senior pastor now. We are in Christian work and have been for years. As the pastor's wife, I am expected to do lots of things and help out with the work at church. Although I can do it, it is really hard for me to be a leader and live up to the role of a minister's wife."

She had a quiet, subdued manner and spoke steadily but softly. Her nature reflected a sensitivity and desire for peaceful situations. She was tactful and polite. These qualities suggested an "S" personality who was a loyal, hard worker and had a hard time saying no. She also had some "C" qualities that gave her high standards to live up to. Her next comments confirmed my conclusions.

"All of the things I am expected to do are really not my nature. It really isn't my personality to do all of those things, but as the pastor's wife, I am expected to, so I try to go ahead and do it anyway."

Knowing that "S" people have trouble acknowledging their true feelings, I asked, "Do you feel guilty saying you don't want to do these things? Is it wrong for you to say no you don't want to live up to these expectations?"

"Oh, yes, I sure do," she replied. "It's like I shouldn't really feel this way. My husband and I talk about it, and I do better for a while, then I fall back in the routine and I get depressed all over again."

Jamie experienced periodic depression as she tried to go against her own personal nature, doing things she honestly was not good at doing and did not want to do. The fact that she was doing God's work did not make a difference. The work she was doing was good, but it did not keep her from depression. Although she had not grown up in a Christian home, she had been verbally abused by her parents and had learned the don't talk and don't-trust-your-own-judgment rules in their home. When she became an adult Christian, her childhood training prepared her to take on the evangelical rules as well, and this led to her depression. She learned to put herself aside and not pay attention to her own wants and personality needs. In her attempt to put God and others first and herself last, she became so depressed she was unable to help anyone.

Betty described how she had experienced a similar conflict, although her husband was a teacher in the Christian school system. She had grown up in a Christian home, but it was not a legalistic one with lots of fear and guilt. That came later, after she married.

"I used to be at church every time the doors opened. I taught Sunday school, led women's groups, helped with the nursery — did everything. And we did all of the rules. It was black and white. One day I looked at my children, who were six and eight, and realized our rules were so black and white they couldn't even think for themselves. I began to realize I didn't grow up this way, and I don't have to be like this."

She had so much to say that she didn't give me a chance to ask how she changed things. She told me anyway. "I finally became more assertive, though my husband didn't support me at first. When I said I wasn't going to a church meeting, he'd get a little upset. But I had made up my mind. I decided that what I think matters more than what everybody else thinks of me. We ended up changing churches, and there are still some people that don't understand. But I am not going to live by all those picky little rules and put my kids through that as well. I hate to think what they'd be like now as teenagers if we had kept on like we were going."

Betty, like Jamie, had tried to put herself aside in favor of church and God's work. She tried not to want for herself but for others, until she ran into trouble — her own unhappiness.

With a smile on her face and a twinkle in her eyes, she added, "Now I can laugh and feel free! And why shouldn't I as a Christian? Some people don't understand me and think I should be sober, serious, and not have any fun as a Christian. Even though we are saved by grace, and I believe God doesn't throw you away, there are still those questions you hear: 'Did you do it properly?' 'Did you say it correctly?' It gets into doing the right things again to keep God happy."

Don't Want Basic Needs Met—Do Want to Sacrifice

The don't want—do want rule often causes Christians to deny, or try to deny, their basic, normal needs, in the name of being spiritual. It can easily cause unnecessary stress and a narrowing of life to the point of being ridiculous. It intrudes upon many minor decisions, including what clothes to wear. I sometimes feel guilty getting rid of an old suit that is in good condition but is no longer stylish. Christian teaching from my early years comes to mind and causes me to wonder if I am being worldly by dumping my outdated clothes for newer fashions. For young people it may be choosing a career or a spouse. Is it acceptable to want a fulfilling career that helps us feel good about ourselves? Or is that selfish? Does God test our dedication by calling us into vocations that we will not like? Does Jamie, the minister's wife, need to continue going against her nature to prove her dedication to God? If she had more faith, would she not get depressed? Is she depressed because she is not accepting God's will for her?

Treva, you will remember, had to wear brown stockings in high school and follow many rules that blocked her normal adolescent needs: she was not allowed to want jewelry, nice clothes, or even to play in the band. Even now Treva has difficulty throwing off that early influence and believing that her adult opinions are as valid as the ones she learned in her younger years.

Nadine, who had several brothers, was the only girl in a Christian family who attended a conservative evangelical church where she learned a little Sunday school song about God being everywhere and watching each move she made. This song made a big impression on her, and now, as a grown woman, she wants to lose weight and look attractive, but feels guilty and selfish. "It somehow doesn't seem right, this idea of wearing makeup. It draws too much attention to me." This is a desire she feels she should not have and should instead want to be plain and unattractive. Does this mean giving up on herself and making herself want only what she believes the church and God want?

Joe is in his early thirties, married, and has two children. He grew up in a Christian home that had a provincial view of the world, whereas his wife grew up in a family whose father worked in construction, and they lived in many places. Joe experienced considerable stifling by his parents, which was especially costly to him because he is an intelligent fellow with many abilities. As we were discussing the impact his family had on his adult life, Joe explained the problem he had acknowledging his personal wishes and aspirations. "People would ask what I wanted in life. Want? That just didn't seem right. I didn't feel I had an option. God would pick what He wanted, and I was supposed to do it. Then the Bible kind of fit right in and supported what I felt: to deny myself—not try for anything.

"Then I met Gothard. He was a pleasant, simple man who said he didn't make a lot of money, and yet he had this big semi-truck with his initials on the side. He looked like he had made it following that way of life. He said his staff never advertised; people just came to him. I heard from other people who had been to his place in Oakbrook that it was nice. That seemed to add to it all—you could succeed thinking his way. After I attended his lectures for a week, people said I looked different. That seemed to say that what I was doing was working."

Joe's experience recalled my own because as I was growing up it seemed it was wrong to want to be successful or to want a good living or nice clothes. There was nothing wrong with money, but it was wrong to want it or try to make money. If God wanted me to be poor, I should do more than just accept it; I should really want it. On the other hand, if circumstances developed in which I made money, then it was somehow all right if I did not intentionally try to make it happen.

However, there were contradictions in this don't want—do want rule that confused me even then. I remember a special missionary campaign where collecting money for missions was the main focus, but the leaders were falling short of the amount needed. It began to look like they would have to close the rally without reaching their goal. In the waning hours of the campaign a member of the denomination who owned a recreational vehicle business came forward and offered the money needed to reach the goal. At the closing service, I was amazed to see what a fuss the leaders made over this fellow and the money he gave.

They even had him make a personal appearance on the platform to receive their official gratitude. As a youngster watching, I remember thinking, "I wish that could happen to me. It seems okay for him to have a successful business and money to give to the church. I wonder whether he tried to make it happen or it just fell in his lap? Does he feel guilty about having a business that makes that much money? How does God decide who makes the money to give to the church?"

I have known people with such feelings who try to make a financial arrangement with God. It goes something like this, "God, I know You don't want me to love money, and I won't, but if You help me succeed and make lots of money, I will give lots of it to Your work." With such an arrangement, the effort is sanctified and becomes a kind of not-wanting because it is really for God, though one may hope to benefit in the process.

Serving God and loving others are two important scriptural goals, but if people are taught to systematically deny their own desires, they may never be able to develop emotionally, and this means trouble. Sensitive "S" and "C" personalities are susceptible to such pressure and will act from duty and obligation rather than from the heart.

It should now be clear how the negative evangelical rules cause so many troublesome emotional splits within ACE individuals, as they are taught to deny parts of themselves and to cultivate certain attitudes and beliefs in spite of their true feelings. The splitting that comes from mastering the rules, as one attempts to live a "holy" life, leads away from wholeness.

PART FOUR

EVANGELICAL RULES AND THE SPLIT BETWEEN "HOLINESS" AND WHOLENESS

13

REACTIONS TO THE RULES

G rowing up in an alcoholic home is a difficult task because there are so many unhealthy elements and destructive patterns, but in the dysfunctional Christian home, it is no picnic either. In fact, the evangelical rules are often harder to contend with than the alcoholic rules because they are put forth in the name of God, backed up with Scripture, and given the potential of determining one's eternal destiny. These are mighty issues for a young person to handle, and the secular alcoholic rules pale by comparison because they lack the weighty spiritual dimension.

At some point those who grow up in the dysfunctional evangelical environment are faced with a decision — often subtle and unconscious — of how to respond to the rules and expectations of their parents. Should they make an effort to master the rules in order to be loved? Do they dare go against the rules and risk disapproval? What will God do if they resist? What can be done about the shame they feel? Choosing to follow the rules and master them is clearly the road toward holiness and acceptance in this context, but choosing that route may lead to an internal split that prevents one from achieving true emotional wholeness and spiritual growth, although one may gain a sense of personal control and satisfaction from the effort.

Roles in Alcoholic Homes

Specialists who have studied the rules in alcoholic homes have suggested four possible roles that children play out in response to this particular home situation. Claudia Black delineates the roles of the responsible one, the adjuster, the placater, and the acting-out child.[1]

Essentially, the responsible ones are just that—responsible. They pick up where the parents don't come through and gain security by learning to set goals and accomplish tasks, organizing and manipulating to make sure that things are accomplished. On the surface they may appear to be the ideal child, but often they have not learned to handle their inner emotions, and they can easily become workaholics.

The adjusters learn to go along and not make a fuss. They handle the uncertainty and chaos by adapting and not fighting back, or trying to argue with the unreasonable parent. Black says that acting without thinking or feeling is typical of an adjuster.

The placaters are, or are seen to be, the most sensitive ones in the family. Because of their sensitivity, they have empathy for others and try to fix others' feelings. They often feel responsible for their parents' problems, are reluctant to disagree with anyone, and develop a reputation for being kind and helpful. By focusing their attention on others, they are able to avoid facing their own pain and anger at the home situation. It is easy for a placater to slip into the role of constantly looking for other people to fix. Today's placaters become tomorrow's co-dependents if they continue their rescuing and fixing roles into adulthood.

Some children act-out in the home situation. In my opinion these youngsters have high "D" qualities in their personality, and instead of internalizing their emotions, they fight back in visible ways. This gets rid of their anger to a degree, although it is not the healthiest way of doing it, and it does bring them attention which they probably would not receive otherwise. This acting-out can often lead to other trouble, even such serious trouble as drug use and criminal activity. These children often receive special attention from schools and parents because they are causing trouble, but the real issues behind their behavior may be overlooked.

Context for Roles in Dysfunctional Christian Homes

How do growing children respond to the evangelical rules? It must be stressed that not all evangelical homes are dysfunctional. God is not dysfunctional, but Christian homes can become dysfunctional when dysfunctional people use God and spiritual truths in a destructive manner. So, the first thing to determine is whether or not a Christian home is truly dysfunctional.

People who grow up in homes with healthy family traits, such as unconditional acceptance, open communication, emotional safety, encouragement, and affirmation, can grow up with healthy outlooks, even when they have been exposed to abusive, negative practices in their church. Having the healthy family environment has protected them from the damage that can come from the heavy guilt and fear tactics used at church and church camps. The home environment makes a key difference.

Personality type also influences the way in which youngsters will respond to the teachings to which they are exposed. The forceful "D" person's reaction is going to be different from an "S" person's. So when we look at the roles people choose in response to dysfunctional Christian environments, we need to also take into consideration the differing personality styles.

Roles in Dysfunctional Christian Homes

The roles Black identifies in the alcoholic home have parallels in the Christian home, but with subtle differences. One category is the rebel, which is particularly disturbing to Christian parents because the resistant, strong-willed behavior is seen as rebellion, when in some cases, it is a healthy self-assertion and resistance to some ill-devised parental schemes. But parents who are emphasizing control see any resistance as bad and sinful and want to extinguish it. The rebels, however, are typically determined enough to continue to fight back openly, refusing to listen to their parents' guilt-inducing admonitions. These are the youngsters that typically leave home as soon as they can, stop going to church, and sometimes venture into drugs and other abusive, antisocial behavior.

A different response is made by the surface-pleasers, those youngsters who want to please their parents by doing the right things and are able to take all they hear with a grain of salt. Surface-pleasers can do and say the right things, but their level of sensitivity is low enough so that, though they are only going through the motions, they are not bothered with feelings of guilt. Once they leave home they forget about the rules and do more or less as they please.

Then there are the strugglers who are characterized by straddling the fence between obliged compliance and the inner desire to break free. Their problem is an inner sensitivity and guilt level sufficiently high enough to keep them from actively resisting the evangelical rules. So they suffer in silence as they try to please and do the right things. As children they are typically seen as well-behaved and compliant, but they are seldom happy or spontaneous. They may feel their own hurt deeply, but they do not yell back at their parents, and they often are willing to absorb hurt themselves rather than hurt someone else. It is easy for the strugglers to slip into a co-dependency pattern of trying to help others in pain to avoid dealing with their own. As adults they are prone to experience anxiety and depression because they try to suppress their true feelings in order to reduce their conflict. Strugglers try to live out their emotional split but are seldom successful in completely silencing their inner resistance to the rules.

The "holy" ones are sensitive youngsters who make a valiant effort to live up to the evangelical rules. They are different from the strugglers because they have less ambivalence. They commit themselves wholeheartedly to mastering the rules, while the strugglers feel some reluctance. As children the "holy" ones are easy to raise because they are obedient, careful, and eager to please. They take pride in doing things correctly and become upset with deviations from the rules or normal routines. As adults they are usually seen as the perfect Christians who never do anything wrong. They work tirelessly in all the church activities and often come across with an element of self-righteousness that is threatening to the strugglers. However, even these "holy" ones often do not understand their own emotions and are not in touch with their honest feelings because they have become experts at splitting their negative feelings away from themselves. Any feeling or thought that contradicts their perfect Christian image must be banished so they can maintain their illusion of personal perfection. Since they cannot tolerate "bad" thoughts or feelings in themselves, they also have difficulty accepting others who do have them. This makes it difficult for them to associate with people who are not as committed as they are. They often justify this by saying that God wants them to be separate from the world. They often live their adult lives as legalistic, duty-bound Christians, and if they become leaders or pastors, they perpetuate the evangelical rules in their area of responsibility.

There are also the whole ones who learn to be open about their feelings and can express their true opinions to their parents. They do not live in fear of breaking the rules. They can acknowledge their own negative thoughts and failures. They usually come from Christian families exhibiting healthy family traits that meet their needs for security and significance. They have learned to live within the context of grace and acceptance, instead of trying to behave and perform to earn approval. As adults they like themselves and are able to relate to their own children in a positive manner.

14

HOW THE RULES INTERFERE
WITH WHOLENESS

I f we examine each of the evangelical rules more carefully, we will
see that when they are systematically applied, they strike at the very
heart of the normal, developmental, God-given processes that people
must experience to grow into emotionally healthy people. In other
words, following the evangelical rules leads to diminished emotional
health because they cut the legs from under healthy development and
wreak havoc with personal boundaries.

Don't Talk — Do Say

Interferes with Communication

Communication is a necessary ingredient in any successful relationship.
Lack of communication is the cause of many marital conflicts, and
many couples who come to me for therapy readily admit that they are
not good at communicating. A common complaint from wives is that
their husbands do not talk to them about their feelings or opinions. Parents complain that they do not know what their children are thinking.

It is obvious that talking is a major component of communication,
and if children are systematically discouraged from talking, they are not
going to develop the ability to communicate as children or as adults.
How are we going to communicate if we have not learned to express

ourselves and put our thoughts, wishes, and frustrations into words? This in itself is a problem, but as an evangelical rule, it has another dimension that is even more destructive on a deeper level.

Promotes Dishonesty

A child is not only taught not to speak his or her mind, but is also instructed what to say instead. Not only does this rule interfere with open communication, it makes any communication practically worthless because it is based on dishonesty. The emphasis is on having children say what parents want to hear and not on what children truly feel and think. When people are not expressing their true opinions, then even though there may be conversation, there is no communication in the real sense of the word. If honesty is not present, then there can be no true relationship or communication at all. Growing children learn to put on an act, and before they realize it, they begin to lose touch with their true selves and try to believe and live the facade they have had to cultivate.

Prevents Intimacy

When honesty is absent from a relationship, true intimacy is also impossible. Being systematically trained to say what is expected does not prepare children for intimacy as youth or as adults. Intimacy is essentially openness to other persons, a willingness to let others see our true selves. This means being able to confess our fears, weaknesses, worries, and hidden faults. The more one is discouraged from expressing true opinions and thoughts, the less one is able to be open. Impressionable children begin to believe that what they want to say is not worthwhile because no one is willing to listen to them. Such learning prevents them from being open about themselves because they think they must say the right things to be accepted, and saying what they really think seems to get them into trouble with their parents. They have learned that intimacy and being open is risky, dangerous, and something to avoid.

Inhibits Personal Growth

There is an old expression that experience is the best teacher, and this maxim applies to talking and conversation. Some call it verbalization, or articulating one's thoughts. Talking about one's ideas helps in thinking them through and gaining a clear idea of what one really thinks and believes. That is why discussion, whether around the family table or at school or somewhere else, is so important. Integration of ideas takes place through the process of talking. The don't talk—do say rule, however, promotes saying what is expected and shelving true thoughts.

Some years ago I tried my hand at sales through a multi-level marketing plan. The idea was for me to sign up other people to sell under me, and I would receive a percentage of all the money generated. Making a sales presentation was outside my natural comfort zone. I realized that even when I had studied the material and thought I understood it perfectly, I found myself floundering and stuttering when I tried to explain it. I suddenly realized the difference between just thinking about the ideas and being able to actually verbalize them. Somehow, saying them out loud helped me learn them in a more concrete way. The talking part helped me realize there were ideas I was trying to sell that I did not completely understand, though when I simply thought about them, I believed I did understand them.

Articulating one's ideas is an important part of learning because it helps one think things through and correct any errors in ideas. This correction can take place through one's own insight or from appropriate feedback from others. When someone is not allowed to express true thoughts, the learning loop is broken.

Psychotherapy uses this concept to help people talk about their situations, think them through, and in so doing, develop new ways of seeing the world in order to make different choices. Most people do not take time to sit down and think through their lives and emotions. The people who come to my office for therapy benefit from articulation of their own feelings, so it is necessary for them to do most of the talking. As I have helped people talk about their lives and situations, I have seen them begin to put together insights and experiences in ways they have never done before. They could not have done it if they had only thought about it. Putting those thoughts into words made the difference and enhanced their learning.

Last year, at a local Christian college, my wife and I taught a condensed class on personal growth and the difference between growing up "holy" and growing up wholly. Our approach was to develop a relationship with the class members, provide a safe environment, present ideas and information, and then encourage discussion of students' reactions as they processed and assimilated the information. Surprisingly these students had difficulty with our approach. They were unaccustomed to identifying and articulating their own opinions. One student showed us the soft spot. "Tell us what you want us to know, then we will know what you want to hear."

"But it doesn't work that way here," I replied. "I don't want you to say what you think I want to hear because then you are not learning anything. I want you to say what you really think."

Still they protested, "In most of our classes, we are supposed to say what the teacher or professor wants to hear. We aren't asked what we think." These students had been taught don't talk—do say, and it was interfering with their personal development. As we became better acquainted with the students, I realized that many of them had grown up with parents who emphasized the don't talk—do say rule also. No wonder they were unaccustomed to expressing their true opinions.

Don't Trust—Do Trust

Stops Attachment

As we looked at this rule, we saw that it consists of two components, and either or both can impact growing children and adults. The first damage occurs when parents do not provide an emotionally safe environment, and children cannot trust the significant people in their lives to meet their needs. The next harm is done when children are taught to distrust their own abilities in thinking and self-development. It is possible for persons to have a trusting relationship with their parents but not with themselves and their own abilities. It is important to keep these two distinctions in mind because they make a difference in the struggles a person will experience.

In our discussion of healthy family traits (see chapter 4), we noted that Erikson lists trust as the first building block in psychological development. Attachment or bonding to parents, or one's primary caretaker, is an essential step. If a person is unable to develop trust in other people, that one will never be able to have a close, meaningful attachment. The attachment provides the security and significance needed for personal growth. When there is healthy attachment, people are able to support one another, exchange information, and attend to one another's needs.

The principle of attachment is strikingly illustrated in the film *Rainman*. The story involves the experiences of two brothers and the effect their relationship has on each one. Raymond is autistic and so emotionally withdrawn that he is unable to make any meaningful emotional attachments. His brother, Charlie, enters the story as a self-centered wheeler-dealer who wants to take Raymond out of his institutional home and use him to gain access to Raymond's inheritance from their father. As the story progresses, Charlie begins to make some personal changes because he emotionally attaches to Raymond and begins to appreciate him for the human being he really is. Gradually he begins to care for him as a brother, rather than an object to be used for his own purposes.

Raymond, on the other hand, is the same throughout the film because he is unable to make emotional attachments. His security lies in his routine and keeping things the same. He has not learned to trust in people and relationships. Consequently, he does not change and grow as his brother does.

In real life this lack of trust often leads one into various addictions. Those who do not learn to seek relief in relationships, because their own experiences have been painful, seek relief in avenues that will not hurt them emotionally. Some people simply withdraw and shut out the entire world as they enter a state of severe emotional disturbance. Other people turn to alcohol because it can soothe their pain and help them forget for a while. Alcohol becomes their reliable friend because it is predictable, and this is important for the person who has had an unpredictable, undependable parent, Christian or non-Christian. Other people turn to sex, drugs, or food. I believe that the increase in addictions and compulsive disorders stems from the increased lack of healthy childhood environments in our society.

The trust factor is also critical for adult spiritual life and development — those who had a distrusting relationship with parents may also have a difficult time trusting God. Those whose parents were warm, dependable, and interested in them do not find it difficult to believe that God can love them also.

Rita had grown up in a Christian home and church, but her father left when she was young, and she was sexually abused by an older brother. Her mother entertained many boyfriends in their home and often took them upstairs to Rita's bedroom. These few remarks make it obvious that her home life did not encourage trust that those around her would take care of her. As we also looked at her spiritual life and the effect her home experiences had on her, she stated with tension in her voice, "I can't totally give my whole life to the Lord. I am afraid to give it all up. I'm afraid He will take it away from me. If I give all of my-self—they might leave me [the people close to me might leave me, and I'd be abandoned]. I feel guilty. I try to read the Bible and I know I have to, but I can't. So I forget the whole thing. People think I'm a good Christian."

Another very important dysfunction that is a related issue prevalent in the evangelical community is a form of attachment that is conditional. There is acceptance and emotional investment from parents when the children behave properly and do what they are supposed to do. When the children do not live up to the rules or submit to the expected control, then the acceptance is withdrawn. This causes insecurity in the child as the attachment waxes and wanes with the degree of acceptable behavior. Consequently, the child maintains an external focus to deal with this un-stable situation, and the emphasis is on trying to behave in order to main-tain attachment with the parents. This state of affairs interferes with nor-mal emotional development as internal splitting is practiced to maintain some security in a conditional relationship. The parents who emphasize control are most likely to create this type of relationship, one which does not mirror God's unconditional acceptance of people through grace.

Interferes with Responsibility

Because the second major application of the don't trust—do trust rule concerns trusting one's own judgment and opinions, it strikes at the heart of learning responsibility. The second half of the rule says do trust what others judge and think instead. This encourages self-doubt, which cripples a person's ability to evaluate situations, make decisions, and develop his or her own personal beliefs. This type of dependent thinking fosters a superficial way of living that consists of doing the right things in order to be loved and accepted. Those who do not learn to be responsible for their own thoughts and judgments later find themselves at the mercy of strange fads and doctrines that come along because they have no firmly rooted belief of their own. Their beliefs are often little more than the platitudes they have had to memorize because they have not analyzed and personalized them.

The self-doubt thus generated interferes with the second stage of personal development indentified by Erikson as autonomy vs. shame and doubt.[1] The person who has been systematically discouraged from developing individual ideas will be reluctant to pursue autonomy for fear of criticism or rejection. This prevents development of one's own separate identity and will, and impedes the ability to question, think, reason, and form conclusions.

Remember Treva, who was afraid to trust her own opinions and judgments? She had studied Scripture and decided that there was no basis there for not wearing jewelry, but she was still afraid to take the initiative and act on her own judgment. Doubt haunted her and made her angry as she continued in the trap of trying to live up to this particular rule.

Don't Feel — Do Feel

Stops Emotional Integration

The don't feel — do feel rule as practiced in control-oriented environments flies in the face of human nature. Emotions are a normal part of every person's makeup, and God has designed people to have them. When children and adults are told not to feel what they do feel, and instead to feel what is acceptable, the stage is being set for future problems. Denying and stuffing one's emotions is one of the primary causes for depression. This rule plays havoc with many areas of a person's life because emotions are such a basic part of being human. Denying one's feelings is denying very real parts of the self.

Remember Cathy, who stopped going to her mother for help because her feelings were not acknowledged? She also talked about part of her still being a little girl who wants to receive affectionate care from a parent. Emotionally, part of her has remained the unloved child waiting for someone to take care of her. Because she has successfully withdrawn her emotions and tried to hide them from herself and her parents, she has slowed her own emotional growth. When emotions are not accepted into our awareness and worked through our psychological system, growth does not take place.

The emotional conflict is intensified when the second part of the rule kicks into play and people are told to feel (or not feel) something that is contrary to their true feelings. This includes feelings of forgiveness, sexual attraction, anger, personal pain, and so on. Satisfying this rule requires double effort as we resist one feeling and try to manufacture another. When this is examined in the light of personal growth, it is sad to realize that so many people put so much effort into feeling or not feeling what they truly feel! Healthy emotional growth requires accepting and processing our true feelings, but don't feel — do feel works in direct contradiction to this principle by promoting splitting.

Promotes Low Self-Esteem

Pressing someone to try to feel what they do not feel promotes a negative self-image and encourages self-dislike. Since one's self-image is a primary regulator of behavior, this disorder is critical; a negative sense of self inevitably deters and inhibits positive emotional growth. We play out our self-image in reality, and the way we feel about ourselves translates into actual behavior. When we do not feel good about ourselves, it will be evident in how we live. Since the effects of this rule can be so crippling, it is ironic that Christian parents can damage their children as much as or more than the alcoholic home.

Karla, the woman in chapter 11 who had to give up her profession due to emotional stresses, grew up in a Christian home, although she can hardly remember her youth. Some of her memory loss is due to past ECT treatments for depression, and some of it is because her childhood was so painful. As a child she experienced consistent verbal abuse from her Christian mother, and her brother says it is a wonder she turned out as well as she has. He remembers their mother brandishing a butcher knife as she chased Karla through the house.

Karla relates that her parents "were seen as good Christian people in the community. Mom was always involved and helping people. If I had ever tried to tell people what she was like at home, they wouldn't believe me. All she ever did was put me down, tell me I was no good and that I would never amount to anything. Now I am so depressed, I think Mom was right. I am no good. I have had to give up my job because I can't handle it. I tried really hard to keep it, but it hurts so much. I shouldn't be angry at my mother. She died last summer, and she's not here anymore. I am just really a bad person." Her self-image has been severely damaged by her mother's verbal lashings which have no basis in reality. Having believed Mom's criticisms, Karla has taken over her mother's job of putting herself down and is now doing a thorough job.

I am often struck with the fact that so many struggling Christians have extremely negative self-images and a good measure of self-hatred for being such bad persons. Incredibly, the churches often promote these negative feelings. When children or adults are encouraged to feel shame and loathing for themselves in the name of God, something is wrong, because the churches are then reinforcing the feelings of badness in people. The gospel declares that people are acceptable and lovable even though they are imperfect. A sense of shame and negative self-worth is the seedbed for many addictions, and it is curious that many churches are stoking the fires of the addictive process by promoting shame in people.

Don't Want — Do Want

Interferes with Autonomy

The don't want — do want rule interferes with the normal developmental process of personal autonomy and purposeful action on one's own behalf. Part of wholeness is the ability to act alone, to have one's own opinions and ideas, specific desires and wants. When the first rule repressing verbal expression and the second rule denying one's ability to reason combine with this rule restraining personal wants and self-assertion, the result is a real shutdown of the ability to act independently.

Impedes Emotional Development

Systematically applied with young children growing up in Christian homes, this rule impedes emotional development, converting them into containers for what their parents and church leaders tell them and say they want. They can become mere puppets with no substance of their own, and their shallow depth makes them fall prey to the stresses they will have to face. Having no idea what they really believe or feel, they lack the necessary confidence and skills to exercise healthy control over their lives and set appropriate boundaries. This is a common problem in Christians who are co-dependent.

Too often those who teach self-denial in the evangelical community do so without understanding these broader implications for human development. We cannot give up something we do not possess or deny ourselves something we do not want. The person who never learns to say no is unable to say yes in any valid sense. Paul Tournier helps clarify this point:

> Before giving up one's selfishness, one has to express it in living. One has to express it, at any rate, to the legitimate extent to which all living beings need to assert their personal lives. This is their right, and even their duty. . . . We must assert ourselves, then, before we deny ourselves. We must know what we want, and struggle to achieve it.[2]

Referring to the control type of evangelical teaching, Tournier concludes, "A negative education of this kind destroys a child's self-confidence and pushes him into neurosis, because it blocks the spontaneous force of life within him."[3]

15

THE DYNAMICS
OF THE INTERNAL SPLIT

M astering the evangelical rules often leads to an internal split that provides a false sense of "holiness" but precludes wholeness as an integrated person. How can people be whole when they are denying feelings, keeping all honest thoughts to themselves, acting as though they have no wants, forcing feelings of forgiveness when they are actually hurt and angry, afraid to admit that they are wrong, suppressing doubts and anger toward God or their parents? Emotionally split people are not dealing with all of themselves. They are neither integrated emotionally nor whole, because parts of themselves are locked inside hidden closets that do not see daylight. No wonder life becomes a burden and a joyless duty.

Tournier obviously observed similar dynamics at work in his patients in Switzerland because his comments touch on the essence of each of the rules and their impact on basic emotional development:

It is by daring to express his desires, tastes, and opinions, and through feeling that they are respected, that the child becomes aware that he exists, of being a person distinct from other persons. It is a violation of the person of the child to try to direct him in everything according to what his parents think best, without heeding his own preferences. He comes to the point where he no longer knows what his desires, tastes, and opinions are, and an individual without any personal desire, taste, or opinion does not feel that he exists, either. This can be observed in families with high moral or religious pretensions. The parents are so sure they have a monopoly of absolute truth that any other view than their own can only be a grievous error in their eyes. They are so sure of their judgment in all matters, that they impose it upon their children — for their own good, they think.[1]

Rosie, whom we met in chapter 6, is an ACE in her early forties. Although she is an attractive woman with naturally silver hair, she does not feel as confident as she appears. Her sensitive nature has suffered many injuries through the years, and it is difficult for her to trust that people will genuinely care for her. Along with her hurt is considerable anger, but she has difficulty dealing with this for several reasons. You will recall that her Christian father, who was active in the local church and enjoyed a reputation as a good Christian man, had a terrible temper and readily exploded whenever he felt like it on the family farm. As a child Rosie watched in fear as he beat her older brother, feeling the pain as keenly as if the blows were falling on her own back. On other occasions she peered from behind the house as he mercilessly beat the horses when they angered him. Seeing such negative and damaging results of her father's anger, Rosie determined not to repeat the example and hurt others as her father had done. Her fear of following in her father's footsteps was reinforced by the lessons she learned at church, which told her that anger was wrong and unacceptable in God's eyes.

As we discussed the pain she experienced at her father's hand, the subject of anger came up. "But I am not angry. I can't be angry because anger is wrong. And if I let myself be angry, I will be sinning, and God will not be pleased with me. I might say or do something I shouldn't."

To live up to the standard she had learned at church about not being angry and her own goal of not being like her father, she had to split her anger away from herself, move it out of her awareness, and not experience it. This would enable her to view herself as a person without anger.

Degrees of Splitting

Rosie's story is one example of how splitting takes place. It can happen with other thoughts and emotions as well. Anything that is or seems to be unacceptable is disowned or split away from the person, so only acceptable feelings and thoughts remain. The degree of splitting can vary from person to person. For some it takes the form of separate feelings that one shouldn't have. The person tries to push them aside, but they keep coming back. The part that is split away is experienced as an undesirable set of feelings. For those who have gone further, the undesirable emotions can feel like a child inside. This child has a set of feelings that usually were not acceptable in the childhood home. This is especially true when a person has been sexually or physically abused as a child.

In extreme cases of splitting, some people actually develop multiple personalities where each personality is so isolated that it is not aware of the others. In some cases a person has taken the normal parts of self— anger, sadness, fear, pleasure — and has split each one into a separate personality, each with its own name. If Sally is the fun part, then the woman shifts into the Sally personality to have fun. But Sally does not have anger, so she shifts into the Josie personality to be angry, and so on.

Lacy came to my office because she was experiencing anxiety and depression which caused her to be ornery with her family and made it difficult to handle her daily reponsibilities. As we began to explore her family background, some important information came to light. Lacy grew up as the only girl among several boys. Her father was a heavy drinker, and he had little use for girls. Boys were all right, but Lacy received very little affirmation from him. Her mother was a high-strung woman whose nerves were easily jangled, and she often insisted that Lacy be quiet. Whenever Lacy did anything that upset her mother's nerves, she was reprimanded and told how bad she was. Lacy never understood what was actually so bad about her actions. Her mother also threatened her by saying, "If you don't straighten up, God will send you to hell!"

Growing up like this was painful for her, especially when she was also sexually abused by both her drunken father and an uncle whom she dearly loved. To survive in this home, she began to split the pain and terror away from herself. She was able to hide behind a tough, I-don't-need-anybody wall until her brother died. As her grief over her brother began to emerge, she remembered that he had also sexually abused her. The pain she had split away from herself was not a separate personality but was the image of a little girl with an ugly, scary face. Sometimes she felt this little girl was following her, and though she could not actually see her in the room, she had a mental image of her which was as real as if she were there. Through therapy Lacy began to recognize that the little girl actually was a part of herself that she had tried to get rid of through splitting. By ridding herself of the pain, she could live and survive more comfortably. Her splitting was more extensive than Rosie's, but not as severe as a multiple personality. The splitting that occurs in the ACE dynamic can cover the continuum from mild to severe, depending on the situation, but the dynamics are identical.

Foundation for Splitting

Splitting has its foundation in the fear and lack of emotional safety, which we have noted as a common element in alcoholic and dysfunctional Christian homes. If the environment does not allow certain feelings to be present, or if certain ideas are unacceptable to the parents or the one in control, then the discerning youngster realizes there is potential rejection if the governing person's rules are violated. This is especially true of the children with sensitive personalities who want to please those in authority in order to be loved. To present an acceptable image, they must disown or split away their true feelings and develop a self devoid of the unacceptable wishes and feelings.

Look at this dynamic from the perspective of a developmental model. There are four basic stages, with the possibility of developing along either side of the equation — the left side is healthy and the right side is unhealthy. Clarifying terms are listed under each stage.

Attachment . . . . (vs.) . . . . **Isolation**	
Accepted	Rejected
Loved	Unloved
Valued	Devalued
Wanted	Abandoned
Affirmed	Shamed
High self-esteem	Low self-esteem

Separation . . . . (vs.) . . . . **Fusion**

Separation	Fusion
One's own person	Doing what others want
Independent thinking	Thinking what others think
Ability to set limits	Run over by others
Comfortable & secure with self	Clinging to people for security

Integration . . . . (vs.) . . . . **Splitting**

Integration	Splitting
Accepting all of oneself	Carving away part of self
Able to see shadings of gray	Seeing things as black or white (all good or all bad)
Attachment in spite of the bad	Cannot tolerate the bad

Adulthood . . . . (vs.) . . . . **Childlike**

Adulthood	Childlike
Internalizes authority	Rejects authority
Responsible for self	Not responsible for self

Although this is a sketchy overview, it will give you a general idea of how people develop.[2] As you can see, the home atmosphere that provides security and significance (grace) is going to allow attachment or acceptance to occur. Relationships that have conditional acceptance (control) are going to bounce a child back and forth between attachment (acceptance) and isolation (rejection). In other words, when a child is behaving, he is accepted. When he misbehaves, he is rejected. Being rejected, he is isolated, feeling emotionally abandoned and shamed. To avoid the shame and isolation, the child must behave to maintain attachment, and any break in good behavior threatens to thrust him into the agony of shame and isolation. When this bouncing back and forth cycle is a regular part of the child's home environment, a pattern of conditional attachment takes hold and the personal focus develops in an external direction so abandonment can be avoided and attachment can be maintained through acceptable behavior. The haunting fear of isolation lingers in the background which makes the conditional attachment insecure and subject to sudden change. This lingering fear is in stark contrast to the security found in the home that emphasizes grace and unconditional love, saying, "You are loved no matter what you do."

Sensitive personalities are especially vulnerable. High "S" and "C" people will work extra hard at maintaining their behavior to preserve relationships. The more self-sufficient "D's" basically attach to themselves and do not strive to attach to the parents who have not provided a safe atmosphere. Without such attachment they can grow up without empathy because they do not know how to relate on an emotional level. The "i's" need social approval, so they also will try to perform, but they typically take it less seriously than "S's" and "C's." Co-dependent, rescuing behavior can develop in the "S's" who are too concerned about keeping others happy in order to be attached, and "C's" work at being perfect to be attached.

The attachment stage is critical, and if the attachment is *conditional,* the person is unable to start the next healthy stage of separation. Having one's own thoughts is in contradiction to pleasing the parents who emphasize control ("Say what I want to hear"), so to please and also continue developing, one enters the fusion stage. This means the youngster fuses with the parents and does just what the parents want, instead of becoming his or her own person. This in turn leads to the next unhealthy stage of splitting, where decisions are not made on the basis of reality, but on what will please the person handing out the love. The things that please the parent are kept because it feels safe to have these ideas and thoughts, while the behavior and thoughts that bring rejection are split away. Unable to form a separate identity and become independently responsible, the person continues childlike in relationship to other people and adults. You can see from this progression how the evangelical rules are tied in with control, emotional stifling, and unhealthy development (see Figure 2).

Healthy Development		Unhealthy Development
Attachment	← ──────────── →	Isolation ↓
Separation		Fusion ↓
Integration	*Blocked*	Splitting ↓
Adulthood		Childlike

Fig. 2: Conditional Attachment

Many of the personal experiences described in these pages exhibit the thread of fear that underscores individual lives and show how the emotional split provides some security in an unsafe setting. As Joe summed it up, "In my family, if any emotion or something came up, I had to put it away. My folks couldn't accept it. 'Just laugh it off!' they told me when kids pushed me in school. So I had to put part of me away." The unacceptable aspects of a person must be gotten out of the way in order to have a relationship with the feared person who is in control and has the love one so desperately wants to receive.

Tournier's description of the typical evangelical home so aptly summarizes what takes place as a child grows up under these rules.

> While still young the child must learn to forget himself, to disregard his personal desires, to behave in accordance with the requirements of others, seeking always to please them rather than himself. Of course, the parents head the list of the "others" who must be pleased and have constant service rendered to them, whereas they themselves scarcely ever bother to gratify any of the child's pleasures which they look upon as mere selfish whims. And they accuse him of selfishness if he manifests any personal aspiration.[3]

Dynamics of Splitting

As we look at the dynamics of the split caused by the evangelical rules, it will help to gather them together in one location so we can clearly visualize them. Notice how they are divided from left to right. All of the "don't do's" are on the left, and the "You're supposed to do" admonitions are on the right. To help your visualization, lean back from this page and concentrate your focus on the two columns.

Rule #1: "Don't talk . . . Do say . . . "

Rule #2: "Don't trust . . . Do trust . . . "

Rule #3: "Don't feel . . . Do feel . . . "

Rule #4: "Don't want . . . Do want . . . "

All of the emphasis on the left is against the self, and the focus on the right is toward others, doing what parents/God want us to do. The evangelical rules define how the split should take place if a person wants to be "holy" or acceptable according to the predominant Christian standard. The rules also determine the basis for the direction of a person's focus. Is the focus internal regarding self-development and awareness, or is it external, concerned with surviving and trying to maintain personal safety because the basic needs of security and significance are unmet?

In terms of emphasis, many of us have been taught that true spirituality consists of being on the right side of the equation (doing what we are supposed to do), while "sin" or being unacceptable to God is when we participate in any fashion on the left side of the equation (doing what we want, feeling what we feel, saying what we think, and trusting ourselves). From this perspective, people risk definite danger if they decide to ignore the left half of the picture (the prohibitions), while safety and true "holiness" lie on right half of the equation (following the rules).

Now before you decide that I am throwing too much of the baby out with the dirty bath water, understand that I am not saying that the points on the right are in error or should not be part of the evangelical picture. The Bible does talk about obeying parents, self-denial, fear of God, and so on. It would be absolutely foolhardy for parents to give up teaching their children Biblical values and principles because children need these values as a foundation for their development. Too often an incorrect, dysfunctional application of these teachings in Christian homes and churches occurs when control is emphasized instead of grace. These teachings must be taught with a proper balance and understanding that takes the personal stages of development into account.

When control is emphasized, there must be a standard against which compliance is measured. This leads to the master-list of sins and the evangelical rules as a practical definition of what is a good Christian and a "holy" life. It follows that the more closely one is able to live up to the list, the more spiritual or "holy" that person will be, and thus more acceptable to parents and to God.

If I want to be loved, I must be sure that my actions and thoughts are in conformity with the image I am expected to portray. The evangelical rules function as a guide for doing this.

Here lies the problem in the evangelical community when control is emphasized. Too often parents and churches use Biblical teachings to instill fear, as a way to motivate and control behavior. This lays the foundation for splitting to become an integral part of one's spiritual life. As Ellens points out in his paper on grace (see Appendix C), this appeals to certain people because they can track their lives on a tangible system of behavior. This is particularly true of the "S" and "C" people who are looking for a secure way of doing things. The "C" people prefer rules and lists anyway, so the splitting process and trying to do it perfectly find a natural mesh with their behavioral style of thinking and functioning.

But pursuing the "holy" route means disowning oneself, which is contrary to wholeness. How can one be a whole person and regularly carve parts of oneself away to fit some external mold? One cannot approach a true sense of wholeness before God when one does not admit to all of the parts of the self that constitute the whole person.

There is also another problem. According to the rules, to have a relationship with God, we must get rid of our anger, our selfish wants, and so on. To have these unacceptable feelings will bring God's rejection and disapproval. If we want His approval, we must make ourselves presentable, but we become unhealthy in the process. When we split away our anger, our hurt, and our sexual feelings as though they are not part of us, God cannot redeem these negative aspects since all we take to Him are our "nice" components and certain acceptable little faults and sins. The Christians who are running around trying to live by the rules and emphasizing control as they shove aside their true motives and feelings cannot experience God's grace at a deep, personal level because they have left a big chunk of themselves outside of their relationship with God.

Avoidance Behavior

According to psychological learning theory, when fear is the motivating force behind our behavior, we are engaging in avoidance behavior. This means we decide to act to avoid pain, punishment, or some other negative consequence. Avoidance behaviors are not deeply personal or from the heart, but are superficial, defensive actions to guard against criticism or rejection. These reactions are developed in response to the threat, and so do not promote personal growth or integration.

A common example occurs when one member of a couple is more affectionate than the other. The wife may complain that her husband does not greet her with a hug when he comes home in the evening. Although the husband is not a hugging type, he does not like to have his wife angry at him, so he begins to give her a hug when he enters the house. This is avoidance behavior. After a week or so, the wife says, "You never give me a kiss when you hug me. Don't you like me?" So the husband adds another behavior to reduce the possibility of his wife's disappointment. As time goes on, the list can become longer and longer, and the husband will have built a repertoire of actions based on avoidance rather than from his own heart.

The same sort of thing can happen in the Christian life. To avoid God's wrath under the control system, people must engage in the right behavior according to the master-list. Reading the Bible, having devotions, witnessing, and even seeking salvation after a frightening sermon may all be actions based on fear of consequences rather than from the heart. It is in fact possible to build one's entire spiritual life out of avoidance behavior, but it leads to a life of duty, lacking the freedom and heartfelt joy that the New Testament describes. This is the dynamic for those ACEs who build their spiritual lives on the list of behaviors to perform and to avoid. A gnawing uneasiness begins to develop about the quality of their spiritual lives. But true to the rules, this feeling also must be dismissed as sinful and unacceptable, when in reality it indicates that things are going wrong.

The husband who comes home with a mental list of things he must do every day to avoid his wife's anger and who dreads that she will add new ones to the list may end up in my office saying, "I just don't feel toward her like I used to. I find myself not wanting to go home while I am driving away from work. Somehow I can't be myself at home. I feel more like myself when I am playing softball with the guys on Tuesday and Thursday nights."

Avoidance behaviors are difficult to change because whenever the fear trigger is hit, even after months or years of no fear, the avoidance reaction immediately returns. I can see this in my own life. It has been over twenty years since I attended a hellfire sermon like those I heard regularly in my home church where altar calls were conducted in fearful atmospheres, but a recent experience made me realize the ease with which avoidance behaviors can return. My family and I visited a church where they unexpectedly had an altar call. Although it was nowhere as intense as the revival calls I had experienced, I found my nervous system reacting automatically. My heart rate jumped, my palms became sweaty, and I found myself doubting my own salvation again. "Should I be going forward? Is my life really in order? Is God going to be angry with me if I just stand here?" In the other corner of my mind, I assured myself that I was in pretty good shape and that I was experiencing a return of an avoidance reaction. Nonetheless I was relieved when the service ended.

The evangelical rules establish an ideal of self that is unrealistic and impossible to attain. However, it is supported with Scripture and has a ring of truth and an appeal that is hard to resist. Essentially, the thrust of the rules is to be against oneself, to distrust one's own judgment, to feel unworthy and shameful, to reject one's feelings and desires. Or, to carry it a step further, to even hate ourselves because we are sinful.

The self-hatred intensifies whenever Christians, and it usually is the sensitive ones who are most conscientious, realize in a moment of honesty that they really do some of the things they have split away. Many struggling Christians have said to me, "I know I am not supposed to be angry, but when I am honest, I really am mad, and I don't want to forgive. My mother really hurt me, and I have lost the chance for a normal childhood. I know I am supposed to forgive, but I can't." Their next statement is always the clincher because it leads to the ultimate destructive end of the rules. "I must really be a bad person. It just proves what I already feel, that I am no good. What kind of person am I if I can't do what the Bible says?"

This same principle happens with any type of thought, motive, or emotion that appears on the forbidden side of the equation. To keep the fear of judgment at bay, the sensitive Christian must pull out the stops in order to banish the threatening truth from God's and his parents' eyes. This is especially true of powerful sexual feelings that are difficult to banish from one's life. Since sexual feelings are generally pleasant, regardless of whether they occur within prescribed limits, the person who experiences this pleasure in an immoral act feels doubly guilty because he or she has enjoyed something that is wrong. This adds immeasurably to the sense of shame and badness. "What kind of person am I to enjoy that which God says is wrong?" Efforts to rid oneself of this guilt sometimes take on spiritual dimensions that are unscriptural.

Rennie came to me because of her consistent death wishes. Her parents were in full-time Christian work, but her older brother had sexually abused her from the time she was ten until she was fourteen. She was a sensitive "S" and "C" person who had internalized most of her emotions, and she recalls often praying to God during her teen years that she would die at an early age. As she passed through her teens and did not die, she began to think more about actually killing herself. And she did begin to make attempts. The night before she came to see me for the first time, she had taken about thirty over-the-counter sleeping pills that did nothing more than give her a dry mouth and stomach pains.

As we discussed her life, it was obvious that her deep sense of shame and worthlessness was eating her up. She was internalizing her anger instead of being angry at her brother for victimizing her and her parents for allowing it to happen. Instead of seeing herself as the victim, she saw herself as the bad person who did not deserve to live. In addition she did not know how to balance certain Scripture against her other feelings. "I don't know what to do with verses that say I should be crucified with Christ, and Paul talks about the self he doesn't want to be in Romans 7. Where is the balance? The Bible says I am supposed to love my neighbor as myself, but I am also supposed to crucify myself? How am I supposed to care about myself and want to crucify myself?"

The idea of being crucified with Christ was supporting the split she was trying to follow, and this is a common error among Christians. She believed that crucifying herself was the route to "holiness" and that the bad part of herself was the part to crucify. Indeed, the Scripture does tell us to be crucified with Christ, but she was engaging in self-crucifixion as preparation for presenting herself to God. She intended to split away the bad so God would approve of her, but this is operating under the control system, rather than the redemption system. Not only was she suffering from a sense of guilt and shame, Scripture was serving to reinforce her sense of unworthiness and conflict.

Shame and Egocentricity of Childhood

Shame and personal feelings of badness can develop easily in children for several reasons. Robert H. Schuller advances the idea that lack of trust and shame are part of Adam's sin that has been passed on to every person.[4] This sense of shame can take the form of low self-esteem, inferiority, a feeling of unlovableness, and a sense of personal badness. The fact that children are the weaker, immature members in a family makes them especially vulnerable to practices that reinforce the shameful feelings.

The irony is that too many of the evangelical practices use God to reinforce feelings of shame and self-loathing in children. These practices are not redemptive at all but are actually destructive to emotional and spiritual development. The don't feel—do feel evangelical rule that eliminates many normal feelings experienced by growing youngsters often encourages negative feelings, or as Hession recommends, helps them to see themselves as worms. Many parents use shame to discipline their children when they get out of line. Remember how Terri's father scolded his grandson by saying, "Jesus doesn't love naughty little boys!" He was obviously emphasizing control and wanted to bring shame down on the little fellow.

When the second half of the evangelical rules are held up as the only acceptable alternative and the road to "holiness," those who take them seriously feel guilty and inferior when they are unable to live a life of perfect faith and practice. These feelings of failure reinforce their sense of worthlessness, weak spirituality, and shame because they have not been able to live up to the expected goal of the rules.

Ray had grown up in a Christian home and tended to be a high "C" personality. His church experiences while he was in high school were largely negative because the pastor at his church was a negative, judgmental person. Ray was generally cautious about most things in his life, and what troubled him were the doubts that kept him from having 100 percent faith. "I think I can get it to 95 percent, but I just can't get it all the way," he would say. This left feelings of inadequacy and concern that his spiritual life was in trouble.

The egocentricity of childhood which further explains why children are prone to develop feelings of shame and of being no good is a generally accepted concept in psychology,. Under the ages of ten or twelve, children are unable to think and reason at an abstract level because the brain structures for that function are not fully developed. This means that children reason differently from adults, have difficulty seeing other points of view, and are prone to misinterpret situations. Consequently, when something goes wrong, the child quite naturally blames himself or herself. This is the egocentricity of childhood.

For example, if a father spends no time with his daughter because he is always at work, the daughter does not reason out that her dad is a workaholic who shows his love by working and earning money so she can have nice clothes and go to summer camp. Because of the egocentricity of childhood, she is more likely to think, "My dad never spends time with me. There must be something wrong with me. If I were a better girl, he would want to be with me. I must be a bad person."

This tendency to blame the self takes on an even more critical dimension when the child is sexually or physically abused. As Lacy was working out the pain related to her sexual abuse, she continually cried out, "But why? Why did they do it to me? If they loved me, how could they do it to me? I must have been really bad for them to do that to me. My mother was right. I really am no good. It had to be me." Because of the egocentricity of childhood, she had been blaming herself for years and continued to blame and hate herself as a grown woman. The idea that she is "bad" took root deep within her, and it will require many therapy sessions to turn that perception around.

Abandonment

Abandonment as a concept has recently been more and more discussed in regard to dysfunctional families.

We have all heard stories about babies that were wrapped in newspaper and placed on a doorstep late at night or the infant found in a city dumpster. This is an obvious form of abandonment, when the parent totally rejects the child, leaving it in some desolate spot.

There is a subtle form of abandonment that can be as destructive psychologically as being abandoned in a dumpster, perhaps more so, and it occurs in good Christian homes. It does not involve physical neglect or desertion; it is the emotional abandonment that consists of not spending time with a child, not being available when the child needs help and support, pushing aside requests for help. In short, treating the child as though he or she does not count.

Have you ever seen an old '56 Chevy parked beside a dilapidated farm building? The hood is missing and weeds are growing up through the engine compartment. The fenders are rusty and the side windows are missing. The windshield has been splintered by someone's rock, and the trunk is gaping open to the world. It is obvious that the car has no value to anyone. The owner simply lost all affection for the car and abandoned it. People don't abandon objects that have value and meaning for them. That '56 Chevy in the hands of an antique car buff would look like new. The chrome would be bright with no rust in sight, and the upholstery squeaky clean. The car has definite value to him.

When children's needs for security and significance are ignored, they feel as abandoned as the old '56 Chevy, but unlike the Chevy, they feel the pain. They feel the sense of worthlessness that comes with being abandoned, of being valued so little by those who are supposed to love them. Unfortunately, there are many children and adults who deep inside feel abandoned, but they are hardly visible in the nice suburban houses with green lawns, new cars, and smiling family members milling about.

Coping with Shame and Unlovableness

Deep feelings of shame and personal badness are so strong and so painful that most people decline to deal with them. As though this were not enough, the inner sense of badness is so vivid to the people who are feeling it, that they are quite certain it is visible to others.

This sets up an impossible dilemma because those who are feeling unlovable desperately want to be accepted and loved. But to be loved, they must develop a relationship and be open about themselves in order to receive the understanding and love that they need. But they fear that if they get close to someone and let themselves be known, they will be rejected since no one can love them as they are.

Bobbi was an attractive single woman in her early thirties who held a responsible, professional job. When she first came for therapy, she seemed so calm and steady that I wondered why she was there. As I learned more about her, I realized that even though this Christian woman appeared relaxed and confident, her inner identity was that of an unlovable person. Her father had died in the war, and her mother was emotionally distant and often unavailable. "I grew up feeling like excess baggage," Bobbi reported matter-of-factly. Obviously her needs for significance and security had not been met as a child, and she began to develop an inner sense of shame and unlovableness as she was growing up.

When she was nine years old, an unfortunate event occurred that confirmed for her how bad she really was. One day when her mother was gone, as often was the case, a teenage boy from the neighborhood came to the house. Although he did not stay very long, he raped her before he left. Already feeling like excess baggage in her mother's life, this experience left her feeling dirty and contaminated. Not only had she been unlovable before, now she was dirtied and even more unlovable. She quite naturally concluded that this horrible secret had to remain hidden or people would reject her for sure. So trying to split away the nasty part of herself and hiding it from others became the focus of her life and governed her relationships with people.

She was uncomfortable in social situations, cautious in making friends, and tended to keep to herself. Her secret was so vivid to her that she felt others could look at her and instantly know it. "There's an awful woman, she has been raped." The extent to which this troubled her is evident in an experience she related. When she took an advanced graduate class at a local university, the instructor divided the class into groups for discussion. To become acquainted, the students within the groups were to take turns making some personal comments. "I was so nervous I about jumped out of my skin," Bobbi said. "When it was my turn, I hardly knew what to say. I was so afraid I might say something that would let it show — that they would know that I was raped by the neigh-

bor guy. It's like they could just look at me and know it had happened."
Bobbi's experience is typical of people who feel they must hide their
bad selves, so they cautiously relate to people without actually being
open about themselves.

To cope with this shame, Bobbi had developed her own set of inner
rules to handle it. "I am an unlovable, dirty person. I will not let people
get close to me or let them know my secret. I can't trust that other
people can love me as I am."

A variety of coping behaviors may come into play, but they are all
designed to meet the needs which were not met in the home: significance and security. The beliefs that Patrick Carnes lists as underpinnings
for sexual addiction fit most people's reactions to their personal unworth: (1) I am basically a bad, unworthy person; (2) No one would
love me as I am; (3) My needs are never going to be met if I have to
depend on others.[5]

Once a person has advanced to this point, the next step is to identify
an avenue for either meeting the unmet needs of love and significance or
a method of finding good feelings and anesthetizing the pain at the same
time. Such persons decide that, since they are unable to trust others to
meet their needs, they will have to do it themselves and meet their needs
in ways that either do not involve others or do not involve emotional risk.

At this juncture many outward symptoms appear. Those who turn to
food for comfort and good feelings develop an eating disorder. Those
who use drugs and alcohol become chemically dependent. Others become workaholics. Sexual addiction and violence is another route. Some
become co-dependents as they try to meet their own needs by submerg-
ing themselves into helping others. Even following some churches' legalistic rules and trying to be "holy" can serve as a form of addictive or
compulsive behavior.

Emma was an attractive college student who was battling an eating
disorder. "My father, my good Christian father, left me when I was ten
years old. I didn't think my folks were having any real problems, and he
just leaves all at once, and there is this other woman who becomes my
stepmom. I can't stand her. It hurt so much, and I found myself just
eating and eating when I became depressed. I would eat until I felt phys-

ically sick, and the sick feeling was stronger than the depression, so I didn't feel depressed anymore."

As a child Dana had been sexually abused by her brother but had split the experience away from herself. To cope with the pain, she developed an eating disorder. The problem became so bad that she had to be hospitalized for treatment. After she returned home, her life seemed to stabilize for a number of months, but she continued to be unhappy. She was overly protective of her own children, and her sexual relationship with her husband had never been normal according to her, so to save her marriage she reentered the hospital. "I thought it would be easy this time. The last time I took care of the eating disorder, and this time I figured I would just take care of the abuse. But now I see there is so much more to work on. I don't like myself and feel dirty and contaminated, and I am afraid my husband is going to get sick of me and leave me. There is just so much, and I end up feeling worse." She was beginning to see more clearly her underlying sense of shame and unlovableness.

At this point of confronting and dealing with shame and unworthiness, the struggle for an ACE becomes different from that of the secular person. Although non-Christians may have a deep sense of personal unworth, they lack the spiritual component that permeates the life of an ACE. Usually the ACE's beliefs reinforce the sense of shame and guilt and intensify the conflict. We have already seen many of the Christian teachings that weigh people down at this point. "Where is God while I am struggling? It seems like He has let me down after I have prayed and prayed. But I feel guilty for being angry at Him." "I was taught that a Christian should not be angry." "Deny yourself—put others first. That is the way to happiness. But nobody cares about me." "The happiest time in my life was when I was having an affair. I know it is wrong, but I don't know if I can live without her. I have tried, but I keep going back. I feel awful about it, but I don't know what I can do." "My body is a temple, but look at this ugly fat. I enjoy eating, what can I say. Every time I look in the mirror I feel guilty, but when I get the urge for that cheesecake, I eat it anyway. I'm not much of a Christian." "I have prayed and prayed about it. It seems like God isn't hearing me. I guess I'm so bad even He has given up on me." As you can see in these remarks that struggling ACEs typically make, the spiritual dimension adds a definite note of seriousness to the conflict.

As a result, ACE Christians feel spiritual failure in addition to the emotional shame and unlovableness that already exists. In despair the Christian falls into the same trap that people with other addictions do. They fall back on the only mechanism they know to relieve the pain of their spiritual failure. Just as the drug addict looks for another fix, the bulimic finds a donut shop, and the sex addict tries to make a connection, the Christian tries harder to be perfect and intensifies splitting in order to be pleasing to others and God.

One may pray for twenty minutes a day instead of ten and read the Bible for thirty minutes instead of fifteen. Another works harder at trusting God and pushes anger deeper down and out of sight. One can deny herself and let people take advantage of her as she turns the other cheek; try harder to be selfless in relationships with her family, co-workers, and friends; and volunteer for more responsibility at church and organize the children's Sunday school.

Another tries harder to have faith and repeats verses he has memorized when doubts and frustrations begin to appear. If there is a particular sin that troubles him, he measures spiritual progress by trying to increase the length of time between sinful episodes. He looks for classes, books, and tapes on being a good Christian with no worries, angry feelings, and sexual urges. If the church has altar calls, he goes forward and requests prayer for his failing spiritual life, but most of all he tries to carve away any thoughts or feelings that he believes are wrong.

In other words, intensified efforts and commitment to living by the evangelical rules are the way to rid oneself of badness. The ACE chooses "holiness" not wholeness. But just as the addict's next fix does not cure his inner pain, increased efforts at "holiness" do not dissolve inner shame and feelings of unlovableness. They only draw one more deeply into the destructive, negative cycle of splitting further and further away from oneself and true wholeness. Figure 3 illustrates this concept.

The futility of trying to solve one's loneliness, guilt, shame, feelings of abandonment, or low self-esteem by trying harder to follow the evan-

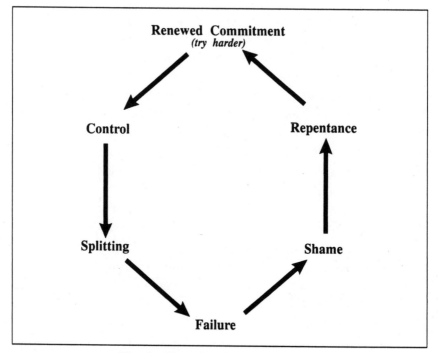

Fig. 3: The ACE Compulsive Cycle

gelical rules often leads to depression. Many Christians live with a constant low-level depression that produces a serious, sober life-style. Though they are conscientious and reliable, people often do not enjoy being around them. Others live tense lives, and some become so seriously depressed and suicidal because they see no hope for improvement that they need professional help.

Physical and Sexual Abuse

There are two additional forms of abuse that add another dimension of emotional difficulty for the ACE. However much one wants to believe that Christian parents would not be abusive to the children God has given them, many Christians who have grown up in apparently Christian homes tell horrifying stories of sexual and physical abuse in their homes.

Terri's story is typical. "Dad was a respected member of the community and had a reputation for being a Christian among his friends. At church he was active in many of the educational and musical activities, but he was different at home. He had a real temper, and he would get so mad at me, even when I hadn't done anything. He would hit me around the face with his fist or grab whatever else was close by. If I had ever told anybody in the community what Dad was like at home, nobody would have believed me." In addition to working out her conflicts with the evangelical rules, her abuse issues complicated her ability to be open and trusting.

Lana, now married with a husband and child, was abused by her father, brother, babysitter, and grandfather. It caused such a deep sense of fear and shame that she split many of her feelings away from herself, especially the pain and anger. She had been able to find meaningful support in her relationship with God, until one day as she was meditating and picturing Christ in her mind, it suddenly occurred to her that He was male. The thought struck a dark chord of fear in her because the primary males in her life had abused her. Could she trust Christ, who was also a male? She decided she could not. This added another dimension to her struggle.

Obviously, physical, sexual, or fierce verbal abuse intensifies the self-hatred, shame, and the sense of unlovableness. Children are already prone to conclude that negative actions against them are their fault, so outrageous abuse is often comprehended in the same way. This intensified shame and negative self-image wreak havoc with the child's mental health and make the difficult task of growing up all the more difficult.

Psychiatrist Roland Summit has developed a concept he calls the Child Sexual Abuse Accommodation Syndrome, which can be applied to all forms of abuse. Essentially, it traces the way a child adjusts to being the unrelenting target of an older adult or child.[6]

- *Secrecy.* The child feels ashamed and guilty about the abuse but does not tell anyone for various reasons. These can include fears of retaliation, not being believed, or loss of love and security. It seems wiser to the child to minimize risk, especially if the fears are strong. Secrecy defines the sexual activity or other unreported abuse as dangerous and bad.

- *Helplessness.* The helplessness felt by the child causes him or her to retreat emotionally, which is the process of keeping the secret. This is critical in the sequence of the accommodation syndrome.

- *Entrapment.* The sense of shame and the various fears combine to entrap and eventually immobilize the child. As the child tries to protect himself or herself by being immobile, he or she begins to feel responsible for what is going on and struggles with the dilemma of whether the abuser is bad or the child is bad. Since the child has neither the power nor the position to judge the abusing adult as bad, the egocentricity of childhood causes the child to accept the self as the one who is bad and deserves punishment. This dynamic is the origin and foundation for self-hate related to all forms of neglect.

- *Accommodation.* A child who is dependent on the abusing adult is still going to need the adult. In order to turn to the abusing parent for this help, the child has to maintain the delusional notion of the adult as a good person. Otherwise, the child would be totally on his or her own for survival. The result is a vertical split with reality: the adult being blameless while the child is bad and at fault. This is mind splitting and is the perception that finalizes the child's adjustment to the abuse so he or she can accommodate to the abuse and continue to see the perpetrator as emotionally available.

In accommodating the abusing adult, the child moves into the fusion stage of development instead of the healthy separation stage because the unhealthy, unconditional attachment with the abusing adult provides insufficient security to develop separateness. The true adult messages are rejecting, isolating ones. This starts the pattern of being used that often continues into adulthood and shows up in abusive relationships and marriages. It is easy for the abused person to misinterpret fusion for attachment because both involve a relationship that can be intense, appear "caring," and include time together. The vertical split that Summit describes reinforces the notion that the fusing "relationship is a good one, but the reason it is not working is because I am bad. Therefore, I must do something to make it better." Consequently, the abused person tries harder to please by doing more splitting and self-hatred as the cycle continues.

It is easy to see from this accommodation syndrome how the sense of badness and shame is intensified under abusive conditions, and unfortunately the Christian community is not immune to this form of abuse. More and more ACEs who present themselves for therapy have such abuse in their backgrounds, and it intensifies and complicates the split produced by the evangelical rules.

Spiritual Abuse

As I have observed people in the ACE category, another phenomenon has puzzled me because I could see it and describe it, but not explain it. There are Christians who can readily attach themselves to God as a resource in their emotional struggles, without reluctance or hesitation. There are other Christians, myself included, who have experienced difficulty viewing God as a supportive ally in dealing with personal conflicts, struggles, and low self-esteem.

My own primary emotion toward God was fear. I was definitely afraid to cross Him, trigger His wrath, or do anything that would send me straight to hell. On the other hand, I also was reluctant to venture too close to Him for fear of what He would do to me if I gave Him the chance. He was not the source of support as I struggled.

I remember a conversation with a minister about my fears and personal struggles. His comments made logical sense but were far afield from where I was in my emotional development. "Why don't you look at yourself in the mirror and say to yourself a number of times, 'God loves me. I am a worthwhile person.'" I just shook my head; here was another person who did not understand where I was in my struggle for wholeness.

For years I assumed that my fear of God was related to the innumerable hellfire sermons I heard as a youngster. Only recently did I gain some helpful insight for understanding this phenomenon which I have observed in myself and other Christians with whom I have worked. I call this phenomenon *spiritual abuse.*

Keeping in mind the sexual and physical abuse model, the fear, emotional damage, shame, and especially the accommodation syndrome, we can see that certain evangelical practices fit into the same conceptual framework. The dynamics and ramifications of spiritual abuse parallel those of physical and sexual abuse. Individuals who have been spiritually abused as children have difficulty seeing God as an ally in their trouble because He is viewed as one of the perpetrators. Of course, God is not a perpetrator, but He is viewed as one because that is how significant adults have presented Him to young children.

Suppose a father approaches his eight-year-old son and while striking him with a length of electrical wire he screams, "You are a bad, stupid person! Only really dumb people do what you did today, and you deserve everything you're getting. I wish you had never been born, and I'll be glad when you're old enough to get out of my sight. I'll beat your butt so bad you won't ever even think about doing that again! If you don't shape up I'll throw you out of the house with my own hands! And don't think you can get out of this by telling anybody about it. I've got you nailed, buddy, and if you try to get out of it, you'll pay for a long time because I won't put up with any of your crap!"

No reasonable person would encourage the little boy to approach this father for emotional support by commanding, "Now your father really loves you and wants the best for you. Go hug him and tell him that you love him, too. He insists that you love him. After all, he gave you life and you live in his house. All you have comes from him, and you owe it to him to please him and to want to spend time with him. You can trust him because he wants to take care of you." The reasonable person would say, "That's ridiculous to think he can go to his dad for comfort. He has been physically beaten, emotionally injured, and verbally abused by his father. How can anyone not realize that he is afraid of his dad and fears what Dad may do to him if he gets too close? He's blaming himself for what his dad does and believes he is a bad person who deserves what he gets."

On the other hand, even reasonable people seldom realize how often parents and churches use God to intimidate their children, to instill intense fear in order to control them; threaten them with frightening stories about God's wrath, final judgment, eternity in hell; and make shaming statements designed to produce submission and obedience. Such treatment constitutes spiritual abuse, just as surely as beatings and threats constitute physical abuse.

I grew up with all these spiritually abusive tactics, and it has been difficult for me to view God as a person who could love me. Because

God was an integral part of the message I heard at church and at home, He was the *instrument* of the abuse in my mind and the primary *reason* for the abuse. After all, the scary stories and threats highlighted the fact that God had certain demands that I must meet, and if I didn't, my soul would be in danger. God was the architect of the entire Biblical plan; how could He not be the perpetrator when He was at the center of everything I heard?

The vertical split is also evident in those Christians who have been spiritually abused. In order to go to God for support, even after they have been beaten down, shamed, and intimidated in His name, they develop a Christian life that is based on the fact that God is perfect and they are the ones who are bad. In order to contain their badness, they put extra effort into splitting away from themselves anything that seems undesirable to God, and they work diligently at mastering the evangelical rules. The little security they possess depends on maintaining the shaky equilibrium of the vertical split. Therefore, they cannot afford to to see that they may not be as bad as they thought because that would mean God is not perfect. And the Bible says that God is perfect, so how can anything be changed? "Maybe we are the ones who are wrong," they begin to wonder, as they feel hopelessly entrapped in their badness and shame.

They are unable to see that the people misrepresenting God are the actual perpetrators, and that God Himself is not involved in abuse. Some Christian denominations clearly teach that people are wicked and shameful, and this only reinforces the negative self-image in a very destructive direction. When ACEs have experienced spiritual abuse, their wounds must be healed before they can relate to God in a healthy manner and move toward wholeness.

PART FIVE

CHOOSING WHOLENESS

16

WHOLENESS IS AN OPTION

For those of us who are ACEs, following the evangelical rules brings a certain amount of security, even though we often struggle intensely with the emotional conflicts that result. Having been told, warned, and sometimes threatened in the name of God that we must follow the rules, how can we choose wholeness by forsaking the rules without risking God's damnation and wrath? How can we understand the Christian perspective in a way that allows us to be ourselves and still be acceptable to God? If we drop the rules, will we also go against the admonition in Hebrews? "Pursue peace with all men, and holiness, without which no one will see the Lord" (12:14).

Allison's observation regarding Christianity's posture in our society may be helpful because it summarizes the thoughts we have been examining.

> However, the vast preponderance of the Christian role was seen to be, overwhelmingly, that of control rather than redemption. . . . A religion of nagging—of exhorting and rebuking, of law and control, of condemnation and fussing-at—is a big part of the picture presented as Christianity, not merely by popular distortions but within the very citadels of scholarly learning.[1]

Control rather than redemption. The evangelical rules that produce ACEs emphasize control, and the key to choosing wholeness lies in grasping and understanding the counterpart of control—redemption also

193

called grace. Grace is the only way out of the performance trap and the spiral of trying to follow the rules to be "holy."

During the course of Cathy's therapy, we had a discussion about her lack of confidence, her sense of personal unworth, and her need to please other people in order to have self-esteem. Although change seemed desirable, it was also somewhat frightening when we considered changing the rules by which she was living. In a tone of mild panic, she said, "My self-worth is tied up in the rules—if I don't do those, then I don't have anything." Though she could admit that the rules were not working, following them provided her with the feeling that at least she was doing something, and that seemed preferable to the vast nothingness she would face if she gave up the rules. "God expects me to keep the rules," she added with a note of finality and resignation.

Although many of us fear that dropping the rules will cause us to lose our standing with God, a closer examination of Scripture indicates otherwise. In fact, choosing to emphasize redemption and grace will not only lead us to wholeness, but a *proper* form of holiness, not a self-righteous perfection that puts us in the Pharisees' company. Choosing wholeness really is an option, and we do not have to drive ourselves into depression trying to follow the evangelical rules.

Grace as the Foundation

A number of Scriptures address the issue of control as opposed to grace and redemption. Paul comes down hard against the Galatians' version of the rule that said people had to be circumcised. Warning them of their error, he asserts that "Christ is useless to you if you are counting on clearing your debt to God by keeping those laws; you are lost from God's grace" (5:4, TLB). This truth is equally applicable to our current version of the evangelical rules.

And there is a familiar verse we all learned as children but then were taught to live as though it did not apply. "For by grace you have been saved through faith, and that not of yourselves; it is the gift of God, not of works, lest anyone should boast" (Ephesians 2:8–9). Paul comes at this point again, "Surely you can't be so idiotic as to think that a man begins his spiritual life in the Spirit and then completes it by reverting to outward observances?" (Galatians 3:3, PHILLIPS). It always puzzled me that I was taught I was saved by grace, but then I had to be extra careful how I behaved so I would not lose my standing with God. Which was really true?

Paul further establishes grace as a foundation when he writes, "For it is good that the heart be established by grace, not with foods which have not profited those who have been occupied with them" (Hebrews 13:9). He also repeats this position in Colossians 2:20–23. He is comparing the Christian process of redemption with that of others who are relying on their actions to bring them salvation. These, plus other Scriptures that could be cited clearly state that grace is the foundation of our faith, not the keeping of rules.

Before we go any further, I would like you to discontinue reading this chapter and turn to Appendix C to read the treatise by Harold Ellens entitled "God's Grace, the Radical Option." Because it is such an excellent piece, I have included it here as an insightful analysis of grace and its role in human behavior. Ellens's comments on grace will serve as a helpful background for the remainder of this book. If you have already read it, you may want to read it again before you continue. As you read, compare his thoughts on grace with the evangelical emphasis on control and the evangelical rules.

Defining Grace

What is grace and what does it look like in everyday life? What constitutes an environment for wholeness? If we want to emphasize grace instead of control in the churches and Christian families, what do we do? We talk about unconditional love, acceptance, support, and so on, but what does it mean in a spiritual sense?

Allison offers some insights that are helpful in defining grace. The English word *impute,* which was more common in the language of the King James Bible than in current English, is a weak and inadequate translation of the Greek word *logidzomai.* Although this concept is crucial for understanding the good news of the gospel, it is difficult to grasp its true essence apart from its Greek meaning. Ineffective attempts to capture its meaning have included such words as *reckon, regard as, account as,* or *think.*

> Jesus himself is the meaning of the word, the action, the event by which we are accepted and to be made whole. . . . The fundamentally essential affirmation of Christianity, then, is that God was indeed "wording" the world in Jesus Christ. . . . We are the objects of this action; regarded, imputed, reckoned, treated, thought of, and "worded" not as we are but as we are to be, whole, "chosen of God, and precious." As we have been and are "worded," so shall we be.[2]

Jesus is the essence of *logidzomai,* and He puts a new label on us that certifies us as acceptable to God, even though we are actually imperfect. As Ellens puts it, "God can't remember that you're a sinner. God honestly thinks that you are a saint, so you are free for self-actualization, free for growth, free to be and to become with alacrity and with abandon."[3]

As the truth of this begins to soak in, we are able to see the freedom it brings to us as Christians and the tremendous difference between living under the concept of *logidzomai,* or a grace that counts us as whole even when we are not, and the system of control to which we are so accustomed. Being reckoned as good, we do not have to stifle our inner selves and our feelings in order to please God or earn His approval. There is no master-list to which I must subscribe. Since God has already known me and expects me to be a sinner, He is not surprised when sin or sinful thoughts appear in my mind. He knew it would happen anyway, and through Christ He has "worded" or counted me as good and whole.

Once we are able to grasp this truth where we live, we can see why Ellens calls it radical and unique to Christianity. It totally eliminates the necessity for having to perform in order to be acceptable to God. It cuts through all the layers of guilt, obligation, and rules and provides a protective covering for our lives as we move forward toward maturity, making our mistakes and committing our sins as we go. The good news is, we are free to experience all of ourselves. God has counted us as acceptable, so we do not have to split the bad parts of ourselves away in an attempt to approach Him looking clean and scrubbed up. We can approach Him with all we are because *logidzomai* says we are okay.

Difficulty Experiencing Grace

For many Christians the concept of grace is familiar in name but not in practice. Most of us can recite the verses and explain their meaning without experiencing grace itself. Unfortunately, it is a foreign concept to many Christians when it comes to everyday living.

One young woman who had adopted the "holy"-one role, as she grew up in a Christian home, came to see me because her father had been abusive to her older siblings until his death when she was eight. Although she had memories of playing in the neighborhood and school, she had no memories of her home life prior to her father's death. "I just always learned to be perfect, work hard, and be a good performer. I never did anything wrong, and I am a perfect employee because I work lots of hours and never give them any hassle. My mother always found something wrong with what I did, though she would only tell me part of what displeased her. Now it is hard for me to believe that other people are not doing the same thing. For six months I thought my boss was upset with my work but wasn't saying anything. When I had my evaluation, he told me I was doing a very good job and that if there was anything he did not like, he would tell me. It is so hard for me to believe that he isn't holding something back because that is what my mom did. I read this book on co-dependence that talked about grace, but I have no idea what grace is. I can't feel it at all."

Her home experiences had created a set of attitudes and feelings that interfered with her experiential knowledge of grace, even though she had been a Christian for years and had grown up in the church. Grace was a familiar term but not a reality. If this is your experience, you are not alone in your inability to claim grace as a primary anchor in your spiritual experience. You can accept the truth that grace is the gateway out of the evangelical performance trap, even if you do not feel it at this moment in your life. Continue your life with the faith that it is possible to eventually experience grace.

The Effects of Labeling

Being labeled as okay has an interesting effect as we begin to understand and experience grace: we begin to shape ourselves to fit the label
God has given us. We all have seen this sort of influence in people
around us. For example, if a youngster is consistently called dumb by
his parents, he soon begins to feel he is dumb and will begin to live and
act like a dumb person. Children tend to live up to the labels placed
upon them. The person who feels he is a born loser will perpetuate this
perception by making choices that cause him to lose. People live out the
truth of their self-images. When it comes to grace and the Christian life,
this same principle holds true as it becomes a reality in our lives. Once
we are able to grasp at a gut level the truth of our positive label, we
begin to conform our behavior to that new image we have of ourselves.
It is the starting point of true wholeness, and also holiness. Allison describes it this way.

> To be treated and reckoned as whole and righteous is to begin to *be-
> come* whole and righteous. . . . Accurately and factually we are sin-
> ners, full of disesteem, guilt, anger, and the fear of death. But God has
> spoken the word that "words" us righteous and whole —
> *logidzomai*. . . . Because we are reckoned by God as good, we are able
> to reckon ourselves good and this reckoning begins to change us into
> the good we are to be.[4]

As we grasp the truth that God reckons us to be good, then we can
see ourselves as good also, instead of bad, as so often happens with the
splitting. God accepts the whole person, which in turn allows us to accept all of ourselves, our good, and our God without fear. We can see
that the long-range effect of grace is going to be positive behavior,
which of course is what the people who emphasize control are wanting
anyway. The difference is in the path leading to such wholesome behavior and the motivation behind it.

These same principles are involved with families' everyday lives,
and it is clearly illustrated in the relationship between fathers and their
daughters. Take, for example, the issue of teenage girls' sexual behavior, which is a concern of most parents. One father, out of his fear, tried
to control his daughter through the use of threats. Upon her return from

a date, he thoroughly checked her clothes and her hair for evidence of disarray. When he spotted questionable evidence he became frightened, and in his fear slapped her as he accused her of being a whore and slut. "I wasn't doing anything, honest, I wasn't," the daughter reported to me. "But after Dad kept accusing me and calling me a whore, I decided that if I'm being accused of it I might as well do it. So I did, and I do." Her father's efforts at control and labeling pushed her into the very immorality he feared.

Another teenage girl faced sexual, as well as other temptations, with a positive rather than a fearful attitude. "My dad has a lot of trust in me, and that means a lot. I want to live up to his belief in me." Her father was practicing *logidzomai*—redemption, grace, and affirmation rather than intimidation and control. His stance tapped into his daughter's desire to live up to his trust.

Grace Promotes Growth

Personal growth also requires personal responsibility at some point. The concept of grace does not eliminate the need to be responsible for what we do, nor does it mean we have no guilt for the actual offenses we commit. There will be confessions to make, situations to correct, and losses to grieve, but all within the concept of grace. "Rebuke, repentance, responsibility, and restitution, yes; but rejection, no! No matter how evil we may feel that we are, God reckons us good in Jesus Christ," Allison declares.[5] When Cathy said, "My self-worth is tied up in the rules," she might as well have said, "My feeling of safety is tied up in the rules." But once she catches hold of grace, she will be able say, "My safety is tied up in the label of grace." She will be free to leave the evangelical rules without fearing rejection from God.

The good news means no condemnation and no rejection in spite of our anger, guilt, twisted motivations, and low-esteem. And because there is no rejection, we can face ourselves in God's true light, confident that He will continue to accept us. This is the freedom to grow and experience ourselves. We do not have to conceal parts of ourselves from God to please Him; we can acknowledge all of ourselves and take responsibility for who we are. As we own our personal motives and feelings,

God can work within us to change us in the direction of the label He has given us. Owning and admitting promotes the personal growth which can lead toward wholeness. The truth of this is evident every day in the offices of those who conduct therapy.

We listen to the painful details of the hurting person's life, but we do not throw up our hands in disgust and proclaim that the person is a total loss to humanity. No! We affirm people's worth and attempt to communicate a sense of value, even though we may not approve of their morals or their actions. Our aim is to help them begin to believe in themselves after having been "good-worded" consistently by us. The people who go through therapy and do not change are the ones who do not admit to their own feelings, their own complicity and wrongdoing. *Logidzomai* provides the security within which we can become responsible in a manner that promotes growth as we face all of our inner thoughts, feelings, and motivations.

Johnny Lingo's Eight-Cow Wife

"What am I worth?" "What is my value?" "What gives me value?" Those are our basic questions. There is a fictional story that illustrates the impact of grace — grace which declares we have definite worth.

Johnny Lingo was a young islander who lived on Nurabandi, not far from the island Kiniwata in the Pacific. Johnny was one of the brightest, strongest, and richest men in the islands, but people shook their heads and smiled about a business deal he had made with a man on Kiniwata. He had paid the unheard-of price of eight cows for a wife who was by any standards unattractive. As one fellow explained, "It would be kindness to call her plain. She was skinny. She walked with her shoulders hunched and her head ducked. She was scared of her own shadow." The amazing fact was that in the islands, two or three cows could buy an average wife, and four or five a highly satisfactory one. Why would Johnny pay eight? Everyone figured Sarita's father, Sam Karoo, had taken young Johnny for a ride, and that is why they smiled whenever they discussed the deal.

The teller of the story finally met Johnny for herself and inquired about his eight-cow purchase of Sarita. She assumed he had done it for his own vanity and reputation — at least she thought this until she saw Sarita. "She was the most beautiful woman I have ever seen. The lift of her shoulders, the tilt of her chin, the sparkle of her eyes all spelled a pride to which no one could deny her the right." Sarita was not the plain girl she had expected, and the explanation lies with Johnny Lingo.

> "Do you ever think," he asked, "what it must mean to a woman to know that her husband settled on the lowest price for which she can be bought? And then later, when the women talk, they boast of what their husbands paid for them. One says four cows, another maybe six. How does she feel, the woman who was sold for one or two? This could not happen to my Sarita."
>
> "Then you did this just to make your wife happy?"
>
> "I wanted Sarita to be happy, yes. But I wanted more than that. This is true. Many things can change a woman. Things that happen inside, things that happen outside. But the thing that matters most is what she thinks about herself. In Kiniwata, Sarita believed she was worth nothing. Now she knows she is worth more than any other woman in the islands."
>
> "Then you wanted — "
>
> "I wanted to marry Sarita. I loved her and no other woman."
>
> "But — " I was close to understanding.
>
> "But," he finished softly, "I wanted an eight-cow wife."[6]

Eight-Cow People

Because Johnny Lingo "reckoned" Sarita to be worth eight cows, she began to act and feel like an eight-cow wife. This transformed her from the shy, plain island girl into a confident, attractive woman who knew she was worth more than any other woman in the islands. Johnny's actions parallel the concept of grace, and for those of us who have grown up in Christian homes, the Biblical account of the principle often has little meaning because it is so familiar. However, God counts people as so worthwhile that He pays an unheard-of price to purchase their redemption. In the economy of the islands, God says we are worth eight cows because He wants eight-cow men and women, and He wants us to believe we are worth more than anything else in the whole world. When we can get hold of this idea, we have touched grace and are on our way toward wholeness.

17

PURSUING WHOLENESS

I f you find that you have grown up more "holy" than wholly, you may want to take stock of the relationships in your life. What type of attachments do you have? Are they conditional or unconditional? Must you continually perform in order to be loved? Are you free to express your honest thoughts and feelings without the threat of rupturing the relationship or being called into question? Do you feel free to be yourself, or do you feel stifled and smothered?

If you are serious about wholeness but do not have an attachment free of conditions, then you will have to find someone with whom you can develop such a relationship. If many of your experiences are similar to those discussed in this book, then you should consider a professional counselor, psychologist, social worker, marriage and family counselor, psychiatrist, or pastoral counselor who has a balanced view of Christian principles and psychological development. They can supply the relationship for growth and development until you are ready to establish other relationships in your own circle of life.

Typical ACE issues can be difficult to iron out by yourself. Even though you may gain many insights by reading and thinking, you need to verbally express your thoughts to another person to work them out. Talking to friends may also be helpful, but I have found that friends can only help to a certain point, and then because they are your friends, they lack the objectivity that you need. Even family members can be helpful, but they often have a hard time being objective about criticism of other family members, and this can quickly become counterproductive for both of you.

Regular counseling sessions can speed things up as you enter a systematic program that encourages and allows you to focus on your particular situation and feelings. Many of us live such active and busy lives, we often do not take the time to sit down and examine our thoughts and feelings. Regular therapy sessions provide the space to think things through and develop. A good counselor can raise ideas and provide shortcuts to insights that one might not hear from friends or family members.

The Importance of Relationship

Eleanor was a single woman in her late twenties whose pastor had referred her to me. She had grown up in a Christian home that certainly had its dysfunctional elements. The father spent very little time with her, was very closed emotionally, and when he did speak, it was usually to criticize. Her mother was a good housekeeper and spent her energies there instead of with the children. There was a definite set of principles to which Eleanor had to adhere in the hope of receiving at least some love and recognition in her Christian home. The basic rules she had to follow to survive emotionally included:

- Don't say no.
- Don't say what I think.
- Don't talk back.
- Remain silent if I disagree.
- *Always* serve others.
- Don't choose my own friends.

It is easy to see why Eleanor struggled with intense feelings of self-hatred. She did not like being female and was very cautious about opening herself to others emotionally. Her depression had increased in the past several months, and her personal physician had prescribed medication to elevate her mood. Progress was slow in therapy as she struggled to face her intense, negative feelings. It was difficult for her to be optimistic about her emotional future, and the notion of wholeness was only a farfetched idea. She had tried to live up to the rules, but even that had not reduced her emotional pain and conflict.

As often happens, events in real life can be as therapeutic as therapy. Jerry, a co-worker, began to take an interest in Eleanor. He was in his second marriage and had two children. He made no pretense about his own feelings and was quite candid as he assessed himself. "I've been divorced and kicked out of the church. They don't want me anymore, and I know I'm not a perfect person. I've given up trying, and if God doesn't like it, well, I guess I'm just going to hell anyway." Having said this of himself, he nevertheless began to treat Eleanor with something very much like Christian grace.

He was attentive and complimented her on her smile. To strengthen their emotional relationship, he insisted, "We are never going to go home after our shift ends angry with each other. You must say whatever you have to say and I will listen and respect it." And he did. He invited her to his house where she was welcomed as a member of the family. She had meals with them, helped fix food in the kitchen, watched videos, and so on. Jerry's affection was a kind of grace.

Eleanor began to change. When she came for her therapy, she was like a breath of sunshine in my office. Her face was literally brighter, her smile was warm, and her eyes twinkled. As months passed she was able to stop taking her medication and maintain her positive attitude. The effects of this grace experience were incredible. Jerry counted her as a worthy person, a valued human being, and she began to live up to the label he had placed upon her. Of course, her problems are not all solved, but she has begun to undo the negativism of her background and is building a healthy foundation for her own life, thanks to this "sinful" fellow who is convinced that he is on God's throwaway list.

Eleanor's positive response to Jerry's acceptance supports Allison's point that "God has spoken the word that 'words' us righteous and whole — *logidzomai*. . . . Because we are reckoned by God as good, we are enabled to reckon ourselves good and this reckoning begins to change us into the good we are to be."[1] Once Eleanor was reckoned good by Jerry, she began to conform to that label. The power of being "worded" is significant in both the emotional and spiritual sense of the word.

Personal growth toward wholeness must have its roots in a relationship in which one can invest emotionally. Personal growth cannot take place without attachment and investment in another person. The labeling that Jerry gave to Eleanor took place within the context of a relationship. Remember Charlie Babbitt and his brother Raymond in the film *Rainman*? Raymond did not grow because he could not attach to anyone. Charlie, on the other hand, invested in Raymond and became more accepting and caring for his brother as the story progressed.

A relationship is extremely important, but not just any version will do. A healing relationship must be unconditional and provide love and acceptance no matter what the other person does or says. So far we have looked at many examples of relationships, but they are mostly unhealthy ones based on performance. Noncompliance with the expected behaviors would have resulted in rejection by family or church. Conditional relationships develop when the parents or persons in authority emphasize control, and control interferes with growth.

Purpose of Relationship

We have seen how control within relationships can lead to stifling and stunted emotional and spiritual life. To experience growth one must have an accepting, encouraging, redemptive environment, providing an atmosphere of security and significance that allows one to develop an attachment or bonding to the other person. This attachment, this knowing that we are loved and accepted for who we are rather than having to earn acceptance, is the basis of healthy relationships, which in turn becomes the foundation for personal growth.

Amy is an attractive young woman in her early twenties who has been struggling with an eating disorder, or at least that is the visible symptom. Her version of "holiness" has been to live up to whatever her mother wants from her since her mother gains most of her significance from Amy. Although she has an attachment to Mom, it is a conditional one, and whenever Amy attempts to pull away, her mother begins to fall apart. This makes Amy feel guilty for upsetting her mother, so she resubmits to keep her mother happy. In doing so she maintains the attachment, but it is not a healthy one that would allow her to grow into the second stage of separateness. She remains conditionally attached, and this leads to fusion (the opposite of separation), a state in which she and her mother are so close that Amy does not have a clear picture of herself as a person distinct from her mother (refer to the developmental model in chapter 15). The eating disorder helps her cope with the conflict and the unhappiness.

As she discusses her situation in our hospital ACE group, she listens carefully to others' ideas and observations. Frequently her eyes light up as she appreciates someone's insights. One day another member of the group who is old enough to be Amy's mother began talking to her like a daughter, encouraging her to become independent, find a job, and build a life for herself. It helped Amy to hear this because she cannot get this kind of advice and feedback from her own mother who is enmeshed in their conditional relationship. In the hospital group, Amy experiences relationships that are not conditional, and this provides a useful comparison to the conditional relationship she has with her mother. By finding professionals outside her family who can provide an unbiased view, Amy is able to develop a clearer picture of her life and what she can do to correct the underlying problems.

Although he does not use the word *relationship*, in one short sentence, Tournier gives us the heart of what good therapy should be. "The essence of psychotherapy is the open-hearted talk, the expression of one's thoughts in the confidence of being really listened to and understood, entry into personal communication and receiving a response — in short, the living experience of dialogue."[2]

Healing Within Relationships

Trusting

Although it may sound simplistic, the essential activities that one needs to perform to find healing within a healthy relationship are the opposite of those in the evangelical rules. One needs to be able to talk about true thoughts and opinions, to trust the other person and one's own judgment, to express feelings of pain, anger, rejection, joy, and one's own wants. Within a healthy relationship that provides security and significance and in which one can honestly talk, one can progress toward wholeness.

Open dialogue can be a real problem for some ACEs who have learned don't talk — do say and don't trust — do trust as they were growing up. It may seem impossible to establish a relationship that requires trusting when one has learned don't trust at home! Usually one who has reached the point of recognizing the need to work on inner issues has experienced enough inner pain to make the issue of trust somewhat secondary. Even though it is hard to trust, the need to get rid of the discomfort makes one willing to try almost anything that will help. If one can find a safe environment, as in counseling or a good support group, it can become easier to open up and to trust than one might have expected.

There are persons, however, who will have difficulty trusting, and this will require some time to overcome. If this is true of you, then be aware of your tendency to distrust and work on it as part of the discussion in the healing relationship, especially if you are seeing a professional person. Remember that the person to whom you are talking is not the parent you could not trust, so your perception that people are not trustworthy quite likely should not apply in this situation. Work gradually at the relationship, sharing a little more about yourself as you risk as much as you can handle, and slowly build the trust a little piece at a time.

Cathy has a hard time trusting and admitting that her guard is up about 75 percent of the time. Writing out her ideas and feelings has been helpful for her because she can bring the written material for me to read, which is easier than saying it all out loud to me. After I have read her remarks, we can discuss her thoughts and feelings.

For an ACE, the goal is to heal the split that developed as you tried to whittle away certain thoughts, feelings, attitudes, etc., in order to live up to the master-list and the evangelical rules. The more successful you were, the more estranged you became from your true self. The goal is to bring all of you into the safety of the new relationship for acceptance and healing.

In fact, this healing relationship is a miniature model of God's grace (*logidzomai*) which counts us as whole even when we are not. As we bring all of us into the light of the relationship and continue to feel accepted — "worded" as okay — we can be more accepting of ourselves and work toward healing as our talking, trusting, feeling, and wanting identify areas in our lives where we were emotionally injured. As we become accepting of all of our inner selves under God's grace, we become the whole persons He wants us to be, and we are freed from having to submit to the control rules to be loved and acceptable.

Let me give an example of how I work with people regarding all of the secret feelings that they have learned to split away from themselves and hide in their emotional closets. Alice was in her early thirties when she came to see me. True to the ACE pattern, she had learned to hide her feelings, especially her anger and resentment toward her parents who had quite thoroughly but unknowingly stifled her, especially when she was in high school. Being an "S" and "C" person, Alice did not fight back with her parents but complied outwardly as she slowly burned inside. Observing that she tried to avoid her anger and split it away from herself, I suggested something that caught her by surprise as I explained an alternative way of handling her emotions.

"You consistently try to push your anger and resentment away from yourself, but it stays with you. I would like you to consider another approach. I want you to be friendly toward your feelings instead of trying to get rid of them." She gave me a quizzical look as I mentioned being friendly to her negative feelings. Trying to explain a little further, I continued. "Try looking at it this way. If someone comes to your house, how are you friendly with them? You invite them in and let them sit at your kitchen table, give them something to drink, and spend some time together. You can do the same with your inner feelings, too. Picture them in your mind as company coming to your house. Invite them into the kitchen, sit down with them, and become better acquainted. I think you can learn to be less afraid of your feelings, and as you become less afraid of them, they will cause you less grief." Although this is a process that takes time, it does work as people learn to become less afraid of the feelings and thoughts they have split away from themselves.

Talking

Since most of the conflict related to the evangelical rules takes place at home and in church, it is obvious that you will need to talk about those early experiences.

First, review the healthy family traits as well as the dysfunctional concepts, and try to analyze your famliy in terms of its focus. Was it someone's drinking habits, physical abuse, a domineering parent who was never wrong, physical disability, the death of a family member, model Christian behavior based on shamed submission, a parent's vocation? How were decisions made? Who made the decisions? Was there input from other family members? Where did your needs fit into the picture? These concepts need to be explored and talked about, including your opinions and feelings about the events that took place.

For some people the focus is quiet and subtle. John is a high "i" college student whose inclination is to be spontaneous and outgoing. Considering his home, he reported:

> Our whole family is serious, and many times I have to repress my feelings to fit in. My brother left home at seventeen to avoid problems with my father. I never argued with his leaving, so I accommodated to my father. As I reflect on my father, it seems most things were done to please him. I feel like I'm living in a set environment created for me, which affects all aspects of my life. I realize now I'll never be happy until I become my own person and make my own decisions.

Jane suffered from being in the shadow of her father's occupation. As a college woman who was in the process of working out her own separation and identity, she put it this way:

> As I was growing up, I always felt the pressure of having to live up to expectations of being a pastor's daughter. Many people would just assume things about me because of my family background, without ever knowing me as a person. I don't think I ever developed a sense of who I really was apart from my family. I never felt like I was just Jane Jacobi. I was always Jane Jacobi, daughter of the pastor.

For Lana it was a deadly combination of two factors, one from her mother and the other from her father and other males in her family. Her mother had a sharp tongue and was quick to use it. Lana, being sensitive by nature, was devastated by her mother's criticism. "Nothing I ever did was right. Nothing! I could never please her, and she would never believe me. I was always wrong. So I would just get quiet and not say anything, and she wouldn't like that either." The focus was avoiding her

Christian mother's verbal abuse. Meanwhile, she suffered repeated sexual abuse, which added another dimension of fear and lack of safety. The overall focus for her was external fear and the need to protect herself as well as she could.

A second area that needs to be talked about and explored includes the personal rules you developed in response to the family focus. These are the rules you have used to guide your behavior and survival strategies. Identifying these personal rules or perceptions is a very important part of the process toward wholeness. They are the key link between what we see and experience in life, and the actions we take in response to those influences. Since we do what makes sense to us, our behavior flows out of our personal rules and perceptions as we learned in chapter 6. Here is a review of the personal rules Cathy developed as she learned to cope in her home. Your own rules may be similar.

- Don't allow yourself to get emotionally close to anyone because you will end up getting hurt. Don't trust.

- If you have an opinion on something, keep it to yourself because nobody really cares what you think.

- Avoid friction with people such as parents. Just agree with them or be quiet.

- Do and say whatever is necessary to keep people happy; and so you don't hurt anybody, do and say the same things they do.

- Always try to do what will make your parents approve of and respect you.

- You can't count on your parents for support because they can be warm or cold and you never know which it will be.

- Spending money and eating make you feel better.

- Try to be perfect. Try to make perfect decisions.

- You can't really trust God because He is going to hurt you in some way by either sending a catastrophe or not giving you what you want.

The split that Cathy experiences is obvious from the rules that she has learned to use in her living. Her focus is pleasing others, not meeting her own legitimate needs, as she attempts to gain affection and avoid the pain of conflict. She cannot trust others emotionally, so she will be cautious in developing a relationship with someone. Her mistrust extends to God, also, which means He will not be a resource to her as she struggles with the difficult issues in her life. Before Cathy can develop a closer relationship with God, she will have to modify her belief that He cannot be trusted. Her actions toward God, which will be in line with her beliefs, will be characterized by reluctance, caution, and lack of openness.

Her second rule, "Do and say whatever is necessary to keep people happy, and so you don't hurt anybody," is going to guide the way she handles her relationships with other people. You can predict that she will be an agreeable person who seldom, if ever, disagrees openly with people. It will be useless to encourage her to speak up to people as long as she has this personal rule. Before she can begin to speak up, she will have to modify her perception that says life goes better if she agrees with everyone. When she can honestly believe, "Life works better for me when I express myself," then she will be free to speak up when she disagrees with someone.

Changing these rules and perceptions is difficult and takes time because we cannot undo in a few weeks what we have practiced for twenty or thirty years. To deal with Cathy's rule against allowing herself to get emotionally close to anyone, I would press her to examine that more closely to see if it is really true, and is it possible that there *are* people who will not hurt her if she is close to them? The purpose is to establish a small window of doubt concerning this rule that she has developed. Once this had taken hold, I would try to make the window larger so that eventually she could attempt more openness with people and move toward wholeness.

A second approach is to figure out where the rule originated. Sometimes the rules are direct statements from one parent. A parental statement of "You can never do anything right" becomes in the person's mind "I can never do anything right." Or "You are always in the way" becomes "I am no good and a bother." In such cases I try to help people see that their parents are actually people just like themselves. And like everyone else, their opinions are just that, opinions. Since they have failures and weaknesses, hopes and feelings, like everyone else, one can begin to challenge the messages learned from them.

Feeling

Along with talking it is important to feel what you experienced through the years. Part of the process toward wholeness is to bring all that we feel into the unconditional relationship where we can experience acceptance no matter what we feel. For many ACEs who have been splitting their pain and anger away from themselves for years, this may take some time.

Bea, who can't remember anything prior to her eighth birthday, has split that part of her life away so well that she doesn't even remember it. During our sessions she can talk about some things very easily, but she has not yet begun to feel the really painful memories. Part of this is due to the inner rules she has established for herself. One is to "avoid pain at all costs," and the other is "feeling gets me into trouble." By my analysis, she is a very sensitive, feeling-oriented person who, according to her mother's observation, "was an affectionate child but turned cold at some time." Bea is not sure when her change occurred, but she does remember being sexually abused by her uncle soon after her dad's funeral when she was eight years old, a memory that came to her mind when I commented on her sensitive nature. She also wonders if her father abused her before he died.

As we continue to talk about the experiences she has had and to uncover the rules she has developed, she has begun to experience some emotion, though it is still vague. At times tears come into her eyes, but she is unsure of the emotion behind it. As we continue therapy, she will eventually begin to feel the painful emotions that have been repressed. But before she can recover her feelings totally, she will need to modify her rules about avoiding pain and feeling.

Lou is a fifty-year-old woman whose father died (it feels like abandonment to her) when she was two years old, and her mother had to go to work to support Lou and her two older siblings. As a result her mother was not around to attend Lou's school activities or give her much attention. The neighbors were supposed to keep an eye out for Lou, but most of the time she was unsupervised. "I was alone all the time, and I have felt alone all of my life!" Lou cried in agony as she recalled her childhood experiences. "My mother was never there for me, and I feel like I didn't have a normal childhood. By the time I was ten years old I could do everything—wash, fix meals, clean the house, and all that stuff. I was always so responsible, right from the beginning. I never did anything for me." She was grieving the loss of the childhood she never had.

As Lou continued to look at her life pattern, she was able to see that she felt unloved, abandoned, and ignored, so she became super-responsible in order to have self-worth. The problem was she tried to fix everything, keep things perfect, and did too much for her children as she neglected her own feelings and well-being. Now in the hospital after attempting suicide, she was beginning to see the pattern that had developed in her life.

"I got my Christianity through my aunt and a church I attended when I was a teenager," Lou stated. "But when my baby died—and he looked so healthy, just like my other children—I began to feel angry at God. That is when I began to move away from God because I felt so guilty for being angry, but I was. How could God do that to me? Why was He punishing me by letting my dad die, not letting me have a childhood, having five pregnancies and losing three of them? Why?" As she sobbed out her pain, some of the depressing burden lifted, and she began to see a glimmer of hope in the future for the first time. She was allowing herself to feel as she brought her past pain into the safety of our relationship. "I never realized that past experiences could affect me this much. I see now that things that happened before I was six years old have been affecting me, and I didn't even know it. I have told you things I have never even told my husband. I can see how this talking it out helps."

Because feelings of unlovableness, shame, and abandonment are difficult to face, we will try any escape route imaginable until we run out of options. Even then, it feels as though life will end when the intense feelings come to the surface, but they can be faced a little at a time in the context of a safe relationship or group where encouragement and support are available. Our inner fear of these painful feelings is like a bogeyman, with no basis in objective reality, but the inner child does not know that because it feels so real. These fears take on huge proportions because children are so vulnerable and experience life as a little person in a big person's world. Being abandoned or ignored at any age hurts deeply, but it can hurt even more for children, who lack the ability to reason it out or to take control of their lives by changing where they live or choosing friends.

We often feed fear by avoiding it. Remember the old saying, If you fall off a horse, get back on right away. If a person falls off a horse and does not remount immediately, the last memory he or she has is falling off, and this memory will color any future thoughts about horseback riding. On the other hand, if the person remounts immediately and rides without falling off, the memory of falling off has been dimmed by the successful ride. The fear has been reduced by facing it immediately.

Suppose there were a large woods behind the house where you grew up, and you were told by your parents that the woods are dangerous. There are scary creatures in there, and if you ever go into the woods, you may never return. As you become older, you begin to wonder what really is in the woods, but your fear kicks into action as you approach. You finally realize that the only way to know for certain whether the woods are actually dangerous is to check it out for yourself. With all of the old fears crowding into your mind, you make your way to the edge of the woods, and your fear tells you that if you go in, you will never return. Facing the anxiety, you enter the woods a little bit at a time, handling only as much as you can. Even though it is frightening, once you have explored the woods and found them safe, you will never fear the woods again.

Facing abandonment, unlovableness, and shame is very much like facing the bogeyman in the woods. Even though the feelings are real, the only way we can reduce their impact on us is to face them a little at a time. Usually we will feel as though we are going to die (or wish we would) as we face the feelings, but once we are through the experience, the fears can never again be as threatening because we have faced them and survived. This is not a one-time event but a gradual process, as we persistently face the bogeyman of fear within a trusting, safe relationship.

The same process applies for the individuals who have been abused and have split parts of themselves away. The little-girl part of Lana's personality contains the abused feelings from her childhood. Often the little girl is absolutely gone, which leaves adult Lana rather numb with no real feelings of her own. In our sessions we invite the feeling part of Lana to come into the relationship, and she does so with dread because she fears the rejection that happened so much in the past. If you have experienced similar feelings — that the little-child feeling is like a separate part of you—you can bring it back into relationship with yourself, but you should do it with a trusted, trained professional who can help you through the process.

Anger is one of the most difficult emotions for ACEs to handle because most of them have been taught that anger is wrong under the control system. Consequently, it is one of the primary emotions to eliminate in order to live up to the rules. As you know, it does not go away but remains and can poison one's inner spirit and cause tension as one tries to maintain the split. Lana, who had to survive with her critical mother and abusive father, found release by writing out her feelings. Regarding her anger toward her parents and the Biblical commandment to honor them, she penned the following description of her inner conflict:

> Honor thy mother and father that thy days
>   may be long . . .
> I have failed here.
> I honor not, in my heart,
> Though I honor with my lips
> And do not dishonor others.
> I don't feel honoring
> Or respecting.
> In fact I feel angry and hurt,
> I have an intense dislike
> That I continue to hide.
> Can one survive
> With a double heart?
> Yet, how can one honor
> Those who hurt, ignored and slayed,
> Day upon day,
> Year upon year,
> So as to crush and destroy
> Their sensitive child.
> In my eyes,
> They're still all-powerful,

All-right,
Yet really
They feel all wrong.
I'm confused, God.

You can see her struggle within the split — the reality of the hurt and anger, but the fear of going against the Bible if she honestly admits to her anger. She needs to empty herself of her anger, and she may do that in our counseling relationship. The commandment to honor our mother and father does not mean we have to stifle anger that comes from the hurt we experience at their hands. However, it is counterproductive to go to them with anger aflame and try to settle things with one outburst.

It is more helpful to express the anger with a third person who can listen without judgment. Working out the anger will eventually lead to a true sense of forgiveness because the first stage of airing our grievances must be accomplished before we can enter the second stage of forgiveness. Forced forgiveness is not likely true forgiveness. The first step prepares for the second, and once we have emptied our anger, forgiveness comes as a natural conclusion.

Paul touches upon the issue of anger between people who are attached to each other. He encourages them to be honest with each other. "Stop lying to each other; tell the truth, for we are parts of each other and when we lie to each other we are hurting ourselves. If you are angry, don't sin by nursing your grudge. Don't let the sun go down with you still angry — get over it quickly; for when you are angry you give a mighty foothold to the devil" (Ephesians 4:25–26, TLB).

He is encouraging honest communication, including appropriate anger. He does not suggest stifling of feelings in order to maintain peace because such dishonesty hurts everyone. The book of Job is a good example of a person expressing his anger toward God for the losses that he suffered, and God in His grace can listen and absorb anger more than anyone else. In fact, appropriate anger is an important part of becoming a whole person.

Wanting

As you can see, the process of becoming whole includes putting all of our hidden thoughts, feelings, and fears on the table within the context of the safe relationship. Remember, we are able to do this under the umbrella of grace which says that God counts us as whole even though we are not. That means God is not going to be angry with us for dumping our inner, raw selves in front of Him because He already knows we are imperfect and has counted us as acceptable anyway. We can place our wants in the open, too.

Identifying our wants is an important part of our development and leads us into the next stage as we become our own persons. If we are in a conditional relationship, then we are only free to want what we are supposed to want. Remember the grandmother who told Angie she didn't want to go away? "Tell Grandma you really want to stay here." Grandma was trying to thwart the child's individuality, and a person who has grown up with a pattern of being placed in a dependent position such as this, and accepts it, grows up without a clear sense of individuality or separateness.

Within the context of the safe relationship, we need to express and explore our wants and our dreams. Bea, who wants to avoid pain at all costs, realizes that she has been living so cautiously that it has been like a slow death. As she explored some of her dreams, her feeling nature began to show. She would like to sing in a Christian rock band and watch the audience react to the impact of the music. Treva, who gave up her career and stayed home because that was the right thing to do, would like to get a "good job and show them that I am worth something." She wants to be a successful woman in her own right.

We need to explore and identify our wants, and God will be able to guide us in which way we should go with them, but to systematically deny all of our own desires is going to cripple us and make us ineffective for kingdom work because we will not be whole persons. Teilhard de Chardin shared an insight that should encourage you to identify your wants.

> Which is better for the Christian, activity or passivity? Life or death? Growth or diminishment? Development or curtailment? Possession or renunciation? . . . Why separate and contrast the two natural phases of a single effort? . . . Develop yourself and take possession of the world *in order to be.* Once this has been accomplished, then is the time to think about renunciation; then is the time to accept diminishment for the sake of *being in another.* . . . First, develop yourself.[3]

Instead of fulfillment and self-denial being polar opposites as the evangelical rules suggest, they are stages in a process. Before we can give something up, we must possess it. Before we can give, we have to receive. It is ridiculous to urge renunciation upon a person who has nothing to renounce. Life is a movement back and forth between assertion and letting go, of possessing and giving up. As we begin to see this truth and realize that God can direct us, we can acknowledge our true desires, which prepares us to be our own persons.[4]

Becoming Your Own Person

Becoming your own person is an important phase of personal development. Once you have established a safe relationship within which you begin to understand yourself, you also begin to see your uniqueness, your wants, your feelings, and the issues that are important to you.

In this stage of development, you begin to take steps that establish you as your own person with your own separate identity.[5] It does not mean you have to cut off your relationships, because if you have a positive, healthy attachment with someone, that person will not stop loving you as you become your own person. If someone does discourage your independence, then you do not have an unconditional relationship with them, and they are not a healthy influence.

Mandi was a college student who had grown up in the church and in a Christian home and who attended my class on personal development. At the beginning of the class, she was experiencing some personal conflict and splitting as she tried to meet her needs of security and significance.

> Before this class started, I had a lot of questions about myself. Why do I turn antisocial when I'm around a lot of people? Why can't I face up to any kind of confrontation? Why do I always lie about how I'm feeling? I was so confused with life in general that I was ready to give up. I have a real hard time being my own person. I tend to wear a mask a lot because I don't want people to see how I'm really feeling. I don't want to risk hurting anyone's feelings. I don't want to lose them as friends.

As we studied personality styles, she learned that she had many "S" traits, which explained her desire to avoid conflict and her fear of showing her true feelings. She discovered that she was more normal than she had thought. There was nothing wrong with her, and she realized she could become her own person:

> I have to learn to be more assertive in all areas of life. I have to tell myself, *You can tell your parents you love them. You can tell your feelings and express your emotions without losing any friends. You don't have to repress anymore. You can trust in God because He does have time to listen to you.* If I write all these down on a piece of paper, I know I'll begin to grow more. I won't have to wear the mask anymore.

Tom was another young fellow who had grown up in a Christian home and had been pushed by his mother to act like a socially dynamic person with an "i" personality, when in reality he was goal-oriented and wanted to do things correctly ("D" and "C" traits). Within the safe atmosphere of the personal growth class, he began to sort out his feelings related to his mother, and then began to see how he could become his own person.

> In the past few days, I have realized how much my mother influenced my understanding of myself. I think there was a real me and a me she wanted me to be. Only recently have I discovered which is truly me, instead of a me that my mother authored. A big step in my personal autonomy was realizing that I am not a high "i" person like my mother wanted. Her intentions were good because she knew high "i" personality styles are popular, but this influenced my feeling that I wasn't worth much because I wasn't naturally what my mother wanted me to be. The way I felt was, "Why aren't my feelings and tendencies good enough, why do I have to change for you to love me?"

As Tom gained a clearer picture of his relationship with his mother, he was able to understand their conflict and see that there was nothing wrong with him. The problem was in the relationship with Mom because she was expecting him to act contrary to his true personality style. Once he could make this connection, he was freed to realize that he has his own unique contribution to make. Once he realized it was okay for him not to be a high "i" like his mother wanted, he could move toward being his own person. His own identity was more clearly defined in relationship to his mother, and he was relieved of the burden to split parts of himself away in order to keep her happy.

There is another way of seeing this autonomy stage. To establish our separateness, we need to take a stand by saying no and meaning it when we need to. In order for our yes to mean anything, we also must be able to say no. Or we might say, "That is not me!" We see an early demonstration of this in two-year-old children as they begin to separate from their parents and say, "No!" to almost everything. To establish their separate sense of self, they take issue with their parents. This gives them the emotional power and satisfaction of having a separate will and identity.

One must be able to say, "No," after we enter adulthood, too. Some people call this setting limits or establishing boundaries, and others simply say, "That's not me. I am not like that. I don't want to be treated that way." As Christians we do need to set limits on bad things that happen to us. Too often people who have grown up as ACEs believe they should absorb all of the pain in their relationships so the other person is not hurt, that it is Christian to do so. Granted, the Bible says we should turn the other cheek, but if a person turns the other cheek out of fear rather than from a position of strength, it has little value. We must first learn to defend ourselves, and then be able to turn the other cheek by choice rather than fear or duty.

Cathy is struggling with this issue. Through the years she has been unable to tell her brothers that she does not like their teasing, and she fears speaking up to her father. "I am afraid if I say something they will like me even less." In order to take a stand as her own person against her brothers, she will have to become less dependent upon them for approval and affection. This means she needs to establish other safe relationships that affirm her personal worth, so, if her family does reject her, she has other supportive attachments in place.

In this stage of development it is helpful to work out the emotional issues with our parents. Remember I said it is unwise to have a big emotional blowup with them. Instead, it requires a process of breaking the dependent tie that we have with them. There are several ways this can be accomplished. For those of us who have tended to go along with parents' wishes instead of expressing our own, we need to be aware of the pattern and see it when the situations arise. To break the pattern and begin establishing ourselves as our own person, we can quietly and systematically begin to take a position by saying, "No, that is not me. I don't think I will do that." As we consistently take a stand over time, we gradually establish ourselves as people with our own thoughts and wishes.

If Cathy were to implement this approach, she would stop going to her parents' house for coffee every Sunday after church because it is a source of irritation for her and is a tangible representation of her dependence on her parents. She would not have to make a major production out of saying, "No." When she is talking to her mother on the phone, she could say, "I don't think we will be over Sunday for coffee. I would like to do some different things on Sunday, so we are going to go straight home from church." If mother has a hard time accepting Cathy's statement, she may press her a little more, and Cathy may have to explain the situation more thoroughly. "Mom, all through the years I have tended to go along with what other people want, or what I believe other people want from me in order to be liked. Even though I can think for myself, doing it for myself is harder. I am not wanting to hurt your feelings, but I usually feel like I have to go to your house for coffee because it is the thing to do, and not what I really want to do. I am realizing that to really stand on my own, I need to begin acting on my own beliefs and be honest with myself and others about what I believe."

If her mother is a wise person, she will be able to accept what Cathy has to say and continue to love her even if she does not show up for coffee. If Mother becomes angry, attacks or criticizes her, Cathy will know her conditional relationship is not going to change. In that case, the relationship is not a healthy one that will promote Cathy's growth.

A second approach is to confront parents with one's hurt but not one's anger, and hurt is usually behind anger. Sensitive persons who keep their feelings to themselves have built up years of hurt because they have not spoken up to their parents and have had little or no experience in saying, "That is not me — I don't like it when you say that to me. It hurts me!"

Once we have sufficiently emptied ourselves of anger with a third person, we can go to our parents and tell them how we have felt in our relationship with them growing up. Among other things, this will bring the relationship into balance. Instead of our doing all the listening, we will finally contribute our own thoughts and feelings to the relationship. It is also a way of establishing ourselves as separate persons, by expressing our true thoughts as opposed to silently going along with whatever we believe our parents want. It is a way of saying, "I am my own person, and I have my own feelings that are important and special to me. I want you to recognize me and my feelings as valid." Third, it clarifies the type of relationship we really have with our parents. If Dad becomes angry and cannot understand what you are saying, then you have a conditional attachment that is not going to change. He is unable to recognize you as a person in your own right, and you will need to accept that this is the way it is. You cannot change him. If he can accept your feelings, then you will have established a more unconditional attachment which can develop into a more meaningful relationship.

If Cathy were to go to her mother, she would need to summarize the painful portion of her relationship into a few sentences so she could make her point clearly and without inappropriate anger. Cathy would need to say something like this: "Mom, when I was growing up I often felt like you did not care about what I was feeling. I felt pushed away like you did not take me seriously. For example, when my brothers would tease me all the time, and I asked you to help out, you told me not to let it bother me. That hurt me. I felt like I had to go along with what you wanted for you to love me." This is an example of confronting her mother with the pain from her childhood, not the anger.

In approaching parents it is important to realize that we have no control over their response, but we can control what we say. The goal is to say what we need to say to experience becoming our own person. How the parents respond is secondary and not really the point of the conversation. We can gain no matter what happens. A positive response is good to receive, but it is only a bonus to the primary goal.

Rodney is a high "C" person who always has been concerned about doing the right thing, and even though he saw many inconsistencies in his parents' Christian home, he continued to attend church. Gradually he realized that church was not very meaningful, and he was attending out of duty. His heart was not in it. As we discussed honesty and being his own person, he realized that most of his life he had done what he was expected to do. As part of his search for his separateness, he decided to discontinue church attendance for a while. There was a problem, however. His family had a tradition of going to his mother's every Sunday after church for coffee, and he was concerned about her reaction once she learned he had not gone to church. Since he wanted to live more honestly, he didn't want to show up wearing his suit, pretending he had been to church, and if he arrived wearing casual clothes, she would question him.

Finally, he decided to talk to his mother about his thoughts, which was risky a step for him. He had never been that open with her. Fearing she would reject him, he went to her house when no other family members were around and began to talk about his feelings. To his surprise and relief, his mother was very understanding, and they had the most meaningful conversation of their lives. He received the bonus, but he was also prepared to take a stand even if she did not have empathy for his struggles.

Even though your parents may not be living, there are other options you can pursue. If your parent has a living sibling, talking to that person can be helpful, since he or she can be a substitute for your parent. Even though the sibling cannot answer totally for your parent, you will have the experience of expressing yourself to another person close to your parent.

One young woman who was working through some final feelings about her father was feeling very hurt and angry. The emotion was welling up within her, and she needed to express it in order to move on emotionally. But her father was no longer living. I suggested that she go to the cemetery where he was buried and talk to him there, as though he were actually alive. Acting on my advice, she drove to the cemetery and found her father's grave. Just being at the grave stimulated her emotions further, and for several hours she poured out her pent-up anger and hurt with sobbing and deep emotion, but the experience was extremely helpful for her.[6]

Accepting All of Me

The master-list tends to externalize evil, meaning that sinfulness is clearly defined in terms of actions we need to avoid. To reduce inner sinfulness, one has only to conform more and more closely to the list.

This tends to divide the world into good and bad, black and white, and encourage "holiness" more than wholeness. Although it can have the appearance of being useful, this system results in a morality based on do's and don'ts rather than on empathy and wisdom. Under the rule-based system, I would not cheat you because it is wrong, but in a healthy relationship, I won't cheat you because I care about you and do not want to hurt you. The control system is a superficial form of morality, living dutifully with no connectedness to other people.

Jesus was critical about this way of life which the Pharisees promoted. "Woe to you, scribes and Pharisees, hypocrites! For you are like whitewashed tombs which indeed appear beautiful outwardly, but inside are full of dead men's bones and all uncleanness. Even so you also outwardly appear righteous to men, but inside you are full of hypocrisy and lawlessness" (Matthew 23:27–28). Even though they were living by the letter of the law, they were missing the entire point about relationships and the kingdom. They had no real connectedness with people.

The goal of wholeness is to have attachment and connectedness to others and to see others as equal to ourselves under grace. This provides a basis for loving others out of a higher scriptural principle of caring—a basis that following the rules could never produce. It is living at a higher level of personal development. The passage in Romans summarizes this point quite clearly:

> Owe no one anything except to love one another, for he who loves another has fulfilled the law. For the commandments, *"You shall not commit adultery," "You shall not murder," "You shall not steal," "You shall not bear false witness," "You shall not covet,"* and if there is any other commandment, are all summed up in this saying, namely, *"You shall love your neighbor as yourself."* Love does no harm to a neighbor; therefore love is the fulfillment of the law. (Romans 13:8–10)

Caring for people from a basis of attachment supersedes living by the rules, but in order to attain this phase of development, we must move beyond the master-list and its view of the world. We must move beyond the tension of splitting the badness away from ourselves in order to live by the rules. As long as we are engaged in splitting, we are maintaining a negative focus on our own failures and denying their existence. If we have not come to terms with our own wrongdoings, we will find it difficult to care about other people who are living the very badness we are trying to deny in ourselves. When I was going to college, I worked during the summers for my uncle's construction company, which exposed me to a part of the world that I had not experienced before. Since I was in my pious, keep-all-the-rules stage of my life, I had not realized or come to terms with my own sinful state. I thought I was pretty spiritual and fairly close to being perfect because I had almost mastered the master-list. Many of the construction workers used foul language, smoked tobacco, and liked to tell dirty jokes. Trying to be "holy," I experienced some inner anxiety as I had to be around these fellows everyday. Feeling a sense of Christian obligation to show I was separate from the world, I tried to look the other way while a dirty joke was in the air so I would not look as though I condoned the activity. I hesitated to become too friendly with these fellows because they were bad people, and I couldn't let their low standards rub off on me. I was living according to the leaven of the Pharisees. The outside of my cup was clean, but inside I was unable to associate with others in a truly caring way. My internal split interfered with my ability to love my fellow workers.

Once my world fell apart and I struggled through my hurt, anger, and sense of shame, I realized that sinfulness is a state of being, not just conscious actions. But this state of being is continually being redeemed by God's grace, and I also realized that, at heart, I am no better than anyone else. God loves everyone equally, and who am I to put myself above the next fellow. My heart is no better than the construction worker's who sneaked the copper wire out of the building we were demolishing so he could sell it for extra cash, or the cement finisher who loved to chew tobacco and tell dirty stories. I came to understand that God is not surprised at our sinfulness (cf. Romans 3:23), and He expects it.

Under grace I realized I do not need to be afraid of my own imperfections and sin. Grace covers it all and counts me as acceptable, so I can forget about the struggle with the master-list and be "free for actualization, free for growth, free to be and to become with alacrity and with abandon," as Ellens says.[7]

In order to achieve this, we must accept our whole self and come to terms with our own inner badness, realizing that there is good and bad in everyone. As we experience this freedom in ourselves, we are able to extend it to others and remain attached to them, even when they commit wrongs because their actions do not threaten us. We have enough connectedness with ourselves, God, and others, to remain in relationship even with people who are doing things we do not condone. Jesus is the perfect example of one who could hang out with the worst of sinners and maintain His own identity and connectedness. He was a whole person. "Love is the fulfillment of the law."

Developing Authority

Being able to assume an appropriate authority over one's life is the fourth stage of growth. It takes years, and some say a person achieves this stage near thirty. As children we saw the world from the perspective of a child, and of course, everything around us was a lot bigger than we were. Life was a series of directives from the big people around us. But as we became older, we were given more and more responsibility. As we accept more responsibility, we begin to exercise authority over our lives and make adult decisions.

One woman who was undernurtured as a child dislikes being a wife, a mother, and a grown woman. She wants to be the little girl she feels inside and have her father take care of her. As we analyzed her life, I could understand more clearly why she was having so much trouble. Emotionally, she is a little girl in a big person's world. She looks like an adult, but inwardly feels like a little girl who is trying to be a mother to other children just a little younger than she feels herself to be. When she is in bed with her husband, she is the little girl having sex with a man. No wonder it is difficult for her. She has not reached the place of taking authority over her own life and cannot take proper authority over her children either.

The persons who resent authority will have trouble with this stage because they will not want to internalize something they hate. The persons who are able to respect authority will be able to submit to a role without having to surrender their autonomy or submit to another person.

Man was not made to worship man, as Jesus pointed out when He said we should not call one another rabbi or father. We are all equal as individuals, without one having authority over the other.

As we accomplish this stage, we will be able to be God's representatives to exercise authority over evil here in the world. We will have grown to the place where we are free to be the type of people God wants us to be — connected, our own persons, accepting of ourselves, and able to assume authority over our lives.

18

FINDING GRACE

I have heard about grace from my earliest childhood, but it has taken years for me to understand it on a personal level, and it continues to be a bit hazy. If you do not have the experience of standing knee-deep in grace, continue your struggle in the belief that it is ultimately attainable.

Parents First

When an ACE comes to me with a spiritual complaint, I immediately begin to look at the family relationships because they are the foundation of adult spiritual life. Our family experiences color our perceptions, which in turn affect our concept of God. As Christians complain about God, I inquire about their families, and they often use identical words to describe their fathers as they use to describe God. When I point this out, they are invariably surprised to realize the connection.

A thirty-year-old man from Colorado called me recently to talk about his high "C" personality. He had read my first book and wanted some direction as he attempted to solve his faith difficulties. "I am a compliant personality (high "C"), and I have struggles with my faith. Although I grew up in a Christian home, it was not a heavy Christian home. When I was in high school, I accepted Christ, and it changed my life. Four or five years later, I really began to struggle in my faith and in my marriage."

Rather than focusing on the faith issue, I asked about his parents. To my questions, he replied, "My mom is loving and kind."

So far, so good.

"What about your dad?" I inquired, figuring there had to be a problem somewhere.

"He was very strong. I was hurt by the ways he treated us." He hesitated on the other end without elaborating, so I asked him to tell me more. "I was not emotionally secure in the family. I can tell one story to help you understand. The day before I started kindergarten, he decided to teach me to tell time. I was supposed to look at the clock and tell him the correct time, and every time I had a wrong answer he whipped me with the belt."

Wondering if this were an isolated incident, I asked, "Was this unusual, or was your dad always like this?"

"He didn't really take time to be involved in my life. It was the way he handled lots of things," he replied.

As we talked on, I pointed out the tension that develops between the fear of isolation and the desire for attachment in children who live in unsafe home environments. Living with his father's attitude, he had grown up with conditional attachment but also the constant fear that he would be punished unexpectedly for reasons he did not understand. He had experienced a form of abuse which was continuing to affect him.

As we discussed his relationship with his father, I could see similarities between this and his spiritual struggles. He was a perfectionist who wanted to do things correctly, and growing up under an unpredictable parent had left him feeling anxious and on edge. He wondered whether he would ever be accepted by his father. The fearful relationship with his dad influenced his relationship with God. It was based on fear, and to counter the fear, he tried to perform more perfectly, but he was unsuccessful. He was into the negative cycle of performance to earn approval.

Before he tackles his spiritual problem, he needs to work out the fear and threat of isolation that has come from his relationship with his father. He is going to have a difficult time jumping into a meaningful grace experience when his primary experience with his father has been conditional attachment and fearful insecurity. No wonder he is emotionally and spiritually anxious.

Sources of Grace: Gates, Tractors, and Sex

"How does one find grace?" I have wondered through the years. As a young person growing up in Indiana and during my YFC days, it always seemed that the people who were the most excited about grace were the ones who had really lived it up and done all of the wild things I could never do, and then had experienced an exciting, life-changing conversion. As much as I would have liked to try that approach, I knew my conscience would never allow it. So I continued my life, struggling the best I could while I told God He would have to help me out if He wanted me to have a more positive grace experience.

Clearing up the distortions that exist in parent-child relationships does pave the way for a more positive relationship with God, and this has happened to me. Through my teen and early adult years, my primary focus was on the unresolved hurts I had experienced with my dad. Since I am a sensitive "S" person, I kept my hurts to myself and did not express my feelings directly when Dad made decisions I did not like. Consequently, the hurts I experienced colored my entire perspective of our relationship, and I was unable to appreciate the positive contributions he had made to my life. After I had resolved the hurts in our relationship, I was free to see our relationship in a new light, and now that I am beginning to gain a firmer grasp on grace, I can see how he actually did convey grace to me.

When I was growing up, I always enjoyed working with wood and even considered being a carpenter. So when my dad needed to build several new wooden gates, I was interested and willing to help. Because the gates controlled the access to the farm lane and the fields, they had to be wide enough to accommodate farm machinery. Each gate consisted of five one-by-six-inch boards twelve-feet long, held in a horizontal position by nailing four one-by-six-inch boards spaced equally and vertically along the length of the gate. My task was to cut the lumber into the correct lengths and nail the pieces into place.

After I had built several gates, I stood back and looked at them with pride, and noticed the clean, smooth appearance of the wood. *Looks pretty good,* I thought to myself as I began to cut the lumber for the last gate. Suddenly, as I began to assemble the last one, I realized that one of the twelve-foot pieces was not long enough. With a sinking sense of horror, I realized I had made a mistake and cut one of the long pieces into a short one. I was unable to finish the gate because my dad had not bought extra lumber. He obviously was not planning for any mistakes.

Fearing my dad's criticism, I finally forced myself to find him and tell him about my error (I was always spanked more than any of my brothers for my wrongdoings). His unexpected response is still imprinted on my mind. "Mistakes like that happen." He added another comment that told me he really understood, "Uncle Eldon says that happens to him, too." To appreciate what this meant to me, you must know that Uncle Eldon was special to me and was also a first-rate professional carpenter. I had tremendous respect for my uncle, and being assured that he made mistakes cutting lumber took away my sense of failure and shame at having made the mistake. My dad gave me grace, even though I had ruined that board for the gate. The gate project was a grace experience, but I was not able to appreciate it until years later.

My dad also had an Allis-Chalmers W-C tractor, built long before ignition switches were used. This one had a foot-operated starter that often malfunctioned. As a teenager I fancied myself a hotshot at running the tractors and figured out a way to get the tractor started even when it was in gear. One hot summer day, I leaped onto the tractor, did my thing with the starter, and the old Allis, already in reverse gear, roared to life. In my hasty confidence, I had overlooked the throttle, which was open several notches. The tractor began speeding backward. This would not have been a problem except the tractor was inside the shed, and I was nowhere near the driver's seat as I was doing my number with the temperamental starter. As the Allis roared backward toward the door, I tried to untangle myself from my start-up position so I could gain control of the steering wheel and swing the rear tires away from the side of the shed door. But the tractor was only eight or nine feet from the door to start, and I had very little time to make my move. Before I could hit the clutch or grab the steering wheel, the tractor wheel weights struck the hand-hewn beam that held up the door. By the time I hit the clutch, the damage was done, and the beam was dangling, knocked off the foundation.

My three brothers soon constituted an interested audience as I climbed off the Allis and surveyed the damage. Since Dad had gone to town at the time, I recruited their boyhood wisdom, and we tried to push the beam back onto the foundation before Dad came home. We tugged and pulled and pried with a huge crowbar, but our efforts were useless. I knew I was doomed and died a thousand deaths as I waited for my dad to return.

To my utter amazement, my dad never said a cross word. He calmly surveyed the situation and told us to nail a piece of two-by-four onto the beam, and then directed us as we raised the beam with a farm jack and swung it back into place. Now I can see that he conveyed grace to me through that incident.

Now, as a parent, I have the opportunity to see life from the other side of the fence. This past year I started to allow our thirteen-year-old daughter to move the car in the driveway when I am washing the family vehicles. Driving the car is big stuff to Amanda and also motivates her to help with the work. One particular day I asked her to back the car out of the garage, warning her to "watch out for the grill that is in the driveway!"

Being forewarned Amanda focused her attention on the grill instead of the garage door. As she turned the steering wheel to avoid the grill, she rammed the right fender into the side of the garage door opening. With a panic-stricken look, she clambered out of the car, anticipating an angry outburst from me. As I turned to see what was happening, I had a flashback to my own teenage experience with the Allis-Chalmers and the shed. Without speaking I jumped into the car and eased it away from the garage to survey the damage. Pondering my own response as I straightened the bent garage door track, I remembered how much I appreciated my dad's forgiveness, so I said to Amanda, "Well, it looks like you had your first accident, and it doesn't look too bad. You'll probably just have to buy a new chrome piece for the car." I thought she needed to be responsible for the damaged chrome, but I wanted to give her a grace experience just as my dad had given me.

My concept of grace has come through relationships with people. The most significant was with my wife. It was with her that I first *felt* accepted just for who I was, and she has been the most important person in my life ever since. Since our daughters were born, I have often stood in the dim glow of the nightlight, gazing at their small, pretty faces as they slept. As I looked at them and felt the overwhelming sense of emotion and attachment, I have wondered, "I know how I feel toward Amanda and Molly as my daughters. Is it really possible that God has these same feelings for *me?*" Out of my relationship with my daughters, I began to reevaluate my own concept of God.

Marcie came to me for therapy, and one of the issues she was struggling with was her tendency to become involved sexually with men. The situation was complicated by the fact that she was married. Analysis of her background indicated that she needed lots of male attention, but no matter how much she received, it was not enough. Her behavior troubled her inner conscience, but the pull toward sexual involvement was so compelling that she could not resist, in spite of repeated, conscious, prayerful efforts. Her compulsion was like an addiction.

In spite of her un-Biblical behavior, she maintained her faith in God. In fact, her faith seemed to grow in spite of, or perhaps I should say because of, what she was doing. "I know what I am doing is wrong," she exclaimed to me, "but I don't know what to do. I have tried to quit; I really have. And I have prayed about it, but the pull just does not go away. I still feel that God loves me; in fact, through this, His grace is becoming more real."

Perhaps her experience illustrates Ellens' point when he asserts, "Grace is grace precisely in the fact that it is exploitable. It is for people who are inclined to exploit it, who are inclined to go on taking advantage of the assurance of grace to avoid growth, to avoid redemption, to avoid healing, to avoid maturity, and to avoid transcendence."[1] Allison expresses a similar belief as he likens parental acceptance of their children's shameful mistakes to God and Christians: "However, this is part of being in the parent business. Similarly, part of being in the 'God-business' is the forgiveness of sins, and there are far more sinister threats to our humanity than the usual things about which people feel so acutely guilty."[2]

Paul's Beetle

Grace did not come to Paul through a person, but it came nevertheless. He grew up in a basically Christian home, but when he was in college, he became involved in a cult which tied up his life for a number of years. Somehow he was able to extricate himself from the group and reenter the mainstream of Christian thinking. When he became a psychologist, he began working with other individuals who needed help overcoming cult experiences. In spite of this, he did not have a firm grasp on the concept of grace.

One day as he was alone in the woods, he noticed a beetle on a branch near him. As he looked at the beetle, he noted its unusual markings. As he examined the beetle more closely, he noticed the intricate, delicate design on its small body and its brilliant, sharply defined colors. As he studied the tiny spectacle of beauty before him, he suddenly realized the insignificance of the tiny beetle in comparison to the total universe. "Here was this tiny little beetle that I could squash with my finger if I wanted to, and it served no really significant purpose in the bigger scheme of things. But God had taken enough time to carefully design this little beetle right down to its intricate markings and bright colors. And for what purpose? If God can be that concerned and do such a precise job with a beetle, what about me? If He cares that much about a little beetle, then He must be able to care for me, too." As he stood alone in the woods, pondering the little beetle, Paul experienced an overwhelming sense of God's grace.

God can work in many ways. If we search for wholeness with a sincere heart and present God with our honest selves, I do believe that He will meet us through a beetle, another person, a surprising experience, or even through our sin. We can find the grace that is available. As ACEs we have grace, whether or not we feel it, and we can search with confidence because "God can't remember that you're a sinner. God honestly thinks that you are a saint, so you are free for self-actualization, free for growth, free to be and to become with alacrity and with abandon."[3]

APPENDIXES

DiSC HIGHLIGHTS

T hese are the highlights of the four behavioral categories.[1] By viewing them together, you can see the differences among the four dimensions. Keep in mind that most people are high on at least one and often two of these categories. When two dimensions are both high, they modify each other. In other words, a person who is high on "C" and "i" will be more organized than a person who is only high on "i."

HIGHLIGHTS			
"D"	**"i"**	**"S"**	**"C"**
High ego	Emotional	Loyal	Perfectionist
Impatient	People-oriented	Family-oriented	Sensitive and intuitive
Desires change	Disorganized	Possessive	Accurate
Fears being taken advantage of	Fears loss of social approval	Fears loss of security	Fears criticism of performance
Needs direct answers	Optimistic	Slow to change	Needs many explanations

(Reprinted by permission of Performax/Carlson Learning Company, Minneapolis, Minnesota, and In His Grace, Inc., Houston, Texas.)

BIBLE CHARACTERS AND THE DiSC PERSONALITY SYSTEM

T he DiSC Biblical Personal Profile adds a unique dimension to our perception of Bible characters, as we begin to see them as real people similar to us. This material is useful as a format for personal Bible study as well as an organized church program. Accompanying workbooks are available which focus on understanding yourself and others, creating loving environments for people, and finding your place of service in the church community. To purchase and use this material, a person must be a certified associate of Performax/Carlson Learning System.

For your additional study, Bible characters and corresponding Scriptures are provided here. Since women did not have a prominent role in Hebrew cultural and societal affairs, the Bible has scanty details on women's activities. Consequently, some of the DiSC links with Biblical women are based on minimal information.

Biblical Personality	Scripture Reference
Martha, Nehemiah, high "D" and "S," work-oriented, either/or	Luke 10:38–42; Nehemiah

Biblical Personality	Scriptural Reference
Abraham, Hannah, high "S" and moderate "i" and "C," seeks harmony, dislikes conflict	Genesis 21, 24; 1 Samuel 1, 2
David, Miriam, high "i" and "C," accomplishes goals through people, highly emotional	1 Samuel 16, 18, 21; Exodus 15:20–21
Abigail, Barnabas, high "i" and "S," encourager, overly tolerant	1 Samuel 25; Acts 4:36–37; 9:26–27; 15:36–41
Michal, Paul, high "D" and "C," brings change, critical spirit	2 Samuel 6:14–23; Acts 15; Galatians 2
Lydia, Solomon, high "D," seeks new horizons, fears boredom	Acts 16:13–15, 40; Ecclesiastes 2; 1 Kings 9:10–28
Apollos, Laban, Stephen, high "i" and "D," strong speaker, manipulates details	Acts 18:24–28; Genesis 29: 15–30; Acts 6, 7
Esther, John, Moses, high "C" and "S," maintains standards, sacrificially loyal	Esther 4; John 19:26–27; Exodus 3, 4, 20, 32
Luke, Mary, Ruth, high "C," medium "S," criticizes and tests, follows directions to the letter	Luke 1:1–4, 26–56; Ruth 2, 3
Anna, Jacob, James, high "S" and "C," determination, remembers wrongs	Luke 2:36–38; Genesis 29, 30, 31, 32; Acts 15:13–21
Peter, Rebekah, high "i," moderate "D," seller, closer (may use verbal deception), overly optimistic	Matthew 14:22–33; 26; Acts 3; Genesis 24

Biblical Personality	Scripture Reference
Deborah, Elijah, Jonah, high "C," moderate "S" and "i," verbalizes correctness, prone to depression	Judges 4, 5; 1 Kings 18, 19; Jonah 4
Aaron, King Saul, high "i," can rally people together, sensitive to social pressure	Exodus 4:14–17; 32; 1 Samuel 15
Joshua, Sarah, high "D" and "i," gets results, can be intimidating	Joshua 1; Genesis 16; 1 Peter 3:5–6
Dorcas, Isaac, high "S," seeks security of family, avoids conflict	Acts 9:36–38; Genesis 26; 27

(Reprinted by permission of Performax/Carlson Learning Company, Minneapolis, Minnesota, and In His Grace, Inc., Houston, Texas.)

GOD'S GRACE, THE RADICAL OPTION

The following article on grace has been excerpted from a lecture given by Dr. J. Harold Ellens at the 1987 CAPS national convention. It also appeared in Perspectives: A Journal of Reformed Thought (Grand Rapids: Reformed Church Press, November 1989, 4–8) and is used by permission of the publisher.

ва ва ва

T he theology of grace has been my all-encompassing preoccupation and the driving force of my existence for at least twenty years. As a pastor and psychotherapist and as a rather neurotic Christian trying to come to terms with his own being, the grace of God is the thing that has saved my life and has made some sense out of it. It has given substance and focus to my work.

Grace as an Alien Idea

Grace is apparently an inherently alien idea to us. Left to ourselves, none of us would ever catch the idea, to say nothing about our bent to think of it as erroneous and impossible. If the idea of grace were not delivered to us with authority, and if it were not so immediately and obviously the thing that changes our lives redemptively—both psychologically and spiritually—we would tolerate none of it. The notion of grace as the unconditional, universal, and total divine acceptance of all of us is inherently at crosswinds with the drive of our own spirits to self-certification and to the achievement of personal stability and meaning. It is the theology of grace which, if allowed to get free from the cultural and historical matrix of the Scripture, is the one thing that can radically change human life.

We do not begin to realize or to appreciate the radical, unconditional, and universal nature of that divine perspective until we begin to acknowledge that grace as God personally articulates it in Scripture certifies you and me as saints in the middle of our brokenness, in the process of our pathology, in spite of ourselves. There's a more striking reality even than that: grace affirms us in our pathogenesis, affirms us in the center of the process of our being sick, sinful, destructive, distorted, and in the process of creating distortion, sickness, and sin in our world. The radical option of grace is that it is precisely because of, and in the middle of, the impossibility of our sinful humanity that God embraces us in spite of ourselves. "While we were yet sinners, Christ died for us" (Romans 5:8).

Until very recently, I have read that particular verse as meaning, "While we're still unwillingly and passively and not too malignantly sinners, Christ died for us. While we were sinners wishing we weren't, Christ died for us." The radical option of grace is that it is precisely in the context of our being sinners who want to be sinners and who are destructively sinners and who insist upon going on being sinners that Christ died for us, in our malignancy.

I want to assert in this connection that Bonhoeffer is wrong. In the introductory paragraphs of his *Cost of Discipleship,* he refers to cheap grace. He presents there a dissertation on the error of imagining that grace can be imposed upon, or taken advantage of, or exploited. Grace is grace precisely in the fact that it is exploitable. It is for people who are inclined to exploit it, who are inclined to go on taking advantage of the assurance of grace to avoid growth, to avoid redemption, to avoid healing, to avoid maturity, and to avoid transcendence.

One side of me always wants to insist that there must be a better option than grace. I resist grace for two reasons. The first is that if it is really true that God is for me unconditionally and in spite of myself, suddenly that revises my entire agenda. That means that if genuine, true, appropriate, ideal, healing, redemptive relationships are unconditional, then my relationship with you can no longer continue to be a conditional relationship. Then I cannot go on saying that if you please me, I will love you; that if you are congenial to me, I will embrace you. If you wear the right clothes, you can come to my church. If you avoid worldly amusements, you can be a certified elder in the congregation. I can no longer operate my life on conditional relationship dynamics if it's really true that grace is unconditional.

Secondly, I resist grace and the theology of grace because if it's really true that grace is as radical as the Bible claims, that means I have to take my hands off the controls. It is no longer possible for me, as it were, to live my life with the subconscious notion that on Saturday night I can reach up and grab God by the collar and say, "OK, God, I did your thing this week and therefore you owe me a favor. I kept to the prescriptions this week. I followed the codes of conduct for worship and for ethics and for theological confession, and I've mouthed the right phrases, and I know how to quote the right Scriptures, and therefore somehow, you've got to recognize that I am justifiable." If grace is grace, then there is no option for me but to cast myself into the arms of God.

There's a story about a Texas rancher, a vigorous, aggressive, achieving fellow, who had made lots of money with a big ranch and had many people working for him. He developed the notion that religion was a good thing for these folks because it kept them in line and it motivated them. So, every Sunday morning he marched his ranch hands off to church. He said, "It will teach them a lesson."

Some years went by and a migrant worker who had parked himself and his family of twelve children just across the fence from the rancher's ranch sneaked under the fence one night and stole a calf. The ranch hands discovered it, gruffly jerked him up before the rancher, and asked, "What shall we do with him?" The owner said, "String him up. It will teach him a lesson."

The rancher died and appeared before God. When the books were opened and the angels read the long record of aggressive behavior, they asked God, "What shall we do with him?" And God said, "Forgive him; it will teach him a lesson."

Most thought concerning the grace of God and the function of grace in human existence is so superficial as to be garish and obscene. I'm always tempted to use the word *pagan* because I believe that's what anything short of radical grace ends up being. All theological formulae which set grace in tension with law or which set mercy in tension with justice have not begun to apprehend the profundity of the truth about grace. Theological formulae that set those tensions are sub-Christian formulae.

Furthermore, all psychological predilections which pose grace and the experience of grace as somewhat short of unconditional are pagan. I want to put the ax to any remnant of psychological or theological predilection that wants somehow still to condition grace with the constraints or requirements of discipline or justice or law. Order and structure and discipline are acts of grace in the form of tough love and therefore are strictly tangential and secondary to grace in God's economy.

The Psychological Insight of Grace

The theology of grace is the most significant psychological information and insight that has ever been experienced by human beings. It has never been superseded or in any way approximated in any alternative vision of God in the history of humanity. It is rooted in the Pentateuch and is these days sometimes referred to as mainstream Old Testament Yahwist theology.

Humans everywhere are moved by their longing for God. Everywhere humans worship. To do so seems intrinsic to our very natures. Liturgies or strategies of worship grow, I believe, out of psychological as well as out of spiritual sources deep within our personalities. Those psychic sources of religion are closely related to the native human anxiety patterns which are so generative in, and discernible from, our personality formation and shape.

Some forms of worship and religion meet the deep human psychic needs and others never meet them. Most religious practices in life and history reinforce the anxiety of human beings through the frustrating dynamics of guilt and the sense of the ultimate helplessness we have in the face of our problems of morality. Most do not provide relief from the threat of our morality.

Authentic Judeo-Christian notions of the theology of grace are unique in history. The Judeo-Christian gospel cuts to the center of the human problem with the guarantee of meaningfulness in this life and the assurance of our immortality. That is to say, grace is the sort of thing that outflanks our inherent inclination to form our personalities in the shape of defensive structures and stategies that are designed to compensate for our universal, generic anxiety about being, identity, and worthiness. Grace neutralizes the need and the possibility for self-justification; grace reaches past our sense of sin and shame. It puts God's hand once and for all on our central distorting hurt. Grace declares that we are saints of God in spite of ourselves.

Consider the marvelous passage in the Old Testament prophet Micah (7:18–20), which says,

> Who is a God like thee, pardoning iniquity and passing over transgression for the remnant of his inheritance? He does not retain his anger for ever because he delights in steadfast love. He will again have compassion upon us, he will tread our iniquities under foot. Thou wilt cast all our sins into the depths of the sea. Thou wilt show faithfulness to Jacob and steadfast love to Abraham, as thou hast sworn to our fathers from the days of old.

God can't remember that you're a sinner. God honestly thinks that you are a saint, so you are free for self-actualization, free for growth, free to be and to become with alacrity and with abandon. . . .

A Healing Intervention . . .

The theology of grace is the most healing intervention ever undertaken for the population of this planet. The nature of grace, therefore, is crucial. It is the Bible's mainstream from the beginning to the end. It is a truth that as Christians we inherit from Judaism. It comes to flower in Jesus Christ in New Testament theology. Only here in all the history of humanity is religion a constructive anxiety-reduction mechanism.

The theology of that Biblical mainstream is a healing option because it cuts through to the heart of our essential lostness. It leads us to Christ. It is not mechanistic or legalistic but dynamic and growth-oriented, not status-oriented. It modifies some of the pain of our symptoms of psycho-spiritual unwholesomeness, but it treats the disease and the dis-ease of our alienation. It does not beat us back to paradise, back to the womb; rather, it puts our hand in the hand of our Father and leads us forward into the kingdom, into the new paradise. When properly mediated, this theology of grace heals human pathology in mind and spirit. It is the most comprehensive and relevant psychological theory and practice ever conceived in human experience.

Unfortunately the history of Judaism and Christianity is not uniformly a demonstration of this. The history of the Christian religion is fraught with the paganism that shapes all other forms of religion. It took the Jews about 1,500 years to destroy Abram's great faith vision of grace and to subvert it to the legalism of the Davidic kingdom. It took the Christians — after Christ cut back through to the essence of that grace perspective — about five hundred to one thousand years to subvert it and to change it into the medieval formula of works-righteousness.

It took the disciples of the Reformers about two centuries to move from the essence of Lutheranism and Calvinism, which did indeed cut back to the ground and root of grace, to distort it into Reformed and Lutheran scholasticism. The further we go, the greater our efficiency for reverting to paganism. Only in the authentic, essential Judaism and Christianity is this radical notion of unconditional and universal grace preserved.

The history of religion has been a patch job, a patch job in orthodox problem solving. The tragedy of it is that orthodoxy is always merely the posture of the arrogance of the elite, the security system of the chosen, the self-certifying and self-justifying system of the in-group. It is an idol substituted for God and his truth. Orthodoxy is always the enemy of the truth; it is always the compulsive and formalistic enemy of grace.

Grace urges egalitarian solidarity with the whole, flawed humanity for whom God is unconditionally in favor.

Theology which implies that I'm okay if I go through correct motions and measure up is pagan. Conditional grace is no grace at all. In that kind of posture we are people who come crawling to God with a rusty cup in our cramped fist. Grace means that we are invited to run in reckless abandon to him with yawning buckets and gaping hearts.

NOTES

Chapter 2: Adult Children of Evangelical Christians

1. Claudia Black, *It Will Never Happen to Me* (Denver: M.A.C. Printing and Publishing Division, 1982), 31–49.

Chapter 3: Personality Makes a Difference

1. John G. Geier, *Personal Profile System Manual* (Minneapolis: Performax/Carlson Learning Company, 1979, rev. 1983).

2. Ken Voges, *Biblical Personal Profile* (Minneapolis: Performax/Carlson Learning Company, 1977, rev. 1979, 1985). Portions of the general highlights material related to Bible characters are based on information in the *Biblical Personal Profile* series. For more indepth information, refer to Appendix B.

3. John G. Geier, *Personal Profile System* (Minneopolis: Performax/Carlson Learning Company, 1978), two audiocassettes.

4. For an excellent discussion of perfectionism from a Christian perspective, see David Stoop, *Hope for the Perfectionist* (Nashville: Oliver-Nelson Books, 1987, 1989).

5. This table is adapted from one compiled by Dan Hendricks, a certified Performax consultant.

Chapter 4: Traits of Healthy Families

1. Delores Curran, *Traits of a Healthy Family* (New York: Ballantine Books, 1983).

2. Curran, *Traits*, 247.

3. Paul Tournier, *A Place for You* (New York: Harper & Row, 1968), 130.

4. Curran, *Traits*, 292.

5. Erik Erikson, *Childhood and Society* (New York: W. W. Norton & Company, 1950, 1963), 247.

6. Curran, *Traits*, 70.

7. Curran, *Traits*, 91.

8. Curran, *Traits*, 266.

9. Curran, *Traits*, 150.

10. Curran, *Traits*, 191.

11. Curran, *Traits*, 242.

Chapter 5: Control or Grace

1. David A. Seamands, *Healing for Damaged Emotions* (Wheaton, IL: Victor Books, 1981), 29–30.

2. Hession as quoted by John D. Carter and Bruce Narramore in *The Integration of Psychology and Theology: An Introduction* (Grand Rapids: Academie Books, Zondervan Publishing House, 1979), 24.

3. Robert H. Schuller, *Self-Esteem: The New Reformation* (Waco: Word Books, 1982), 61.

4. Schuller, *Self-Esteem*, 65–69.

5. C. FitzSimons Allison, *Guilt, Anger, and God, The Patterns of Our Discontents* (New York: The Seabury Press, 1972), 34, 35, 37.

6. Allison, *Guilt*, 36, 37.

7. Allison, *Guilt*, 40.

Chapter 6: Making Rules for Living

1. For a thorough discussion on the relationship between perception and behavior, especially as it relates to therapy, see Kenneth Urial Gutsch and Jacob Virgil Ritenour, II, *Nexus Psychotherapy: Between Humanism and Behaviorism* (Springfield: Charles C. Thomas Publisher, 1978).

2. The ideas presented here were taken from an abnormal psychology class taught by Marian Kinget, Ph.D. at Michigan State University, Spring 1968.

Chapter 7: The Family Focus

1. Seamands, *Healing*, 70–71.

2. Seamands, *Healing*, 49.

3. Denis Waitley, *The Psychology of Winning* (Chicago: Nightingale-Conant Corporation, 1978), audiocassettes, tape 3.

4. Waitley, *Winning*, tape 3.

5. Patrick Carnes, *Out of the Shadows* (Minneapolis: CompCare Publishers, 1983), 82–84.

Chapter 10: Rule 2: Don't Trust — Do Trust

1. Black, *It Will Never Happen to Me*, 40.

Chapter 11: Rule 3: Don't Feel — Do Feel

1. Black, *It Will Never Happen to Me*, 46.

2. Tournier, *Place*, 122.

3. Waitley, *Winning*, tape 3.

4. Seamands, *Healing*, 70.

Chapter 13: Reaction to the Rules

1. Black, *It Will Never Happen to Me*, 53–64.

Chapter 14: How the Rules Interfere with Wholeness

1. Erikson, *Childhood*, 251–254.

2. Tournier, *Place*, 108, 112.

3. Tournier, *Place*, 115.

Chapter 15: The Dynamics of the Internal Split

1. Tournier, *Place*, 107–8.

2. For a more detailed discussion of these stages from a Christian perspective, see Henry Cloud, *When Your World Makes No Sense* (Nashville: Oliver-Nelson, 1990).

3. Tournier, *Place*, 108.

4. Schuller, *Self-Esteem*, 61–99.

5. Carnes, *Shadows*, 82–84.

6. Roland C. Summit, "The Child Sexual Abuse Accommodation Syndrome," *Child Abuse and Neglect*, volume 7 (Elmsford, NY: Pergamon Press Ltd., 1983), 177–193.

Chapter 16: Wholeness Is an Option

1. Allison, *Guilt*, 35, 37.

2. Allison, *Guilt*, 46–47.

3. Dr. J. Harold Ellens, "God's Grace, the Radical Option," in *Perspectives* (Grand Rapids: Reformed Church Press, 1989), 5.

4. Allison, *Guilt*, 47, 49.

5. Allison, *Guilt*, 50.

6. Patricia McGerr, "Johnny Lingo's Eight-Cow Wife," *Reader's Digest*, February 1988, 138–41.

Chapter 17: Pursuing Wholeness

1. Allison, *Guilt*, 47, 49.

2. Tournier, *Place*, 106.

3. Chardin quoted by Tournier, *Place*, 100.

4. For an excellent treatise on this critical issue, read *A Place for You* by Paul Tournier. Since the book is out of print, it may take some searching, but its insights are worth the effort. This same topic is discussed in more detail in *The Dangers of Growing Up in a Christian Home*.

5. For more detailed information on the developmental stages from a Biblical viewpoint, refer to Henry Cloud, *When Your World Makes No Sense* (Nashville: Oliver-Nelson Publishers, 1990).

6. For additional information regarding becoming your own person, refer to Donald E. Sloat, *The Dangers of Growing Up in a Christian Home* (Nashville: Thomas Nelson Publishers, 1986), 199-250.

7. Ellens, "God's Grace," 5.

Chapter 18: Finding Grace

1. Ellens, "God's Grace", 4.

2. Allison, *Guilt*, 66.

3. Ellens, "God's Grace", 5.

Appendix A: DiSC Highlights

1. John G. Geier, *The Personal Profile System* (Minneapolis: Performax/Carlson Learning Company, 1978), two audiocassettes.

SELECTED BIBLIOGRAPHY

Buhler, Rich. *Pain and Pretending.* Nashville: Thomas Nelson Publishers, 1988.

Cloud, Henry. *When Your World Makes No Sense.* Nashville: Oliver-Nelson Books, 1990.

Helmfelt, Robert, Frank Minirth, and Paul Meier. *Love Is A Choice: Recovery for codependent relationships.* Nashville: Thomas Nelson Publishers, 1989.

Seamands, David A. *Healing Grace.* Wheaton: Victor Books, 1988.

Sell, Charles. *Unfinished Business.* Portland: Multnomah Press, 1989.

Sloat, Donald E. *The Dangers of Growing Up in a Christian Home.* Nashville: Thomas Nelson Publishers, 1986.

Stoop, David. *Hope for the Perfectionist.* Nashville: Oliver-Nelson Books, 1987, 1989.

Thurman, Chris. *The Lies We Believe.* Nashville: Thomas Nelson Publishers, 1989.

Tournier, Paul. *A Place for You.* New York: Harper & Row Publishers, 1968.

ABOUT THE AUTHOR

D r. Donald E. Sloat has earned a B.A. degree from Bethel College in Biblical Literature with a minor in theology, a M.A. degree in counseling at Michigan State University, and a Ph.D. degree from the University of Southern Mississippi.

Following his master's internship at Pine Rest Christian Hospital in Grand Rapids, Michigan, he was hired as a member of the Pine Rest psychology department. He also worked as a therapist at an adolescent mental health and drug abuse center before he began his doctoral program. After earning his doctorate, he was the clinical director of an outpatient drug abuse program in Flint, Michigan, and started a private practice in Owosso. Employment as a program supervisor and staff psychologist for Ottawa County Community Health in Holland, Michigan, preceded his development of a private practice in Grand Rapids.

In his private practice, he works with adolescents and adults, specializing in adult children of evangelicals. As a member of Forest View Psychiatric Hospital's affiliate staff, he has developed and conducts a specialty inpatient Christian care program. In addition to being an author with two books and over fifteen published articles, he has taught personal development courses and developed multi-media programs. He and his wife, Linda, have two daughters, Amanda and Molly.

He is a certified Performax consultant and is licensed as a psychologist in Arizona, California, and Michigan. His professional affiliations include the American Psychological Association and the Christian Association for Psychological Studies.

The typeface for the text of this book is *Times Roman*. In 1930, typographer Stanley Morison joined the staff of *The Times* (London) to supervise design of a typeface for the reformatting of this renowned English daily. Morison had overseen type-library reforms at Cambridge University Press in 1925, but this new task would prove a formidable challenge despite a decade of experience in paleography, calligraphy, and typography. *Times New Roman* was credited as coming from Morison's original pencil renderings in the first years of the 1930s, but the typeface went through numerous changes under the scrutiny of a critical committee of dissatisfied *Times* staffers and editors. The resulting typeface, *Times Roman*, has been called the most used, most successful typeface of this century. The design is of enduring value to English and American printers and publishers, who choose the typeface for its readability and economy when run on today's high-speed presses.

Substantive Editing:
Michael S. Hyatt

Copy Editing:
Susan Kirby

Cover Design:
Steve Diggs & Friends
Nashville, Tennessee

Page Composition:
Xerox Ventura Publisher
Printware 720 IQ Laser Printer

Printing and Binding:
Maple-Vail Book Manufacturing Group
York, Pennsylvania

Cover Printing:
Strine Printing Company
York, Pennsylvania